Social Care Practice in Context

Malcolm Payne

palgrave
macmillan

First published 2009 by
PALGRAVE MACMILLAN

Palgrave Macmillan in the UK is an imprint of Macmillan Publishers Limited, registered in England, company number 785998, of Houndmills, Basingstoke, Hampshire RG21 6XS

Palgrave Macmillan in the US is a division of St Martin's Press LLC, 175 Fifth Avenue, New York, NY 10010.

Palgrave Macmillan is the global academic imprint of the above companies and has companies and representatives throughout the world.

Palgrave® and Macmillan® are registered trademarks in the United States, the United Kingdom, Europe and other countries.

ISBN-13: 978–0–230–52181–0
ISBN-10: 0–230–52181–9

This book is printed on paper suitable for recycling and made from fully managed and sustained forest sources. Logging, pulping and manufacturing processes are expected to conform to the environmental regulations of the country of origin.

A catalogue record for this book is available from the British Library.

A catalog record for this book is available from the Library of Congress.

10 9 8 7 6 5 4 3 2 1
18 17 16 15 14 13 12 11 10 09

Printed and bound in China

Reshaping Social Work Series

Series Editors: **Robert Adams, Lena Dominelli and Malcolm Payne**

The **Reshaping Social Work** series aims to develop the knowledge base for critical, reflective practitioners. Each book is designed to support students on qualifying social work programmes and update practitioners on crucial issues in today's social work, strengthening research knowledge, critical analysis and skilled practice to shape social work to meet future challenges.

Published titles

Critical Issues in Social Work with Older People Mo Ray, Judith Phillips and Miriam Bernard
Social Work and Power Roger Smith
Social Work Research for Social Justice Beth Humphries

Forthcoming titles

Anti-Racist Practice in Social Work Kish Bhatti-Sinclair
Social Work and Spirituality Margaret Holloway and Bernard Moss

Invitation to authors

The Series Editors welcome proposals for new books within the *Reshaping Social Work* series. Please contact one of the series editors for an initial discussion:

- Robert Adams at rvadams@rvadams.karoo.co.uk
- Lena Dominelli at lena.dominelli@durham.ac.uk
- Malcol   g.uk

Reshaping Social Work
Series Editors: **Robert Adams, Lena Dominelli and Malcolm Payne**
Series Standing Order ISBN 1–4039–4878–X
(outside North America only)

You can receive future titles in this series as they are published by placing a standing order. Please contact your bookseller or, in the case of difficulty, write to us at the address below with your name and address, the title of the series and the ISBN quoted above.

Customer Services Department
Macmillan Distribution Ltd
Houndmills
Basingstoke
Hampshire
RG21 6XS
England

Contents

Figures

Research boxes

Tables

Introduction

Aim

The aim of this book is to identify the significant expertise required to practise in social care and to place it in a theoretical and policy context. I think that social care is a valuable form of social work, but much social work thinking neglects social care tasks in favour of behaviour and social change. Yet social care is an important part of the lives of people receiving it, as carers and as service users or both. We must be ambitious about what we want to achieve, or we condemn an important part of our population to the not-very-good, the as-cheap-as-we-can-get-away-with. Social care needs the financial and human resources to achieve good quality of life for people needing these services, but also to develop the best practice in engaging with, relating to, intervening and participating with them. If we aim to enable citizens to feel secure that we will respond consistently to their social care needs, we must plan to be there with the best we can do.

So, in this book I present social care as a social profession alongside social work within the UK. We might see social care and social work as related to each other in three different ways, with social care being:

- 'Not-social work', a separate but possibly related activity, developing autonomy as an occupational group
- An aspect of social work, which is in the process of differentiating its own particular characteristics
- An overarching social intervention, which includes social work.

Social care developed from residential and day care work and coordination and collaboration practices in social work. Residential, day care and field social workers share many objectives for service users, each taking different parts in the overall provision. Field social workers have usually had more professional autonomy and better conditions of service in local government, so residential and day care workers and other social care workers have often aspired to social work qualification, to be able to move into field practice. Social care emphasizes the differences between residential and day care work and field social work, and seeks to establish, define and develop a practice that expresses that difference in both aim and method.

Alongside the social care practice that has come from residential and day care work, the major source of social care fieldwork is the care management that emerged from community care reforms in the 1990s. While this is similar to field and therapeutic social work in that it is a face-to-face practice working with individuals and families in the community, it is different in that it focuses on service provision aspects of social services. These have been neglected or rejected in therapeutic social work, or are perceived as a deprofessionalization and bureaucratization of therapeutic social work. This is because care management replaces practice discretion with official procedures designed to achieve managerial control of practice. Moreover, its objectives seem to have only superficial connection with discretionary social work's aim to benefit individuals, since care management is mainly concerned with management processes to ration services and constrain increases in expenditure.

However, care management techniques originally developed from social work, and sought to improve coordination and collaboration. They therefore potentially offer a broad range of techniques to benefit service users (Payne, 1995). Moreover, the fact that a social work practice has been incorporated into government provision in a way that does not use its full potential, or diverges from its professional objectives, does not necessarily invalidate the practice. Discretionary, interpersonal elements of social work are often needed to implement care management successfully; this is the case with Mrs Envall.

practice example

Mrs Envall, a frail older person coming out of hospital, could be moved to a care home by going to her bedside, telling her that she will be discharged soon, and going through a list of factors in her life that mean that she needs to move to a care home and the only available one is Oaklands. However, it is more humane and effective to discuss with the service user her own and her family's uncertainties and work through with her the sense of loss of independence and her own home, which will be a part of the decision-making for her. Other options from her family may emerge to be examined, and she and her family will be able to prepare better for the move. They may also be helped to understand the resource constraints and pressures, and will often be sympathetic to them. Thus, effective social care needs good social work within family and personal relationships and is consistent with it. Performing tasks to achieve only the agency's management objectives may sometimes be sufficient. Mrs Envall may be aware that, with a heavy heart, she must go to a care home. If she has no family or friends, there will probably be little fuss in accepting the care system's decision. If she has such supports, they will often rally round to make sure it will work. But it is not good social care.

In summary, then, the points to be made about the relationship between social care and social work are as follows:

- Social work is a well-established, recognized profession, with an international body of knowledge. Social care, on the other hand, is a British development responding to UK political and service systems. Seen as part of social professions in the world, social care is a UK social profession alongside professions such as social pedagogy, social education or social development, which exist in other countries.
- Social care draws on knowledge and skills recognized internationally as part of social work and developed as part of academic social work.
- It also draws on knowledge from and practice traditions within management, groupwork, community work, residential care, counselling and psychotherapy.

Social care has developed elements of practice, explored more fully in Chapter 2, relevant to settings that organize and provide long-term care, with the overall aim of maintaining social cohesion and inclusion.

Important themes in social care practice

A number of important themes run through the book, which reflect my position on current debates in social care. An important theme is the development of personalization as an approach to social care; this is often presented as being concerned mainly with providing direct payments or independent budgeting so that people can control how their own social care services are organized and provided.

In this book, I argue that it needs to offer more than that. Personalization can only be a part of other important qualities in social care. I show how these develop from a clear understanding of the nature of caring, that it is both receptive and developmental, about strengthening people's connections with others around them and with the organizations and social institutions they are part of. It does involve intrusion and surveillance particularly where it deals with risk and protection. A good quality of life for users and carers is an important outcome of social care, and to achieve this, care needs to be appropriate in time and place and connect with people's cultural, social and spiritual values.

Another set of important themes concerns the way we organize social care. There is a lot of talk about agency partnerships, but organizations don't partner, people do, and our focus should be on practice skills alongside organizational requirements of partnership. However, good social care practice is not just about fitting in with everyone else, it includes effective advocacy, based on good understanding of users' and carers' values and wishes.

A third group of themes is about the equal importance of users and carers in our practice. Social care should deal holistically with both users and carers in their social networks, not as bundles of needs to be assessed for highly rationed services.

The book's argument and organization

Building on these themes, I argue in this book that social work must accept the challenge of understanding and integrating care work into its practice, and value it, because caring values, and is valued by, service users and carers.

The first three chapters set the scene for a discussion of social care practice later in the book. In Chapter 1, I examine how we may understand a service that seeks to be caring and concerned with the social. These ideas provide the benchmark for evaluating whether a social care service is doing a good job. Emerging from ideas about what is caring and social, Chapter 2 argues that central to a social caring service is valuing its users and the people who are involved in caring for them. This also means that caring services must be normalizing, that is, they offer a good quality of life that most people would value. This chapter then goes on to look at the ideas that are emerging about what the elements of a social care service are. Chapter 3 asks what sort of organization and policy provides a good social care service, and examines some aspects of the present agency system. Chapters 4 to 7 move through the process of social care practice, starting with socially caring engagement and assessment in Chapter 4. Chapter 5 looks at relationships with other agencies and colleagues to advocate and negotiate for service users and their carers and mobilize appropriate services. Chapter 6 examines developments that aim to achieve socially caring practice interventions, and Chapter 7 explores appropriate endings; examining reviewing, auditing and researching practice as part of our work. Chapter 8 proposes that, to be caring, practice must support the development of practitioners and services and moves on to discuss where social care practice is going over the next few years, bearing in mind my argument about the need for caring being an integrated part of what its practitioners do.

Stop and think

In the chapters that follow, I include a 'stop and think' activity to help you to reflect on and apply what you have read. I also list some publications and websites that might help you to take the chapter topics further. As a first reflection, it may help you to prepare for the discussions about caring as the basis for social care in Chapter 1 by reviewing the discussion in this Introduction, and then listing the main points of difference and similarity between social care and social work as you see them or in your experience.

What is social care practice?

What is social care?

Social care is a difficult concept to understand, because the term is used in different places with different meanings. The three main usages refer to:

- Social work practice in residential, day care and other group care settings (for example the Social Care Association)
- A British term referring to services, including social work, provided in the field of social welfare. Used like this, the term often connects with 'healthcare'. 'Social care' has replaced 'the social services' and 'the personal social services' in UK government terminology, and official documents often refer to an omnibus term: 'health and social care'. Talking about 'social care' emphasizes that providing effective services is a crucial part of social work, which in turn is part of social care
- Practice and training for practice in the 'care sector' of the economy and in state welfare services, often in group care settings, as distinct from therapeutic social work designed to enhance personal growth and self-understanding (Payne, 2006).

The underlying reason for using 'social care' in these ways is the same: it reflects a political and professional shift to emphasize caring, and to distinguish the responsibility to be caring in these services from other responsibilities. In particular, social care aims to focus practice on caring attitudes and caring services, because service users and carers value that. Many professions concerned with well-being emphasize psychological or counselling therapies that help people with difficult feelings or emotions, thinking or cognitions and relationships. Social care's development, therefore, is a policy shift. It says to practitioners that, whatever therapeutic or educational work they do, care runs alongside it and should be integrated into it.

The political shift towards talking about 'social care' implies that practical caring tasks may be low-status and relatively unskilled – there is debate about that – but they must nevertheless always be part of services aimed at well-being. If that is so, practitioners such as social workers must integrate low-status, unskilled care work into what they do and have a concern for it as part of their services, even if they do not do it personally. In related professions, such as nursing and teaching, relatively low-skilled tasks are performed by assistants or ancillaries, but the professional practitioner still has responsibility for what such staff do. In social work, too, practitioners do not just 'assess' for a care package or 'manage' a care home, they are responsible for the caring that users and informal carers experience.

A number of formal definitions of social care exist, and some are quoted in Table 1.1; looking at these suggests that the idea is not yet well developed. The Platt Report (2007) on the status of social care usefully points out that service users prefer definitions that refer to what the services aim to achieve for them, as well as what they consist of. The English Department of Health (DH), which is responsible for adult social care, is using the term 'social care' alongside 'healthcare' to emphasize both the connection and also the administrative and legal differences between them in the UK system; in fact mainly in the system in England and Wales. Another important report, the Wanless Report (2006) on the social care of older people, starts from social care policy and its interaction with social security and healthcare policies.

Table 1.1 Definitions of social care

Department of Health White Paper Our Health, Our Care, Our Say
...the wide range of services designed to support people to maintain their independence, enable them to play a fuller part in society, protect them in vulnerable situations and manage complex relationships. (DH, 2006a: 1.29)
Department of Health social care website
Social care is one of the major public service areas. In England, the responsibility to provide social care services rests principally with local councils. At any one time, up to 1.5 million of the most vulnerable people in society are relying on social workers and support staff for help. Social care services also make a major contribution to tackling social exclusion. Currently, modernizing social services is a national priority, and to have the greatest effect this must happen in conjunction with the modernization of the NHS. (DH, 2007a)
BBC Q&A social care
There is no simple definition of social care. However, it is agreed it covers a wide range of services provided by local authorities and the independent sector to elderly people either in their own homes or in a care home. It also covers day centres which help people with daily living. Services like help with washing, dressing, feeding or assistance in going to the toilet are also included, as are meals-on-wheels and home-help for people with disabilities. It does not cover nursing care, which is defined as care that has to be provided or supervised by a registered nurse. (BBC, 2007)
Platt Report The Status of Social Care: A Review 2007
The group of services that provide personal care and support to people in a social situation – such as family; the community; a communal setting; to help them achieve independence and to promote their positive contribution as citizens. (Platt, 2007)

Examples of recent formal change referring to social care are the Care Standards Act 2000 and equivalents such as the Regulation of Care (Scotland) Act 2001, which set up the regulators of social work in the UK. These are the General Social Care Council in England, the Care Council for Wales, and the Northern Ireland Social Care Council, although the Scottish equivalent is the Scottish Social Services Council. The Social Care Institute for Excellence (SCIE, 2006) and its Scottish equivalent the Scottish Institute for Excellence in Social Work Education (SIESWE, 2006), were also established to develop and disseminate knowledge and research about social care; again, though, the Scottish terminology is different, referring to 'social work'. The main government website on social services, produced by the DH, also refers to 'social care' describing social work as a small part of social care, mainly because there are a small number of qualified and registered social workers compared with the number of people who work in social care altogether. Does this mean that looking after children in public care is not now social care? Does it mean that children and families work is the only role of social work; that ensuring the well-being of adults is not social work but something different? No, because practice in services for children and families still has to be caring, and is often called 'children's social care'. Also, social care services for adults still require considerable professional social work skill.

Social work is nevertheless part of the social care system; in changing the name from 'social services', the DH wants to emphasize the importance of caring responsibilities in social work. In most other countries, 'social work' and 'social services' are still the overall terms, and would include both services and practice that in the UK might be called 'social care'. Therefore, most international literature refers to social work when referring to actions and services that in the UK would normally be called social care. At the end of this chapter, therefore, I examine the interaction between social work and social care as practices and as professions.

Is this a real change or just talk? The late 1990s and early 2000s were a time of 'spin'; politics and the media aimed to renew and modernize the image of public services by presenting them more positively, so you might be cynical about the reasons for this change. However, the change in language reflects an important, valuable change in perspective, organization and practice, in the following ways:

- Dealing with people's *problems* by social and behaviour change shifted towards responding to care needs for effective, responsive *services* (the perspective change)
- Planned service *structures* shifted towards flexible responses to service users' assessed *needs* (the organizational change)
- Concern for interpersonal *processes* shifted towards achieving effective, planned care *outcomes* (the practice change).

These are changes in focus, not a complete u-turn. What we are moving from (a problem focus, a focus on organizational structures, and a focus on interpersonal processes) have not become less important. Rather, they have been placed in a new service and practice context. It is helpful to understand these changes as a recognition that social services need to be more personalized in order to meet the duty to respond in the best way possible to the needs that citizens present to be dealt with by their public social services.

Social care, citizenship and social services

Citizenship and state social care

A historic shift during the last half of the 20th century moved care for sick, disabled and vulnerable people out of institutions and into 'the community'. This shift is an international movement and is the origin of UK social care. The shift to caring emphasizes that one of the ways that states achieve social cohesion is through taking responsibility for caring for people who are its citizens. Citizens in a modern state are in social relationships, connected with each other within a community of people who have shared interests and responsibility for each other's well-being.

Social work is part of achieving social well-being and cohesion, but, in the 20th century, it was mainly about behavioural adaptation and social change. From the 1990s onwards, social work with children and families progressively separated from 'adult social services' in the English social services departments (SSDs) that had been established in local government during the 1970s; this split was formalized in the early 2000s, although it is still not completely universal. Many non-local government social work agencies are not divided like this. For example, I work in a hospice, where the social work team works with both children and adults.

Social care services and workers

Social care is provided within a range of services for adults and children, which cost English local councils £14.06bn and £4.49bn respectively in 2005–6, providing a service for 1.72 million adults in 2004–5 (CSCI, 2006: 3.3, 3.10). Data about children is collected differently: 60,900 were 'looked after' by English councils in 2004–5 (CSCI, 2006: 3.52). During the financial year April 2004 to March 2005, about 584,000 adults used home care, 267,240 were assisted to live in residential care, and, of the 1.96 million new contacts from adults to English councils, 649,000 people had completed assessments for care. Table 1.2 lists the services inspected by the Commission for Social Care Inspection (CSCI) with a summary of what each service provides drawn from its descriptions; this clarifies the official view of what these services consist of. As this book is published the CSCI will merge with the healthcare regulator, but at the time of writing we do not know the details. Services in the home include a range of practical care, including the provision of meals. Day care services are also provided for many different groups. This book aims to identify principles of care provision in these services, rather than the services themselves or the policy that leads to them, although the next two chapters briefly examine the organizational and policy context of social care.

Table 1.2 Social care provision

Adult services	Children's services	Description
Care homes and settings	Children's homes	Provide accommodation, meals and personal care
	Schools and colleges	Schools and colleges that also provide care, such as boarding schools, further education colleges and schools where children with learning disabilities are taught
Care in your own home		Care workers provide help with washing, dressing and eating and other practical tasks in people's own homes
Direct payment support schemes		Help with cash payments made direct by local councils to enable people to buy assistance with care
Nurses' agencies		Organize nurses to visit people who need care, possibly in their own homes, but mostly in care homes or hospitals
Adult support schemes	Fostering agencies	Organize to provide people in need with a family life in the carers' homes
	Adoption agencies	Adoption agencies organize families to take permanent legal responsibility for a child
Specialist services		Care homes or day centres that provide for specific ethnic minority groups
	Residential family centres	Temporary accommodation for families where parents are receiving help with parenting skills

SOURCE: CSCI (2007).

A range of people work in these services. We distinguish between:

- Paid workers, including a group of qualified social workers; I use the term 'practitioners'
- Informal carers, who are often members of the families of service users, or part of their informal social networks. Various terms are used for this group; I adopt the British convention of calling them carers.

Both these aspects of care services are important, since they interact with each other in providing care for people, and there are important distinctions between them, considered below in 'Care and caring'.

Where does the term 'social care' come from?

The term 'social care' has been used in the UK since at least 1982, when 'social care planning' was described in the Barclay Report (1982) on the 'role and tasks of social work' as one of the two roles (the other was 'counselling') of social work. After the Report, people began to use 'social care' to refer to 'indirect' social work in contrast to direct work in relationships with service users and their families. Examples of indirect work include organizing services or advocating on behalf of service users with other agencies.

As Goldberg and Connelly (1982: 2) wrote:

> The term 'social care', meaning 'the social as distinct from the economic ways in which people look after each other, directly or indirectly' … seems to convey more adequately these recent developments in the personal social services. The concept embraces not only social work and other statutory personal social services but also all kinds of voluntary activities as well as self-help and mutual help.

The 'Social Care Association' was set up in 1985, mainly drawing its membership from the former 'Residential Care Association' (SCA, 2006). This move aimed to broaden the organization's focus to care work in people's homes and in other community settings as well as in residential and day care.

Also during the 1980s, private residential care expanded, and the 'for-profit' sector became the most important provider of residential care and a big employer of staff. Previously, most residential care had been in local authority (LA) social services departments (SSDs). A new term was needed to distinguish a sector of social provision from SSDs. It became a sector of the economy, an 'industry', at a time when traditional manufacturing industries were being displaced in the economy by service industries.

Concern about training for staff in care work in residential care grew out of the development of 'industry-wide' training in all sectors of the economy during the 1990s. Qualifying social work education, already well established, became universal during the 1980s for fieldwork practitioners. Many agencies moved to emphasize wider training needs in all economic sectors, the term 'social care sector' was preferred to 'social services' which by that time had become associated with LA SSDs. By the end of the 1990s 'social care' was the most inclusive term. However, this is a British development; most of the rest of the world uses social work as the overarching term, including effective service provision within that.

Social care's alternative aims

The term 'social care' came into wide use as an alternative to the existing services. Therefore, referring to 'social care' implies that social care is different from social work or social services. The implications are as follows.

Social care is multi-sectoral

It includes private sector or 'for-profit' provision and voluntary, not-for-profit or 'third-sector' provision alongside government, state or local authority provision. 'Third-sector' is an American term for voluntary or not-for-profit organizations, implying that the first two sectors are the private and state sectors. It follows from the fact that social care is multi-sectoral that it includes a private sector, and therefore incorporates market-based approaches to providing services, not only public services.

Social care is provision

From the 1980s, governments have separated providing a service to service users, 'service provision', from the task of planning and paying for the services in an area, 'commissioning'. This is part of the arrangements for multi-sectoral services, since there has to be an administrative arrangement for choosing between services in the different sectors. Commissioning means giving or authorizing a person or organization to carry out their responsibilities, usually referring to official responsibilities. It is a military analogy: senior officers in the army are 'commissioned' when they are given their posts. It is also sometimes used to refer to getting a new building or service running after the planning stage.

In principle, separating commissioning from provision should be more flexible than the local authority providing everything, because services can be offered in different combinations. In practice, this division of responsibility may confuse users and workers with complex arrangements. In adult community care, for example, a care manager employed by an LA usually assesses people's needs and organizes a 'care package' to meet the needs, although there are other ways of managing this process (Payne, 1995). The services in the care package may be provided by agencies, from different sectors, including the LA. Similarly, in child care, a child protection or child and families worker usually decides, usually as part of a case conference or review, when a child needs residential care or a school for children with emotional and behavioural disorders (EBD). However, the people providing the care are usually managed separately within the LA, or work for a specialist residential or EBD care agency; they are part of implementing 'social care' including some social work practice.

practice example

Harris is a young person 'looked after' (the legal term) by the LA in residential care. Daily responsibility for his personal development falls to the staff of the care home, and consequently their relationships are important to him. On the other hand, strategic decisions, for example about whether he is in a care home at all, and if so where, lie with his social worker whom he rarely sees. The social worker's decisions reflect policy, availability of wider services or intended outcomes that differ from the daily issues concerning Harris and the residential care staff who care for him. A periodic case conference or review, involving Harris and his parents, takes the decisions. Both care workers and Harris may find it hard to see who has the most influence in the meetings. Also, he finds it hard to look back afterwards to see why decisions were made.

Commissioning care in packages sometimes makes it hard to identify who is responsible for decisions. One of the important tasks of social care is, therefore, to keep track of the decisions made about packages of services and help users to understand and make the best use of them. Harris is an example of the need for this role.

Social care is about providing services

From the 1940s onwards, social work's main purpose was to deal with people who were seen as having problems, or as being a problem for other people or for society in general. Social services were not a universal service, like healthcare or education, that everyone might use, but were stigmatized as being for people who could not manage independently. As Webb and Wistow (1987: 215), reviewing 'the rise of social care', put it: 'Compared with the unflattering popular image of field social work, the social care services have appeared as providers of direct practical support to individuals in need.'

A DH study in 2001 (Research Box 1.1) confirms this impression. Most people have a negative picture of social work and social care, because the people social workers deal with are troubled or troublesome and difficult to deal with. Consequently, other people do not like being part of a service that works with such stigmatized people. People with a serious disability or who are very frail because of old age have an acceptable call on the state's social services, but most people prefer not to have to ask for that help. Also, most people would prefer not to provide that help, sometimes struggling over long periods. Another point is that healthcare and education are free for most people, whereas people receiving help from social security and social services either have to pay or be subjected to a means test, a check that they have not got the income or capital (the 'means') to pay a charge.

As a result, social work and social care are stigmatized because they are not universal, but only offered to difficult people with difficult problems. Calling on social care services implies that someone has managed their life or problems badly. Because richer people pay for their own help rather than calling on state help, many people feel that social care services are not in their control and that officialdom will interfere in their private affairs because the state is paying. In this way, social work and social services are a public intervention, interpreted as public interference, in private life, rather than an exchange for citizens' contributions to their community and family in the past, or for payment. In addition, many people think that 'doing' caring may be necessary but is undesirable work, whether done voluntarily or as employment; this is one of the reasons why it has low status.

research box 1.1

Public perceptions of social work and social care

Why the study was carried out – There were concerns about recruitment to social work, because of a shortage of trained staff and a fall in applications to social work courses.

Methods – An independent market research company studied the views of focus groups of people who had little knowledge or experience of the social services. Focus groups are a good way of stimulating people to express ideas about a topic that they are unfamiliar with.

Results – Public perception of social work was unfavourable for two reasons:

1. Social workers dealt with intractable situations, involving unpleasant issues and disapproved people, in particular child abuse.
2. They were seen as hemmed in by large workloads and bureaucratic procedures.

Public perception of social care was that it consisted of mainly practical tasks caring for elderly people, carried out by women. Both roles were stressful, difficult and unpleasant, requiring a sense of vocation.

Outcomes – The government developed an advertising campaign, emphasizing the interest, complexity and social value of social work, which successfully increased applications to courses.

Source: Research Works (2001).

Social care provides care, not therapy or change

The centre of social work practice has been to help people fit in better to society, either by changing people's social relationships and behaviour or by working to change elements of social provision or social organization. These are broadly therapeutic or social change objectives. Social care focuses on what Davies (1994) calls 'maintenance' in social work, that is, helping people to maintain their functioning and quality of life when it would otherwise have deteriorated.

Social care works with long-term conditions

Because it has this maintenance role, social care often works with people who have long-term conditions, or situations in which they need continuing involvement. Social work increasingly uses short-term techniques like task-centred or cognitive-behavioural work to change behaviour. It assesses people for services and plans work, while social care services do the daily work of caring, with social workers playing limited roles. Part of the reason for this is that healthcare services have focused on curing acute conditions, transferring long-term care to social care.

Social care works with all groups of service users

While we often think of services for adults as social care and services for children and families as social work, social care broadly means work with people that includes substantial elements of caring, and children and families work is often called 'children's social care'. The Social Care Association grew out of professional bodies in children's residential care. Social care with all user groups uses similar principles and knowledge and raises similar issues, and its ideas draw on residential care ideas.

Social care: implications for practice

In summary, social care aims, within broader social provision, to deliver care services in all sectors of the economy for groups of service users with long-term conditions or needs. Being multi-sectoral means that social care practice has to emphasize the interaction of organizations and being long term means that practice must be concerned with consistency over long periods across those organizations. This means that social care practice has to develop continuing relationships with service users and carers and integrate the work of different organizations. Social work has different aims, about behavioural and social change, and evidence suggests that the best social work is often focused on specific issues in people's lives and works well through brief contacts. The organization of, and policy of, social care services has failed to recognize the practice implications of social care's aim and content of consistent long-term care. Therefore in exploring and formulating the requirements of social care practice, this book argues that some current organization and policy is a barrier to good practice, because it does not foster continuing caring relationships.

In the next two sections, I examine the two crucial elements of social care: the idea of care and the idea of the social. If social care is a policy shift that emphasizes the importance of caring, we need to understand in detail what that might mean.

Care and caring

Informal caring arises as people accept responsibility for caring for others as a natural part of their family and social networks. Social care is distinct, although it connects with informal caring. Like 'medical care' or 'nursing care', it refers to services from paid workers provided to people because of citizenship in a society. Citizen caring is part of the social capital, the accumulated resources, of a society, promoting social cohesion by accepting that a society has a responsibility for organizing care for its citizens. Social care contributes to social capital in two ways. First, it contributes caring provision: organized caring as part of the state and the economy. Thus, its second contribution to social capital is caring support. Social care supports the social cohesion generated by informal caring and it extends caring beyond interpersonal responsibility into social responsibility.

If, as I have argued, social care is a new approach to the social services, bringing caring into the duties that we accept within our state and social responsibilities to citizens, we must mean that the public and service users are entitled to expect citizen caring to be like informal caring in important ways and to complain when it is not. Therefore, understanding *care* and *being caring* is an important basis for social care. It provides values that define our practice and objectives, and expectations and clarity about what being caring means for our services. The public and service users compare citizen caring with the benchmark of informal caring. We cannot, therefore, cut paid social care services off from the general understood concept of caring by saying that citizen caring is different.

This section aims to introduce ideas about care and being caring as basic concepts that underlie the rest of this book. I start from informal caring, and then compare and contrast citizen caring with it, examining how caring services need to be organized to make their contribution to informal caring.

I often ask groups or audiences what image they have of caring. A common image is of mothers and children or, particularly in healthcare audiences, 'mopping the fevered brow' as someone put it recently, that is, physical help in illness that is not specialized nursing aimed at cure. The image of caring that connects it with the 'mother–child' relationship has implications for care services, because the maternal care relationship has particular features: the child is very dependent and a close emotional attachment is usually formed between mother and child. These features are not necessarily the same in other caring relationships. Illness may be a transitory condition, and physical help may not be all that is required, so, again, we should be careful of assuming that the images we have are relevant for all caring.

Personal caring

Important ideas in caring are derived from Enlightenment thinkers of the 17th century. The assumption is that citizens within a society are connected, they have moral duty to reduce suffering and, as people who are free to decide on their own course of action, can nevertheless determine through reason that maintaining social connections generates general social benefits. This leads to ideas such as:

- Altruism, the idea that we should have regard for others' needs as a principle in deciding how to act
- Beneficence, the idea that people should help others who need help
- Duty or obligation, the idea that we have a duty to help others

- Tradition, the idea that we should comply with expected behaviour in societies, because this leads to certainty and efficiency
- Reciprocity, the idea that we should return care that others have given to us, or more broadly return to society care that we have received through social relationships (Bulmer, 1987: chapter 5).

All these are aspects of the motivation of people to care, be caring and be cared for and the acceptance that this is morally good and practically useful.

There are two ways of seeing this moral aspect of caring in Western society. One point is that caring is an essential part of being moral; you cannot be a moral person without being caring. It follows from this that a service provided between two people, in a personal relationship or a more formal relationship because they are citizens, must be caring to be moral. A connected but different point is that caring is a moral act, a good act. Therefore providing social care services, like any other caring is a virtuous act; to be virtuous, it must have the accepted features of caring. We therefore have to ask what this caring consists of.

All caring incorporates two aspects, which Noddings (1984) sees as feminine and masculine. The feminine aspect is about connectedness between the carer and others in society and receptiveness to the other person. The masculine aspect is an active commitment on the part of the carer to the other person.

Examples of the masculine aspect are represented in Mayeroff's (1971) account of the characteristics of personal caring. He starts from the principle: 'To care for another person, in the most significant sense, is to help him grow or actualize himself' (p. 1), going on to say: 'To help another grow is to help him care for something outside himself and to be able to care for himself' (p. 6, *sic*; Mayeroff includes women in the personal pronouns 'him' and 'himself'). An important point of Mayeroff's work for social care is that the focus on helping people towards self-actualization proposes a direction and priorities in carrying out caring tasks, and a way of deciding among various possibilities of what to do. Foucault (1986) emphasized how individual self-actualization as a social priority gives importance to the individual in Western society, and values private over public and community life. A related view is that of Tronto (1993) who argues that, to be ethical, care must involve attentiveness to the needs of the cared-for person, responsibility for taking action to meet their needs, competence in doing so and responsiveness to needs that may lead to risk.

The feminine aspect of caring is represented in Noddings's (1984) account of caring. She sees caring as 'engrossment', that is a mental state of being burdened by concern for another person, anxious, fearful or solicitous about their well-being. She criticizes Mayeroff's approach as too rational, too concerned about the carer and the extent to which they are committed. She focuses instead not on projecting ourselves into the other person's shoes, but on receptiveness, being related to and responsive to the other person. The idea of connection is also important in Gilligan's (1993) psychological research into children's moral development. She argues that where there is solidarity in society, people have an 'ethics of care', that is, we see it as a moral good if people care for each other. One view of moral development leads to a rational, rule-making approach to what is good and bad, and leads to a concern about fairness and justice. Her study shows that this is typical of the way boys are brought up, and this leads them to be more concerned to find out who is right, or which argument 'wins' in moral debate. The alternative view, more typical of the way we bring up girls, sees it as more important to care for each other in interdependent relationships. Gilligan (1993: 160) refers to women's accounts of their lives:

> in all of the women's descriptions, identity is defined in a context of relationship and judged by a standard of responsibility and care. Similarly, morality is seen by these women as arising from the experience of connection and conceived as a problem of inclusion rather than one of balancing claims.

The implications of this work for gender relations have led to considerable debate. Feminist writers, in particular, suggest that these different attitudes to the ethics of care might be connected with the tendency for women to be seen as the main carers in social relationships. Thinking more broadly, I suggested above that states provide social care services because they value this social connection between people as a contribution to a nation's social capital and order through generating social solidarity.

practice example

I work in a hospice, with people who know they are going to die soon and with their families. At the end of life, people want to do something useful with the limited time that they have left. This may involve completing life tasks and rounding off relationships that are important to them, reminiscing or recording memories for children or grandchildren, or learning something new. By being concerned with others in this way, or developing themselves, they feel they are achieving something useful, even though they may be too ill to carry on with their ordinary pursuits. In doing this, they are remaining mentally healthy, that is caring for themselves, by caring for others in their family. The hospice, providing a palliative care service, is providing caring support in helping people achieve these important human tasks of caring for others and thereby caring for themselves.

Extending this example to other social provision, children need help to grow and develop in the best possible way. One of the reasons that the child care system has been regarded as poor caring provision is that children in care have poor educational attainment compared with other similar children. People assume that it cannot be caring if it does not achieve children's development. Disabled people, people with learning disabilities and mentally ill people all need the opportunity to make the best of their abilities, because their disabilities may limit them in achieving what they might like or prefer. Older people may be disappointed, isolated or depressed because they have fewer opportunities than in their past to pursue self-actualization and it may be hard for carers or practitioners to think of them as needing personal development and growth.

Practical and emotional care

Care includes conceptually distinct practical and emotional elements. Parker and Lawton's (1994) study of care activities identified in the General Household Survey (Research Box 1.2) showed how people think about different aspects of care. The researchers re-analysed a government survey of family life, which examined informal carers. They showed that most people differentiate caring tasks, which are clustered into caring roles. Different groups of people were found to give different sorts of care. Extensive personal care is the preserve of marriages and other close relationships. Personal care without practical care was largely provided by spouses and children, and most often received by men. Physical help that is not personal is more provided by men and by parents. What this suggests is that different sorts of care needs are met by people in different relationships. Practical help is mainly provided to older people and may be provided by men and non-relatives.

research box 1.2

Caring activities

Why the study was undertaken – To analyse public perceptions of caring.

Methods – Secondary analysis (that is, looking again at existing data from a general survey and analysing it in a new way).

Caring activity	Description
Personal care	Dressing, bathing, toileting
Physical help	Walking, getting in and out of bed
Paperwork/financial matters	
Other practical help	Preparing meals, shopping, housework, household repairs
Keeping someone company	
Taking someone out	
Giving medicine	Including injections, dressings
Keeping an eye on someone	Checking that that they are safe

Source: Parker and Lawton (1994).

While this suggests a potential hierarchy of care from the most to the least personal, people may not value one kind of care more than another. It is partly a matter of need and relationship. Intimate relationships are likely to include caring. Any form of caring might contribute to the intimacy of the relationship and be valued for that reason. If you have a need, for example to have your shopping or disability pension collected, you might value that form of care, even though it is not particularly intimate.

Dalley (1988), reviewing ideologies of caring in community care policies, distinguishes between:

- 'Caring for' someone in a practical way; Parker (1981) calls this 'tending'
- 'Caring about' which is concerned with feelings for another person.

Graham (1983) argued that the identification of women's psychological make-up as being 'caring' focuses on caring about rather than caring for. Parsloe (1989) argued that we should only refer to caring where carers demonstrate love and affection alongside their tending. Hochschild (2004) contends that present-day society demands new forms of 'emotional management', in which we generate 'emotional capital' through relationships, so that we build up the personal strength to be caring and, on the other hand, limit the expenditure of emotional capital by, for example, avoiding less-important relationships.

Mayeroff (1971), however, suggests a process by which, in all care, the practical becomes emotional because the nature of tending or 'caring for' leads to 'caring about'. By caring practically, carers grow committed to the care-receiver's needs for self-actualization. This is important for social care, because it connects informal care with citizen care. A paid carer with, for example, no emotional link through a family relationship, can develop an emotional commitment to caring for a particular person through their practical work. Although citizen care, where the state accepts responsibility for providing caring services, is distinguished from informal care, where emotional commitment comes from personal relationships, they are connected because citizen care generates emotional commitment and connectedness between carer and care-receiver through engagement in achieving the self-actualization of the cared-for person, although it may only do so if there is continuity and good practice.

From personal caring to social care

Personal and citizen caring are, therefore, clearly linked. Ackroyd (1997) suggests that in the UK, caring has two important features:

- As utilitarian and practical, rather than being seen as a moral virtue; the research in Research Box 1.1 supports this
- A contribution to the social order and integration of society.

Right-wing or conservative attitudes see caring for others as part of a movement towards social integration, national solidarity and the foundation of economic prosperity. Socially liberal philosophies see caring as an *expression of* social harmony, rather than as *contributing to* it. Both of these political positions about caring, however, emphasize how an ethics of care through connection between people is seen as part of the solidarity of a society.

Consequently, Western societies have developed practical arrangements that use the concept of care to describe what they are doing (McBeath and Webb, 1997). Professions, such as medicine, nursing, social work and counselling became increasingly socially important (Halmos, 1965, 1970) to meet the moral need to reduce suffering. They all require relationships between individuals as private citizens, state institutions and economic markets. The state and the market intervene in and regulate hitherto private lives and make public the private, individual care relationships. Care practitioners' jobs are made more difficult by this social tension between privacy and intervention.

State care is connected with the state's responsibility to maintain a stable social order through various means of social control (Close, 1992). This has two implications. First, caring responsibilities exert various forms of state control; at least people may fear this. Second, in under-taking state care, the state replicates an existing social order. However, seeing social care as mainly about social control equates social control with the arbitrary exercise of power by an elite (Cowger and Atherton, 1974). Irvine (1978) argues that social work, and by implication social care, relies on much milder social processes. It should be contrasted with non-intervention and its possible outcomes. Day (1981) argues that practitioners face a dilemma between caring as a means of development and self- and social fulfilment and responsibilities for social control of behaviour by persuasion and coercion, which requires them to main-tain a practical balance. For example, it might be controlling to visit a person with learning disabilities at home each day, but failing to do so might leave them unable to care for themselves properly.

Part of that intervention and regulation is the development of policy about informal care, which distinguishes it from and gives it priority over formal citizen care. Bytheway and Johnson (1998) show that, before the 1960s, caring was not differentiated from other social rela-tionships, particularly within families. In the UK, awareness grew that increasing numbers of people were providing care for elderly depend-ents. Policy developed in response, for example the first social security allowance for carers, an invalid care allowance (ICA) in 1975. The growth of lobbying groups led to legislation (see Table 5.2). This required the definition of people as carers in official language and procedures. Since the 1980s, people who are informal 'carers' of others have been identified and distinguished from related ideas in English social policy (Barnes, 2006). During this period, citizen care has increasingly been seen as supplementing informal care, bringing state inter-vention into the private domain.

Such an attitude is still commonplace: I once used the professional jargon 'carer' with a man, to receive the reply: 'Oh no, I'm not her carer, I'm her husband'. However, people do sometimes see the distinction. One of my colleagues recently organized a week's stay with his wife in a nursing home for a very disabled man with a progressive (that is, contin-ually worsening) neurological disease. She returned saying what a wonder-ful opportunity it had been to be a wife again, instead of being a 'carer'.

Providing enough care of the right quality is never possible. A 'care deficit', that is a gap between the amount and type of care that people might ideally want or need, has been commonplace throughout history (Hochschild, 1995). Therefore, economic factors and the need to ration inadequate provision are important ways in which citizen care leads the state to intervene in the private domain. There may also be a question of balance between quality and quantity. One man I worked with put up with the female staff in his care home, but preferred the one male carer on the staff and delayed some personal physical care tasks until the male carer was on duty. This suggests that it may be possible to improve the experience of caring for people where resources are not good enough by improving quality in a way that connects with users' wishes and values.

After childhood, people are normally self-caring in meeting these needs. While people cannot self-care all the time, it is rare to need caring for everything all the time. Connected with this, people's ideas about what is caring come from family and cultural expectations. This is because they are such a natural and universal aspect of everybody's lives that everyone assumes that the way it is in their culture or family is the way it should be. Their idea of caring is integral to who they are as human beings, and to their social background and culture. That is another way in which caring is 'social'. Our understanding of it comes from our closest interpersonal relationships and from the depths of our cultural background.

When we care for someone, we become knowing about them and their needs, we make special efforts to be with them, we do things to them and we enable them to do things themselves. Knowing, being, doing and enabling emphasize the human interaction aspect of caring, although of course we can give them jargon labels such as assessment and intervention.

A related idea is the concept of 'caring presence'. Engebretson (2000) explores a range of nursing writing that emphasizes a non-instrumental 'overt physical presence' (p. 243), by being open, receptive, ready and available, as an important part of caring. This involves:

■ An orientation to time that focuses on the present, rather than future or past

- Use of silence as part of communication and interaction, conveying sincerity and paying attention to the person as a whole, rather than using words to concentrate on cognitive or thinking aspects of the relationship
- Being physically present with someone and doing things with them, as well as psychological presence in focusing on both people being together
- Focusing on immaterial and immeasurable things, not just those that can be measured and described
- Concentrating on detail and subtle aspects of the relationship.

Many of these accounts of good care echo Tronto's (1993) ethical elements of care, discussed above.

Caring: implications for practice

In summary, informal care arises in interpersonal relationships in family and social networks where people have emotional commitments to each other. Social care is a form of citizen care where the state and the market contribute care services to informal care, intervening in private and personal domains. Merely 'providing' or 'delivering' services without the context of strong interpersonal relationships does not meet the requirements of being caring. Therefore, social care practice must both recognize its distinction from personal caring, but remain connected to it by incorporating personal and emotional elements into relationships.

There are two aspects of caring: developmental caring, an active, committed responsibility for another person's development (masculine) and a receptive, connected aspect, an availability to another's needs arising from connectedness between human beings within society (feminine). Both of these aspects are required in social care, because it involves a connected society, through a social care service, taking responsibility for the service user and informal carer, and also doing so in a way that is receptive, by offering a caring presence. Social care gains its direction from the self-fulfilment of the person being cared for, and thus gaining emotional commitment to meeting their needs. This means providing for physical needs, because these always occur in a social context, in which social and cultural expectations provide a basic understanding that caring means receptiveness to both physical and emotional needs. Therefore, the receptiveness element of caring provides a practice method.

We have seen that approaches to caring derive from important intellectual traditions in Western society and people's understanding and expectations about caring come from their social and cultural traditions. Being a practitioner in social care, therefore, means understanding something of the social context in which caring takes place. I therefore turn to the 'social' in social care.

The social

What is 'the social'?

A 'social' is an event in which people meet each other informally over drinks and snacks. 'Social life' is that aspect of leisure where we build relationships with people and do things that we like, rather than relationships with people we work with. 'Social networking' websites are virtual locations for making connections between people in their social lives. 'Social' refers in all these phrases to activities where relationship connections are more important than material things; it is the same in care and caring. Social relationships are organized into patterns, so that we can see people in groups with similarities, either similar interests or similar characteristics.

The 'social' is important in social care because it focuses on:
■ The impact of services such as health and education on people's personal social relations
■ Recruiting social institutions to help people with their problems, including both social institutions that are widely established sets of relationships within which it is accepted people deal with personal distress, such as families and communities, and also organizations such as home care agencies and locations such as care homes and day centres
■ Social and cultural expectations and assumptions about how care should be provided.

For example, most people would see the hospice where I work as a healthcare institution, a social institution of the 'organization' type, employing healthcare staff such as doctors and nurses to help people with advanced and serious illnesses remain self-caring for as long as possible. Most of the work involves managing physical symptoms and maintaining physical functioning. However, patients and their families, social institutions of the 'relationship' type, have to organize themselves to deal with the problems that arise from one of its members being seriously ill; they often come together as that social institution 'the family' more than at other times. Patients and their families have emotional and relationship difficulties: they must deal with the prospect that someone close to them will die soon, they may well want to sort out past problems in relationships with that person, or say 'goodbye' or 'I love you' to them. They may have practical difficulties in applying for appropriate social benefits and organizing additional services at home to care for someone who is very ill and disabled. None of these requirements are centrally about what healthcare staff provide, and are mainly the function of social work and social care staff who focus on interpersonal interactions within social institutions and dealing with organizations (Payne, 2004).

Biological explanations of the social emphasize that human beings are 'social animals' like many other creatures. That is, they live together in groups because cooperating is a more effective way of surviving than being isolated and fighting for yourself. An important aspect of surviving in this way is caring about and caring for others in the group and the survival of the group as a whole. Like many other traits of human behaviour, caring is probably ingrained by many millennia of experience and evolution that make it a worthwhile survival mechanism. We develop those biological preferences by socializing our children into ways of behaving that connect with that caring human nature, but also create social structures that make sense in the interpersonal relationships that societies are built up from. The social therefore refers to more than the evolved biological nature of human beings including:

- Recurring social structures into which human relationships and networks are fitted
- Ways of conducting and organizing social relationships and connections
- Psychological ways of understanding and thinking about social relationships and structures.

These elements of society are part of what Habermas (1984) calls the *lifeworld*. This comprises such aspects of society and social relationships as family, community, value commitments, social cohesion and inclusion and face-to-face communication. Social care, because of its focus on care, is the aspect of government, education and healthcare services that represents the lifeworld as opposed to what Habermas calls the *system world*. This comprises state capitalism with its large bureaucratic and capitalist organizations and an emphasis on the technical rather than the personal and cultural.

Social care is also, however, part of the system world, because of its position as part of large government agencies and increasingly because of its role in managing a quasi-market system of service provision. Thus, it represents both the state and capitalism. However, one of its roles is to humanize the system world with aspects of the lifeworld. It is, therefore, both an aspect of and in tension with the system world. This tension is the source of many of the conflicts and ambiguities in social care work that we have been discussing. Caring is positioned within private, localized, emotionalized social relationships, while as citizen caring, social care joins the more public, and often the official, with the private. This joining of the public, the social, and the formal with the private, the individual and the informal is a central tension of social care practice, because practitioners have to deal with the fact that social care leads to the intrusion of the public into the private. We have seen that practitioners do this by incorporating important generic elements of caring into its intrusion.

The cultural

All these social and organizational matters are crucially affected by culture. Smith (2001) suggests that culture may have a variety of meanings:

- The totality or sum of the social life of a particular nation or identifiable social group
- A heritage passed from one generation to another that provides identity to a particular social group or nation
- A set of values or rules of life that shape behaviour or social expectations
- A set of ways of solving problems by allowing people to communicate and share understanding of emotional needs
- An abstraction referring to a set of ideals or beliefs that define the identity of a particular social group
- An account of how particular ways of human interaction or intergenerational transmission of values or heritage developed as a way of expressing a group's social identity.

Ideas about studying culture developed from the study of literature as writers identified particular values and ideals expressed through literature and the arts. This then led to studies of how different social groups react to various ideals and values, for example the suggestion that working-class communities or particular age groups such as young people have values or social preferences that differed from those of other groups (During, 1993). Working-class people have different gender relationships between the sexes from middle-class people and each generation of young people preferred different kinds of music to older generations. Cultural studies have also examined trends arising from social change and changing values. Important recent cultural trends that have had an impact on social care are as follows.

- Changing attitudes to risk mean that Western societies are more risk-averse, because people have become used to the state managing natural and social events to avoid risk of injury and problems (Beck, 1992; Adam et al., 2000; Cvetkovich and Löfstedt, 1999; Denney, 2005; Webb, 2004). However, in social care, risks are inevitable to enable people to develop freely. Risk therefore needs to be embraced in social care practice as a desirable given in people's lives in a political and social context where risk is avoided. Effective engagement and assessment (Chapter 4) are crucial to this.
- Modern Western societies emphasize expectations of increasing material wealth, possessions and better services, and people enjoy a lifestyle of increasing consumption, generating continuing economic development in a globalized economy. Collective services in this context become alienating because they are not individualized. This promotes a search for individualization, selfishness and competition, rather than collective participation in shared community concerns (Payne and Askeland,

2008). Thus, social care practice has to find ways of respecting individual aspirations in a context of collective service provision. The New Labour government's 'modernization' agenda in public services is substantially about finding ways of doing this through enabling people to have choices in the way their services are provided, and social care is integral to this policy of personalizing the collective. Good care planning (Chapter 5) is an important way of doing this.

■ Social capital derived from citizens' participation in collective community development is lost and people unable to participate in the global economy because of illness, disability or age are excluded from participation in social relations. Social care practice has to maintain people's participation in social relations that are important to them as far as possible. It may also be useful to maintain a sense of inclusion by enabling participation in self-care, in involving informal carers and in managing social care services, since these are so important in the lives of people with long-term disabilities. Aspects of the services that promote self-direction, in particular direct payments, advocacy and personalization (Chapters 5 and 6) are important in social care practice because of this.

■ The state becomes increasingly managerialist, with political responsibility for managing the 'delivery' of effective services to consumers, rather than promoting shared commitment to enabling citizens to receive services as rights. Communitarian values are also prevalent, meaning that people must earn their care by past contributions or present commitment to work or other contributions to society. Social care practice can develop collaboration and communication with colleagues and agencies to personalize the managerial (Chapter 5) and carry out assessment, care management and planning and ending and review processes (Chapters 4, 6 and 7) to combat these cultural trends.

■ Faith and social commitments become individualized and competitive personal belief systems, rather than shared ideologies that require commitment to the common good. Difference becomes politicized and conflictual. Aspects of personal identity such as ethnicity, gender, nationality, sexuality and political and social views as well as characteristics such as mental illness, disability and age that are directly the focus of social care become politicized. This raises concern about potential discrimination on grounds of aspects of personal identity. It therefore becomes an important role of social care both to avoid discrimination on these grounds and more broadly to promote inclusion and equality. Indeed placing services in a context of securing greater equality has become an important aspect of public policy (Equalities Review, 2007).

■ Economic and political globalization lead to migration from poor to rich countries, regions and parts of towns, and bring people of different cultures and social expectations in touch with each other. This means that people and social care practitioners have to deal with challenges to people's self-identity or clashes of culture and faith, and experience the uncertainties of societies affected by constant change.

Such differences between social groups may connect with political or faith allegiances, economic interests or broad social trends. Cultural concerns interconnect with inequalities between social groups. For example, people from lower socio-economic groups die earlier than people in higher socio-economic groups. This is associated, among other things, with cultural preferences for less healthy behaviour than higher socio-economic groups and experiencing more stress in their jobs than middle-class people because they have less control over their work (Siegrist and Theorell, 2006).

The social and cultural: implications for social care practice

Social care's focus on the social and cultural underlines the importance of developing and maintaining consistent and responsive interpersonal relationships as the basis of practice. However, the social and cultural emphasizes that focusing on people's social and cultural identities is a specifically 'lifeworld' perspective on society that social care incorporates into a wide range of other practices in education and healthcare. In doing so it engages in and responds to social trends such as a focus on risk, material consumption, social exclusion, managerialist and communitarian values and the prevalence of inequality and discrimination. Creating a balance of risk and opportunity, personalizing provision, promoting inclusion and participation, collaboration and equality thus become crucial elements of social care practice.

Social care and social work

Social work describes a job, usually regarded as a profession. Its professional status comes from its established roles as a middle-class occupation in government and other public services, requiring higher education and interacting with similar groups such as teachers and nurses to provide complex services requiring knowledge, discretion and a degree of altruism (Payne, 2006).

Social care emerged in the 1990s, as the Introduction argued, developing two aspects of the social services in which social work was the dominant profession:

- An expansion and institutionalization of caring within residential and day settings as a separate occupational group
- The development of care management in organizing packages of service provision in community settings.

These developments provide a renewed and redirected focus for social work. For the first time in social work, they emphasize the importance of both caring tasks and also effective service provision as part of social work. Previously, service provision was seen as an adjunct to therapeutic social work, which aimed at social and behaviour change. It was something social workers did because social work was the main profession leading wider social services and because advocating for services and making services available supported their social and behaviour change objectives. Professional development focused on therapeutic social work, as a 'professionalization project' in which social work, particularly in the USA, sought to achieve professional status in the first half of the 20th century (Payne, 2006).

Internationally, there is a range of social professions. These include, within Europe, the social pedagogue or social *éducateur*, and, in developing countries, the practice of social development work. Thus, in many countries, there are, alongside social work, different patterns of professional organization among occupational groups that work within the 'social'. In the UK, the separate profession of youth and community work is allied to education, whereas in many countries it would be regarded as part of social work. It is, therefore, common for a country to contain a number of social professions, responding to the particular organization of welfare that derives from that country's history and culture.

Conclusion

The discussion above of the ideas of 'care' and 'caring' draws attention to the way in which it must always be 'social':
- Care and caring come from social and cultural expectations. How people understand them changes as social expectations and understanding alter. Experience in particular historical contexts influences relationships and therefore affects how people see and 'do' care.
- Care takes place in relationships that are important to the people involved for reasons other than the provision of care.
- Care is connected with important social structures and ideas, in particular family, community, social network and citizenship.

Therefore, social care emphasizes those aspects of any social services concerned with:
- Social connections and relationships
- Strengthening social institutions and groups important in interpersonal connections and relationships
- Connections between social groups and organizations
- Responses to social and cultural trends.

Social care practice constantly draws on these ideas, and if it fails to do so, it is not good social care practice.

- Social care is a valuable change in focus within social work and social services, and we need to understand the practice and theory changes that result.

- What is social care? – a sector of the economy, a professional practice, a part of health and social care, a type of social work, and therefore a social profession.

- Caring aims to help people grow or actualize themselves, tending to their practical needs and engaging with them emotionally.

- Informal care takes place in family and social networks deriving from personal relationships.

- Citizen care, of which social care is an example, derives from the state accepting responsibility for providing caring services to citizens.

stop and think

- What does your own experience and analysis tell you about care?
- What is the main image you have of someone caring for another person and what kind of behaviour do you think of as caring?
- In what ways does care involve social aspects of life?
- If you are able to share your answers with a group, discuss what implications the alternative views might have for care services.

- Balloch, S. and Hill, M. (eds) (2007) *Care, Community and Citizenship: Research and Practice in a Changing Policy Context*. Bristol: Policy Press.
- Fink, J. (ed.) (2004) *Care: Personal Lives and Social Policy*. Bristol: Policy Press.
- Hugman, R., Peelo, M. and Soothill, K. (eds) (1997) *Concepts of Care: Development in Health and Social Welfare*. London: Arnold.

Websites

- An authoritative official source is the social care website of the Department of Health: http://www.dh.gov.uk/en/Policyandguidance/Healthandsocialcaretopics/Socialcare/.
- Regular news and information about social care is published in the journal *Community Care* and its associated website: http://www.communitycare.co.uk.
- CSCI annual reports are available from http://www.csci.org.uk/

2 Valuing users and carers

Normalizing and valuing: objectives in the caring arena

In this chapter, I argue that an important social care aim is to normalize caring in the social context of the places where people live. Normalization, also called 'social role valorization', is derived from work with people with learning disabilities. It means providing a living environment that offers a quality of life and social roles that would be valued by most people (Ramon, 1991; Race, 2003). Most people value connectedness with their community, family and social network, so care should maintain and enhance their connections. Social care services have a history and social role that often hinders the achievement of normalization.

Chapter 1 suggested that social care provision exists because people expect that the state will provide for its citizens' care needs. I showed that responding to people's emotional and social needs means receptiveness and skilled presence to help people develop through their lives. These seem desirable and unexceptional ideas, so why do people dislike social care? Part of the reason for this is the attitudes revealed in Research Box 1.1: social care is seen as virtuous, but hard, unpleasant work. People needing social care may be pitied, and most people hope that they will neither need this kind of care nor have to provide it.

Therefore, when people use or, as a carer, call on social care, they must adjust to a new identity as 'social care user'. Children receiving care or supervision are marked out from other children. An older person may be forced to realize that their life, certainly their independence, is coming to an end. A disabled person may be separated into specialist accommodation, or have their home adapted for safety or care. A carer is doing things that people mostly do not want to do, involving unpleasant physical contacts, or a regular commitment that becomes a burden. Instead of being a spouse where bodily contact is for companionship, love and sex, for carers, bodily contact is often about tending to physical needs. Practitioners present people with the reality that they must accept this unsought change in identity and have to help people accept being 'users'. A crucial aspect of social care practice, therefore, is understanding and dealing with how people's identities change as they become social care service users, and the people in their social networks become carers.

Identity is a person's sense of self; it comes from their experience of the culture and social relationships around them. The sense of self that identity confers is continuous: it links past, present and hoped for futures with the values that someone has acquired from their social and cultural experience. Those links are often with a place. Most people try to maintain a two-way connectedness with what was valuable in their past lives and an exchange with other people in their family, community and social network. That connectedness promotes a sense of identity, shared values and mutual support for everyone involved. Those interconnections are also with a locality, a place, that seems normal to them in their present identity.

Many people fear needing social care, because these changes in social identity for service users and their informal carers turn their interconnectedness and interdependence into isolation and dependence. It is worse if they also lose their connectedness with the place that contributes to their identity. No longer independent and self-caring, they worry about needing other people to do what we usually expect to do for ourselves. Users need 'help', 'supervision' or 'support'. All of this implies that they cannot help themselves, cannot be trusted alone, cannot do things they need to do. They become an object of someone else's decisions and priorities, not their own. They become dependent on a stranger for doing things that normally they do themselves or that people with whom they have continuing social relationships do for them. Strangers may enter and disturb a user's private territory, home, even bedroom and toilet. Users may have to leave their home, leaving a secure and connected place, share a residential home with strangers or take part in programmed activities in a day centre. They fit with someone else's timetable and priorities.

In social care, that intrusion into privacy is organized and paid for by the state. This is particularly true of disruptions in place that come about because of care needs. A child may be taken by compulsion away from their parents or usual home area. Mentally ill people may be compelled to enter a hospital. In both cases, this may be connected with criminality, and the process involves legal actions. Disabled and elderly people may be forced by circumstances to use special accommodation. Even people who can afford to buy the accommodation or care they need, do so in the market for social care, which they are unaccustomed to and hoped to avoid. People hear that it has poor standards. They may fear loss of privacy through a means test, or having to move and sell their home, their *place*, to pay for care. Others who are independent disdain many care services. The history of residential care makes it a punishment or a criticism if you have to use it; it is devalued as a place for living and caring.

Social care practice, therefore, has to be concerned with sustaining and changing users' and carers' social and place identities. Also, social care is undertaken in a *caring arena*, where a care organization, represented by its practitioners, intersects with and intrudes upon the community, life and relationships of a person receiving care. Figure 2.1 shows this as a diagram, and it is developed in Figure 3.1, there seen as part of agency structure. The caring arena is a specialized place, even if it is the user's own home, where users and people around them interact with care provision. There may be special equipment, or a safe place that confines the user; they may have to sleep downstairs or use a stairlift; their private room or bathroom becomes a place where strangers do care tasks. None of the participants in care is fully in control of the caring arena, neither practitioner nor user and carer; others decide the places that users have to move to, or the equipment supplied.

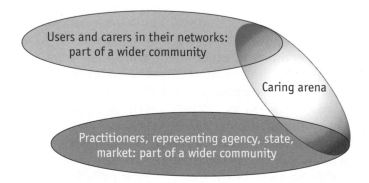

Figure 2.1 The caring arena

Identity and place are crucial aspects of working in social care for two reasons. First, the social relationships and contexts in which care is given and received create how care is and how the participants think about it. If caring arenas are devalued because they involve intrusion, the care provided will also be devalued. Practitioners have to prevent or deal with the impact of this. Social care practice has to connect with the caring values of the people it serves. If it fails to do so, it will attack the connectedness and integrity of their identity with the places and identities that they value. Instead, social care will be associated with the caring arenas that cut them off from valued identities and which, therefore, devalue them.

Second, social care is often provided in social settings, such as residential care, devalued by their history and context. Social care practice, therefore, has to create caring relationships with people in a context hostile to caring relationships. Social care practice, therefore, must ensure that family or community remain caring, even though they have been intruded upon, and building-based institutions such as residential or day care become valued caring arenas. An essential aim of social care is to normalize the caring arenas where the care system and people's community lives intersect.

Because social care must normalize and value the connectedness of the people it works with, understanding people's identity as part of their communities is a crucial aspect of our work. This means gaining an awareness of the social factors affecting them, because:

- To be receptive, social care requires knowing and understanding and is therefore based on knowledge and evidence
- Social care aims to help people grow, and so provides an environment in which they can do so
- Social care involves working collectively with service users, informal carers and colleagues in social care and colleagues in other professions, and this means working through and understanding both social and residential institutions.

Agencies and policies that form them are dealt with in Chapter 3. This chapter refers to social factors and the main elements of care services that create users' identities and form the care arena. Practitioners need understanding of these to be able to value and normalize the experience of users, carers and their communities in the caring arena.

General social factors

Since social care is *social*, we need to understand how social factors influence the demands made upon us, and the interpersonal reactions of users and carers. Otherwise, social care would be a form of counselling or psychotherapy. What gives social care its special character is its regard for the importance of the social on the personal, and the commitment for empowering the personal to respond to the social. Among the range of general social factors that social care workers need to consider are:

- Demographic and population change
- Social structures such as family, community and social network
- Cultural, political and philosophical changes in society.

This section explores ways of keeping in touch with thinking about these issues. Social care practice needs to understand users' and carers' social values, so that care services incorporate those values as normal and acceptable.

Demographic and population change

The demographic changes most relevant to social care concern ageing, health information and information about children. The following information is summarized from the UK National Statistics Office website (see the list of websites at the end of the chapter). The UK population is growing and getting older; this is also true of many other developed countries. The overall population grew by about 8% between 1971 and 2005, and the proportion of children and young people under 16 fell from 25% to 19% of the population in the same period. The overall population is expected to grow by a further 12% between 2004 and 2031, an increase of 7.2 million people. The percentage 65 years old and above grew from 13% to 16%, and is expected to grow to 23% by 2031. The population aged between 65 and 85 grew from 7% to 12% between 1971 and 2005. In 2005, there were 1.2 million people over 85 years in the population. The population will continue to age during the first half of the 21st century. Most of these trends come from changes in births during the 20th century, but there is also a decline in the proportion of deaths in the population. The demographic support ratio will also change: in 2004 there were 3.33 people of working age for every person over 65 years while in 2031, there will be only 2.62. The increases are likely to be highest in England; other UK countries have different patterns and are likely to have less population growth. There has been a general pattern in recent years of high in-migration and out-migration, but the net inflow of migrants has been higher than the outflow since 1994.

These population changes have both a general impact on our society and also on how families operate and care for each other. In particular, there is political concern in many countries about the growing proportion of older people and the decline in the proportion of children, because this might mean that there will be increasing problems in caring for older people who are unable to care for themselves. However, historically, it is unclear whether population change leads to social change or whether social and cultural changes lead to population changes to accommodate the wishes of people living at the time. Probably, the influence of these factors on each other is complex. Social care practitioners need to understand the perceptions that users and carers have of the changes in the community and respond to the expectations that these create.

practice example

I recently met an older couple who enjoyed the colour and excitement of the vibrancy with which their community had been renewed by African Caribbean families moving to their locality. 'I remember how dull it was just after the war', the husband said to me. However, they were aware of how changes in familiar shops and life on the streets had frightened neighbours who became isolated because many friends had died or moved away. This example illustrates that we must try to understand both the social change itself and also how people react to it and the consequences for their relationships.

Among the most useful websites for finding out about population change are government statistics organizations. Statistics websites for the UK, Europe and the USA are listed at the end of this chapter. Other websites that often offer useful statistical information are the government websites for the particular service you are involved in. Finally, academic websites may provide additional information, or findings that allow you to be critical of the information obtained from official sources.

Family and social networks

The social context in which most care, both informal and paid, is provided is people's own home environments. These are strongly influenced by the closest relationships around them: the social networks of their family and communities in the locality and of people who share the same interests and concerns. A social network is the connections between individuals created by interpersonal contacts and relationships. These links may support or hinder people in their lives and care services in their work. Therefore, understanding and working with people's communities and networks is a crucial part of social care.

People debate how to understand what a family is and its importance in social life. A traditional nuclear family consists of two parents and their children, an extended family may include grandparents, grandchildren, uncles and aunts, and often comprises several nuclear families. Different ethnic groups may have varying views about whether the nuclear or extended family should be the main focus of the family and of care. Questions have also arisen about whether variations from a conventional pattern are still a family. A childless couple, a single-parent household, an older couple whose children have left home or a gay or lesbian couple with or without children: are these families? Judgements about this have become politicized, as, for example, accepting gay and lesbian couples as parents is assumed to reflect acceptance of a gay or lesbian lifestyle as 'normal'. This has consequences for social care because if it is an acceptable lifestyle, such people might also have recognized public responsibilities, such as fostering or adopting children.

Working around such debates, Morgan (1996: 11) suggests that the term 'family' should be used to refer to 'sets of practices which deal in chosen ways with ideas of parenthood, kinship and marriage – like the expectations and obligations which are associated with those practices'. Taking this view while doing assessments, people's social relationships and practices help decide if and how they are carrying out some of the responsibilities of being a family. For example, a divorced couple might both take part in parenting, but there is no standard way of organizing this. One important aspect of family relationships is caring for each other. Generally, but not always, people in family relationships take more responsibility for care of each other than people who are not. However, complex social negotiations take place about this, building on a developing commitment to each other, as the study in Research Box 2.1 shows. Practitioners, therefore, need to think about valued patterns of relationships in the families of users that they work with, and try to attain care patterns that respect those values.

Negotiating family responsibilities

Why this study was undertaken – To understand why and by what social processes some family members accepted responsibility for the care of others in a family.

Methods – A two-stage method involved, first, a survey of 978 people, asking questions about their response to vignettes, brief accounts of situations involving personal care, accommodation and financial help. A further qualitative study by interviewing 88 people provided more detailed information about the views of Asian and African Caribbean people.

Results – Kin relationships are significant sources of people's social support, but there are no specific duties associated with particular relationships. A sense of responsibility grew over time, as people developed commitments by exchanging help in different situations. In particular instances, there were informal and sometimes inexplicit negotiations. People's personal identity, as a 'good' son or 'caring' daughter, was bound up in their commitments. There were general social rules about the factors that should be taken into account in the negotiation. For example, parent–child commitments were strongest 'downwards', from parent to child, but less strong 'upwards', because other responsibilities of an adult child balance a commitment to care for an older parent. While such commitments might develop between people other than kin, genealogical links are more likely to generate commitments of a more personal kind.

Source: Finch and Mason (1993).

Social networks are another way of understanding support that comes from connections between people. Network connections may be relationships in which there is regular interpersonal communication, or more distant connections. People's social networks include their families and range more widely. Social network ideas are relevant to caring relationships, both because they support family caring and because they may be alternatives to aspects of it. Social networks shade off into the community, and promoting them often advances the strength and resilience of communities and partnerships between agencies and community organizations (Trevillion, 1999). Networking assumes that people are interdependent. The direction and degree to which they are interdependent can be seen by the flow of resources between them. The environment in which relationships take place helps or hinders interdependencies. People identify networks as social structures where interdependent links have existed over a long period of time, for example between family members or long-standing community members (Trevillion, 1999: 18).

Practitioners need to identify networks that are valued by service users and again seek to incorporate them into the care that they provide, not isolating or excluding people from valued networks. This brings us to the idea of community as a way of understanding interconnectedness between people.

Community

Communities are established and institutionalized connections between people. There are two basic ideas about community: as an association with a locality that carries emotional commitment and as an association with other people who share common interests, a community of interest. 'Community', although originally implying 'of the common people', is a 'warmly persuasive word' (Williams, 1983: 66). It has no countervailing opposite and so always carries positive connotations. The most influential idea is that there is or should or might be a form of living that feels warm and supportive to its participants. In this way of living, there is solidarity between people who share interests or aspects of their lives; solidarity implies both connectedness and commitment to the connections. Often this solidarity is supported by proximity: life is carried on in the same locality. Networks, the social links between people, are closely integrated, so that people in a community see and interact with each other a lot and in several ways. An important aspect of political debate about this concept of community is the assumption that it once existed in many places and has been lost to a greater or lesser extent.

Confusion about ideas of community has been an aspect of social and political debate since the 19th century. Important landmarks of this debate are as follows:

- Tönnies's (1955 – originally 1887) formulation of the ideas of 'community' (*gemeinschaft*) and 'association' (*gesellschaft*). The first implies closely integrated groups of people, the second fragmented and divided societies, with the implication that the former is preferable.
- Studies of communities in the 1950s and '60s using anthropological methods, many summarized in Klein (1965). These have led to the suggestion that some traditional communities that had been in existence a long time created a warmer and more integrated style of living, in which families and neighbours supported one another closely. Crow and Allan (1994) argued that these have been disproportionately influential in developing ideas of 'community'.
- Anxiety from the 1930s onwards that because of changes in housing and economic changes such as the decline of traditional industries, the quality of this supposed traditional community life was being damaged; planning mechanisms sought to control physical development of towns to preserve communities.
- Consequently, sociologists have been concerned that as a result of the

political, policy and social implications of the use of 'community' as a universally positive notion, it could not be used as the basis for rigorous study of social life (see, for example, Stacey, 1969).

- Attempts to respond to social pressures in inner cities by special projects to develop a mutually supportive community where it was presumed not to exist, and through 'community politics' focused on local issues. The most famous of these projects were the 'community development projects' of the 1970s.
- Community can, therefore, be an arena for social conflict, rather than a source of cohesion and order. For example, communities may be the location of tensions that arise because different social groups suffer from inequalities or social oppression, and suffer the effects of such economic restructuring as the loss of work in manufacturing industries in favour of low-paid, part-time service industries (Day, 2006: chapter 6).
- Communities increasingly pursue their relationships in virtual ways. Young people may communicate by texting to build relationships and arrange contacts, rather than by meeting in youth clubs or other locations. Solid relationships among people with shared interests may be built up through emailing or the internet (Day, 2006: chapter 8).

'Community' can also mean 'non-institutional' and informal rather than officially organized care. These are distinctions noted by Bayley (1973) as meaning care *in* the community in smaller institutions but still by professional staff as opposed to care *by* the community outside institutions but by informal carers.

Finally, 'community' is used as a political and ideological term. Willmott (1989) shows how it is frequently attached to services that have elements of local organization to exact commitment from people by offering a feeling of involvement and connection. While this sometimes gains approval for official services by emphasizing their 'community' nature, it may also seek to emphasize the element of personal commitment and action expected of citizens.

These ideas have influenced social care. Social and political debate presumes that if community were present, social care would be less needed, so the social objective of creating or recreating community has become part of many public services, including social care. Moreover, the 'warm, persuasive' terminology has been taken into social work and various therapies. We talk about 'therapeutic communities', for example, to refer to a particular way of organizing residential and day care establishments and hospitals (Millard, 1992). Within social work and social policy, there are a number of distinctive meanings of 'community' to be aware of.

One meaning of community distinguishes it from the state, meaning an expression through organized political structures of the will of the people, and the community as an expression of people's collective actions.

In this distinction, 'community' implies ownership by the people involved rather than the separateness implied by provision through organized, politically defined collective provision. Related to this within community care and other community policies is a shift from collective provision, which is often associated with more socialist ideologies. A move towards more personal responsibility associated with 'New Right' ideologies was influential in the Conservative governments of the 1980s and '90s. Mayo (1994) notes how changes towards a 'mixed economy' of welfare imply different conceptualizations of 'community'. For example, government policy and user campaigning emphasize independence and participation by users and carers in services, and ideas such as personalization, rather than wider 'community involvement' in social care services.

Cultural and value changes

Chapter 1 examined some cultural assumptions that affect social care services. In this section, I draw out some cultural issues relevant to defining caring arenas, as follows:

- Personal and social identity comes from people's association with social and cultural groups. This includes socio-economic status and social class, ethnicity, gender, sexuality and our family and community background. Thus, what people see as important in social care derives from social and cultural experiences.
- Identity is also affected by being defined as within particular user groups and as carers. Thus, the social and cultural experiences of older people, people with learning disabilities or mental illness, and people with physical disabilities are partly defined by their special needs, other people's perception of them and their experience of services and institutions.
- Part of the experience of their needs and services is the experience of exclusion, either as a result of the needs that push people outside networks of relationships that most people value being part of, or because they belong to identifiable stigmatized social groups, such as minority ethnic groups, minority faith groups or groups with visible disabilities. Various associations create identity.

practice example

Karla was born Deaf, into a family where inherited Deafness meant that several people were part of the deaf community, and denoted their Deafness with a capital 'D' because they saw themselves as different from people who became deafened through accident or ageing. They communicated using sign language and much of her social life as a child was in organizations for Deaf people. At around her eighth birthday, she was offered a new operation that would give her some capacity for hearing. Proud of their participation in the Deaf community, some members of the family did not see this as a 'cure' for a disability, but as a potential loss of identity and social relationships. Karla's mother was involved in a doubtful debate about what this would mean for relationships in the family and in Karla's future life. She felt considerable anxiety deciding about the operation. Her doctor felt that it would be child neglect to fail to carry out the operation, and referred Karla to a social worker for assessment.

The social worker who dealt with this first acknowledged the strength of the feelings and the importance of family and social relationships to Karla and other family members. She also acknowledged how valuable the operation might be to Karla in her future life and career. Her approach to this, using some techniques from cognitive-behavioural theory, was to get Karla's mother and important members of the family to do 'homework' to think out in pairs some of the alternative realities of what might happen. In this family, Karla would not lose the opportunity or signing skills to participate, but she might gain other opportunities if she had the operation.

This example illustrates how disabilities and social experiences can create identities and communities that are important to the people involved. It also illustrates the social model of disability. Disabilities are not only the physical effects of Karla's impairment, compared with most people's hearing capacity. The social relationships that created a community for her and her family also excluded her from other communities, who might be prejudiced and lack understanding of things that they valued. Increasingly, political and social identities are associated with cultural, ethnic and faith values in this way.

Social, family, community and culture: implications for social care practice

Understanding social, family, community and cultural identities of users and carers is crucial to social care, because only by understanding can practitioners value users' personal and social identities, and only by valuing can they manage and provide services that normalize users' values in their practice. The caring arena of social care services brings the social policy and organizational framework outlined in Chapter 3 into contact with users' and carers' social lives. To be caring, in the sense described in Chapter 1, social care practitioners need to reduce the impact of intrusion into users' and carers' communities as networks.

Long-term care

Social care services often fail to normalize users' and carers' values because their main users are people who have long-term care needs and those who provide informal care for them. Parker's (1981) groundbreaking paper on 'tending' points out that duration, intensity, complexity and prognosis are crucial dimensions of the type of care required. People who are very physically, psychologically or emotionally dependent will need care:

- for long periods of the day
- over a long timescale
- covering many aspects of their lives.

It will also be care in caring arenas that makes the relationships between carer, the market, the state and the service user complicated; it is not the customer relationship of buying from a shop. Also, it is likely that their care needs will grow over time.

The fact that social care is long term, not a quick in-and-out therapeutic intervention or occasional advice and information, has important consequences for social care practice, making it different from social work, the psychotherapies or information services. For users, needing social care is often a life sentence, certainly a long one. Carers, family, network and community can expect a long-term and growing commitment. Long-term responsibility for an unknown, difficult situation means fear for the future and uncertainty. Once social care services are involved, people grow increasingly certain that a long-term commitment will be needed; they can never know the time or effort that will be required. Even for looked-after children it may lead to care and supervision for most of their childhood, and long-term effects into adulthood. Therefore, in the same way that in child care we plan for permanency and stability, so it should be in social care more generally.

Social care is mainly delivered in people's homes or in housing, care homes and day centre environments that pursue, even if they do not achieve, a policy of normalization. That is, social care services try to make the environment of care one that would be socially valued by most people. This has implications for practice, because part of the work of social care practice is to respond to identity change by creating socially valued institutions and environments as well as being caring. This institutional and environmental change is partly intended to reduce the stigmatizing effects of state intrusion in private lives, but it also increases official surveillance and control of private lives. Practice, therefore, has to focus also on increasing user and carer control of the environment to balance the consequences of intrusion and surveillance.

The elements of social care

How have social care services evolved to seek normalization? The current pattern of social care services reflects shifts in expectation and social attitudes during the 20th century, primarily about the place in which care is provided. Five factors have all had impact on the form and nature of social care and contribute to current efforts to change and develop social care so that it normalizes and values users' and carers' choices:

- Withdrawal from residential care

- Consequent emphasis on risk and protection in the community
- Organizing greater connectedness through day care provision
- Emphasis on family, home and carer support
- Development of independent living.

Withdrawal from devaluing institutional care

Institutional care has always existed alongside care in ordinary living situations. A long-term shift in favour of residential care took place in Europe from the 17th century onwards, mainly because of concern about social disorder (Payne, 2005). In its turn, social care is partly a current expression of the reaction against residential care. Therefore, to understand social care, we have to understand why residential care is devalued by people, and is itself devaluing.

The earliest forms of care in residential institutions were help given alongside religious communities, for example in monasteries and convents. Also, rich people made residential provision in their homes or estates for servants, slaves and people too old to work, in almshouses for instance, and local communities. The skilled trades helped people who were too old or disabled to work or had fallen on hard times. To give two examples of religious responsibility: in Christianity, helping others dignified the donor, and giving a proportion of income as charity to benefit family and community is integral to Islam. This history is important because it draws attention to the way in which residential care for the poor was provided by powerful elites in society, the aristocracy, the merchants and the church, both to demonstrate their religious and social responsibility and also to protect them from social disorder.

Disorder was feared from two sources. Initially, institutions and workhouses were set up to reduce the impact of destitution because poor people unable to work travelled, lost social and moral supports and could be disruptive in new communities. This provision served small, mainly rural communities and proved inadequate when large-scale change resulted from epidemics, war or other disruption. Later, the concern was urban disorder because the moral control of the Christian churches declined in Western societies when urbanization and industrialization led to large populations living in towns.

Urbanization also led to large institutions. Private madhouses were displaced by large state lunatic asylums and colonies for idiots and imbeciles, and local parish work schemes were displaced by large workhouses covering each urban area and coordinated nationally. In criminal justice, small local prisons became larger, regional and national, and industrial schools were set up for young offenders who were causing trouble and developed into Home Office 'approved schools' (in Scotland List D schools). An important aspect of the institutional system was, therefore, to affect the beliefs and regulate the attitudes and behaviour of working-class people to avoid these problems (Parker, 1988). These developments took place in a context, however, where it was assumed that the normal way of getting the necessities for maintaining life and health was through employment regulated by the economic market. Therefore, in this period, residential care maintained the economic and social order against the risk that poor people would disrupt it.

Institutional care has thus become associated with 'badness' and with dependence. Parker (1988: 8) suggests that all residential care has had a 'persistent image', being 'viewed with repugnance' by many people because:

- A repellent image has been deliberately cultivated, care a punishment or last resort, or, as in the case of workhouses, regimes being unpleasant to deter people from incurring costs for the state by using them.
- There has always been abuse of inmates. Corby et al. (2001) review the long history of public inquiries into abuse of children in residential care, and Martin (1984) examined the history of concerns about long-term care in hospitals.
- People in residential life are forced into live-in relationships with others whom they do not choose, and have to fit into enforced routines.
- Compulsion is commonplace. Many inmates are not free to leave. This may be because of legal compulsion or because of de facto restrictions. For example, rented accommodation in the community may be lost on admission to hospital or residential care, or a user may have to sell their home to pay for their care.

Parker (1988), reviewing the historical literature and contemporary investigations, shows that there was considerable variety and divergence in residential care institutions. Labour market assumptions that people had to be forced to work were the main factor in the development of the workhouses. This assumption began to be questioned in economic downturns, and the workhouses were completely overwhelmed by the destitution experienced in the economic depression of the 1930s.

Welfare state policies at the end of the Poor Law in 1948 allowed residential care to become a welfare service. Many of the pre-existing buildings continued in use, in the NHS as long-stay hospitals and in LAs as children's homes and homes for other groups, particularly older people (see: 'Social care, children's services and healthcare' in Chapter 3). However, professional thinking moved away from residential provision and towards a policy of community care (see: 'Community care and child care policy' in Chapter 3). Consequently, the NHS shifted away from long-stay care, closing most of its long-stay provision for people with learning disabilities, mental illnesses and older people between 1970 and 2000.

Residential care for young people has also declined in the last part of the 20th century (Berridge and Brodie, 1998), from about a third of children in care in 1980 to around 11% in 2005–6; the proportion in the 21st century has remained stable for some years (DfES, 2006c). Now children's residential care focuses on troubled young people or those who have special needs. However, children's residential care in particular has given rise to a large literature and important conceptualizations of caring relevant to and applied in social care (Clough, 2000; Ward, 2006). The role of social care practice in residential care is reflected in the two most recent extensive studies, published in late 1998 (Research Boxes 2.2 and 2.3). These show that concordance of social care aims between the official position and the staff culture is important in maintaining stability and good quality care. Box 2.3 particularly illustrates the importance of the developmental aspect of caring discussed in Chapter 1, including helping children to develop and move forward through successful relationships with social care staff. It also shows the importance of receptiveness to children's needs and valuing their good points.

Although there has been a longstanding policy to avoid residential care placements for disabled children, poor investment in suitable replacements means that many children are placed unsuitably. McConkey et al.'s (2004) survey of looked-after disabled children in Northern Ireland found that about a third were in residential placements, mostly in undesirable accommodation such as hospitals and residential homes for adults with learning disabilities. Also, home carers, who were mainly parents, had only limited respite and needs and numbers were underestimated.

research box 2.2

Structure and culture of children's homes

Why this study was undertaken – To understand how the structure and culture of the regimes in children's homes affected outcomes of care for the children in them.

Methods – Nine LA, voluntary and private sector children's homes were studied. There were two three-day visits a year apart, with six-weekly one-day visits in between, and regular telephone contact. Documentary information about the homes, residents and (to a lesser extent) staff was collected, there were two interviews with managers and then non-participant observation of practice in each home. Outcomes for residents on admission were identified from files and compared with what was achieved.

Results – All the homes changed physically (including one complete move) during the 12 months of the study. Individual and staff philosophy and practice also changed. Three homes were forward-looking and consistently worked well. Three fluctuated but managed to maintain ideals and aims. Two homes deteriorated, gradually losing a sense of aims and purpose. One fitted none of these patterns. All the changes were opportunist responses to resource availability or other opportunities, not to strategic decisions or through partnership with residents or other stakeholders. A sense of a 'treatment' service was lacking. Homes worked well if social, formal and belief goals were in concordance, and worked less well where there was dissonance. Where there was concordance, the staff culture was supportive of the children, who then also developed a positive culture of mutual support, which then led to good outcomes. Clear guidance on how to behave in dealing with common needs and incidents is identified that can help establish agreed cultures.

Source: Brown et al. (1998).

research box 2.3

Working in children's homes

Why this study was undertaken – To identify how the work of staff affected the life of residents in children's residential care homes through the culture and group dynamics in the homes.

Methods – A questionnaire survey of 39 homes and interviews with the manager. This was followed by a longitudinal study of six homes among that number, two from each of three LAs through monthly group meetings with staff over a period of at least several months and less than three years. The longitudinal study used an action research model, which fed back early results to help participants improve or change their behaviour, which was then studied in later stages.

Results – Residential work took place on three 'fronts' between staff and young people:

- Containing and controlling them so that they led an orderly life and to encourage acceptable behaviour
- Working individually with young people to meet needs that will allow their life situations to improve
- Providing experiences that repaired experiences that they have missed or lost.

Staff did this by trying to increase the occurrence of group situations that help residents and by reducing occurrences of group situations that were damaging and repairing the consequences of group situations that had produced difficulties. Their practice tried to avoid mixes of residents that might cause difficulties, noted and responded to early warning signs of difficulties in group relations and avoided behaving in ways that might escalate a difficult situation.

Good practice in achieving this involved creating orderly but flexible structures and routines for daily living, creating situations in which residents could demonstrate or learn skills, calling participative meetings to deal with difficulties, arranging enjoyable treats making sure that reasonable sanctions to manage difficulties were well understood by residents, and having activities in mind to divert difficulties before they arose. Consulting with residents, staff worked with individual residents to define goals that identified desired improvements, and took opportunities to work towards those goals, being flexible about how to achieve them, but persevering. Reparative experiences meant understanding what needed repair, disconfirming unhelpful fixed beliefs (for example that all adults are untrustworthy), finding daily experiences that confirmed progress, being ready to listen, while being sensitive to readiness to talk, combining non-verbal symbols and explicit acts of caring and valuing successes, through occasional celebrations. With groups, the work provided opportunities for activities that helped residents learn to work together, handle relationships with others successfully, gain self-respect and be valued by others.

Source: Whitaker et al. (1998).

Adult services for all user groups expanded, and changes in the 1980s led to a large private sector in residential care, where users paid their own fees, or were means-tested for LA support. The Wagner Report (1987) presented residential care as part of a continuum of care services, which should be a 'positive choice' for those who used it. The picture of residential care in the early 2000s, therefore, is of free acute care in the NHS, separated from paid-for, long-stay residential care for adult users in social care. Although part of the Wagner continuum, residential care is still a last resort, because of historical perceptions of being for mad, bad or dependent people, because it was expensive and of poor quality, and because people fear loss of control in their lives (Wanless Report, 2006). Thus, although claiming to provide 'care' it was often unable to provide continuity and connectedness with family and community and a focus on users' personal development, rather than poor quality 'warehousing' for people unable to manage in their own homes with home care.

The view is only slightly different with residential care for children, which is mainly in specialist homes for assessment, for care while children are in transit between adoption or foster care placements, and for treatment of young people with emotional and behavioural disorders. The temporary and specialist nature of residential care for children compromises long-term caring continuity, connectedness and receptiveness to their development. Not surprisingly, therefore, withdrawal from residential care for children continues, and, when needed, residential care is often not adequately caring.

Risk and protection

Residential care originally developed to protect residents, but failed partly because of the risk of abuse and poor care of residents. As residential care declined, focus on risk switched to concern about risks in the community. The neglect and abuse of children in foster care and under the care of their own parents has been a constant theme of scandals in social care, increasing in impact and pace since community provision for children in need has become the main provision (Parton et al., 1997). Reith (1998) argues, drawing on mental health inquiries, that with an increase in community care such scandals have transferred into inquiries into failings of community services. Since the 1980s, abuse of older people and vulnerable adults generally has also increased in profile (Tomlin, 1989; Pritchard, 2001).

Abuse and neglect of vulnerable children and adults have probably not increased, but the withdrawal from residential care has brought this issue into the domain of community services. The reduction of residential care provision also makes the plight of people at risk more apparent to the public around them; large-scale residential care in the 19th century protected the public from awareness and responsibility. Abuse in an era of community care takes place in private, in people's own homes, mainly by their relatives or carers. Public responsibility for doing something about it can only be achieved by intervention in people's private domains. Community caring services, therefore, must incorporate the role of surveillance to protect, as well as to care; this makes the practice of caring more complex, because the motives for intervention become ambiguous. Practitioners, carers and receivers of care are all aware that official engagement must in part include the questioning of private actions. It is hard for a practitioner to demonstrate unambiguous valuation of users and carers.

Work and day care

Increasing provision of day care is another social care response to the shift from institutions. Institutional care provides 24-hour care and surveillance. Day care aims primarily to provide occupation and a time structure to the day that mimics the pattern of working. In this way it supports the social expectation of employment as the main way of providing for life needs, demonstrating that if employment is not available, it should be prepared for or replaced by something similar.

It was not always so. Before the 19th century, fewer clear distinctions were drawn between occupation and community and family life. What people did for income was interwoven with the rest of their life's activities. 'Unemployment' arose during the 19th century as work shifted to be a separate activity carried out for employers in places of employment (Burnett, 1994). Out-of-school children's leisure came only after compulsory schooling in the 1870s. Before this, children would have been employed alongside members of the family in agricultural or home-based trades, or in service (Petrie et al., 2000). Associated with this social change, demands for child protection both in daily life and in employment led to protective legislation and to growing provision in care homes and through fostering.

Because of these social changes, people's lives were structured into occupations carried out during the day, such as schooling and employment, with leisure, family and community life being separated and undertaken mainly at other times. To some degree, there was also a gender split, so that men undertook employment outside the home, and women were more likely to be occupied caring for children and dependent members of the family. Unlike men, women were based mainly in the home, family and community, with paid work as a lower priority in their lives. Retirement pensions, established in the early 20th century, reinforced distinctions between work life, during which men worked and women were home carers and marginal workers, and retirement, during which people did not work and focused their lives in leisure, family and community. The welfare system established in 1948 recognized this, by providing social security benefits based on employment for men, with women dependent on their husband's employment for benefits.

Day provision in some areas of health and social care grew up, responding to the social trend towards work and home life being separated in time and place. The place- and time-structure of daily living separates these activities from family, leisure and general social life, which are valued for different reasons. This even affects retired people, since social life for the non-retired population structures everyone's time into the daytime, evening and weekend divisions created by work life. The 'occupation' of people in care is being treated so that they get well, or at least return to being self-caring, and can resume normal life, with its work/leisure splitting of time. Since care professionals are mainly employed along normal work–life divisions, there is more treatment activity during the day, with users mainly resting at night.

Day care development has been particularly important for people with learning disabilities and with mental illness. It developed early for people with learning disabilities because of the lack of occupation, personal and therapeutic development and satisfactory quality of life in the large colonies housing the 'feeble-minded' at the beginning of the 20th century. Decades of development led to employment-based day training centres or education-based social education centres, prime examples of a tendency to see day care separating aspects of life defined as work or education from leisure and care.

Mental health day care, originating in Russia in the 1930s, spread to the USA and Europe in the 1940s and '50s, reaching a peak in the 1970s. It involved day hospitals providing treatment substituting for in-patient care, vocational rehabilitation for people disabled by mental illness or by long-term institutionalization, and support for outpatient or community care (Marshall et al., 2001; Marshall, 2003). In addition, informal social support for people recovering from mental illness grew, often provided by local community and voluntary organizations. A systematic review has also shown that vocational rehabilitation of mentally ill people is more effective if it directly supports patients at work, rather than providing pre-vocational training in a hospital or day care environment. Day hospital provision was also found to improve psychiatric symptoms more effectively than outpatient care, but at no cost saving. The systematic review could find no studies of informal day provision that met the study criteria (Marshall et al., 2001). A failing of the research reviewed is that it focuses on relief of psychiatric symptoms rather than broader social objectives, which informal social day care might seek to respond to.

Home, family and carer support

The withdrawal from residential care has also meant an increasing focus on care and support for people in their own homes. For adults, this has developed from the provision of home care services. These emerged during the first and second world wars of the 20th century from services provided to support women required to work in the war effort but who were also caring for dependent children and older people. Support included home helps to do domestic and basic caring work, delivery of meals to dependents' homes (meals on wheels or mobile meals) and nurseries for early-years children. These facilities were retained and extended to a wide range of disabled and older people. They became part of LA public health services and becoming integrated into LA social services departments established in the 1970s (Means and Smith, 1998). With greater emphasis on caring tasks, they became a crucial element of community care services as they developed (Means et al., 2003). However, as it became apparent that the majority of caring tasks in people's homes were undertaken by informal carers, who were often women, a movement to provide services to carers as well as service users became a significant element of care legislation in the 1990s.

For disabled and older people, a significant home care service emerged from public health provision to assist people who become disabled while living at home. Practical supports and suitable equipment were developed. Post-war provision for disabled servicemen gave the design and provision of artificial limbs and other special equipment a boost. A further thrust came from campaigns for more consistent provision across the country, enacted in the Chronically Sick and Disabled Persons Act 1989, which required LAs to register and provide services and aids for disabled people. All these moves eventually led to disabled people having the possibility of greater independence, and to the social disability and independent living movements (see the next subsection).

Two important aspects of family care for children and young people are family support services and adoption and foster care. Family support covers a range of advice, advocacy and practical services to assist families in caring for children appropriately, emerging from war-time day nursery provision and community projects to support deprived children. The aim is partly to prevent children needing more full-time public care. One source of this work was the creation of family centres in the 1980s; parents, particularly mothers, come with their children, for early-years care and guidance and training on effective parenting (Stones, 1994; Gardner, 1998). A variety of community projects built on this experience (Gibbons, 1990). Research on these reinforced a move in the Children Act 1989 to focus on supporting parental responsibility. The Labour government of the late 1990s pushed this forward again, as Homestart projects tried to improve the life chances of children in deprived environments. Dolan et al. (2006: 14) suggest that useful elements of family support are concrete practical support, emotional support through empathy and listening to problems, advice and 'esteem' support, which shows parents how their efforts are valued. Thus, while family support provides a range of care directly for children, ideas such as esteem and emotional support for parents again connect with receptive and development caring, discussed in Chapter 1.

Adoption and foster care services occupy an uneasy position between being services caring for 'children in need', the legal formulation, and being services for childless couples wanting to parent children. Fostering is care for children and young people on behalf of their parents, usually through the LA, where it has assumed their care for various reasons. In the 1970s and '80s, evidence accumulated that many children in LA care ('looked after' by LAs in the current terminology) drifted from placement to placement with little clarity about long-term aims. This was partly because social workers sought to reunite them with birth parents. Securing 'permanency', early decisions about direction and permanent placements for looked-after children, has therefore become an important policy aim. Adoption started as a service for childless couples, but as fewer babies and young children have been available for adoption, it has become the most permanent and secure of placements for young children in the care system. In this way, adoption expresses the normalization and valuing strategy in child care, since it normalizes and values the adopters and the looked-after child.

Sellick and Howell (2004) surveyed foster care extensively in the early 21st century. While most foster care in the UK was organized through LAs, the private sector offered some provision, and voluntary organizations were influential, being historically important. Much of the work involves recruitment, training and retention of foster carers, who may be regarded as social carers, providing care in their own homes to children in need.

There were also special projects for children with complex and special needs. Among innovative provisions was a pension scheme for foster carers, whose role has often been seen as an uneasy mix of volunteering and paid work, where carers lose opportunities for pension provision and other benefits of employment. There were also information and support centres for foster carers, bonuses for long service and support for the birth children of foster carers, who of course also contribute to the care.

Development of independent living

Independent living has two elements: an ordinary living environment or ordinary housing, and user-controlled care.

Housing is a special place for most people, because it is private, being segregated from public spaces and is where private activities are carried out There are different types: for example, in big cities, in Scotland and mainland Europe people often live in flats, while in England living in houses is more common. There are also different types of tenure, that is the legal basis by which people have the right to use the house. The most common types of tenure are ownership, usually achieved by taking out a long-term loan called a mortgage, and renting. Families with low incomes gain security by renting 'social housing' from LAs and housing associations, which are voluntary sector housing providers. People with higher incomes, or unable to gain access to social housing, rent from private landlords (Pickvance, 2003).

Sheltered and supported housing includes elements of care, enabling people who would not be self-caring in independent accommodation to continue to have the privacy and control of their own housing rather than living in residential care. Thus, the focus of supported housing is the privacy of housing, rather than the collectivity of care. Usually, this is social housing, but some owner-occupied supported or sheltered housing schemes exist, mainly for older people. Providing care in sheltered or supported housing is a form of social care, and is usually organized as an aspect of housing welfare by LAs or housing associations.

Sheltered housing schemes are groups of homes adapted for older or disabled people. They are often therefore bungalows or flatlets with good access for people with impaired mobility. They are in groups to encourage mutual support and also to facilitate regular visits and contacts by a warden, who might carry out basic care tasks for residents, check on their safety regularly and respond to emergency calls for assistance. The original reason for grouping the housing was that alarm systems required wiring to be connected to each house. Improvements in technology, whereby people can wear radio alarms round their necks and call for assistance or receive a safety check, mean that siting housing together is less necessary. In some areas where sheltered housing schemes with alarm systems were not built, wardens or volunteers are employed to check on older people regularly, and electronic systems have been a useful development.

Supported housing began to emerge in the 1980s, when community care policy led to many people being discharged from psychiatric and learning disability hospitals. An early development was of group homes (Malin, 1983; Pritlove, 1985; Sinson, 1993), where a group of former patients lived together, with varying levels of support. However, as more disabled people began to be discharged, higher levels of support were required, and these included providing drop-in day care and a visiting team of support workers covering areas in which former patients lived in individual housing. This kind of provision retains the privacy of housing, while incorporating some of the intrusion of social care. These schemes were often not grouped together both because this might have led to increased stigmatization of the residents and also because the use of wired alarms was not necessary for this group of people. These developments led to a policy of 'ordinary housing' (Bayliss, 1987). That is, the aim was to enable residents to live in housing with the same degree of independence, self-caring and control of housing that would be preferred by non-disabled people. Since supported housing usually receives only periodic checks that residents are safe and that housing needs are met, support workers employed by LAs or housing associations are often supplemented with care workers from social care agencies providing long-term care, whose aims are personal development and social competence. For example, the government 'supporting people' scheme aimed at homeless people, offenders and others without a settled way of life, refers to 'housing-related support' (ODPM, 2004: 2) of a fairly routine kind.

Independent living derives from a movement by people with physical disabilities to reject collective living such as residential care, because formal services gained excessive control of the lifestyle choices of disabled people (Morris, 1993). The social model of disability proposes that physical impairments become disabilities because social expectations of normal physical functioning restrict disabled people's potential and freedom of action, excluding them from mainstream activities and discriminating against them in many areas of life (Barnes and Mercer, 2005). The commonplace example is the way stairs prevent wheelchair users from gaining access to buildings; non-wheelchair users would not be prevented from participation in ordinary activities. This view proposes that society should be organized to meet the rights of disabled people to participate as citizens in an ordinary life (Barnes and Mercer, 2002). One of those rights is to live in ordinary housing. LAs' responsibility to provide equipment and adaptations to houses to facilitate independent living under the Chronically Sick and Disabled Persons Act 1989 came together with the ordinary housing movement to provide a means by which disabled people could live independently. However, care to assist disabled people in their own homes was limited by the inflexibility and limited funding of LA community care. This led disabled people to campaign for legislation against disability discrimination during the 1990s and early 2000s.

Summary: the elements of social care

The elements of social care come partly from historical trends: they reflect a withdrawal from or reaction against, in particular, residential care. To replace residential care, a pattern of services has developed that provides limited residential care for specialist or complex needs. However, it has been replaced by care in small-scale care environments that increasingly focus on day care, so that people do not live where their care is, and the pattern of division between work and leisure typical of private sector employment since the 19th century is maintained in care services. It has also been replaced by care in people's own homes, largely by their own families, with support for the carers doing this work. Increasingly, social care has moved towards independent living in ordinary housing.

practice example

An example of this development of services is the first person with learning disabilities that I worked with in 1972, a woman in her late 50s. She had been classified as a 'moral imbecile' because she had an illegitimate child in the 1930s and had been living in what was then a mental handicap hospital for nearly 40 years. She was not particularly intellectually impaired. I arranged for her discharge to a rehabilitation care home and she subsequently lived an ordinary life in a group home.

Social care now

This account of the elements of social care shows how its present direction comes from the interaction of moves in professional attitudes influenced in the late 20th century by user campaigns. Examples are the reaction against residential care and the shift to independent living, and the arrangements made for particular user groups. It is clear that a model of social care practice is emerging from a lengthy history of social service provision. That model seeks to implement in many respects the ideas about caring explored in Chapter 1, focusing on supporting independence alongside a degree of intrusion and surveillance justified by the need for care. A pattern of services is developing in which that practice is carried out. Perhaps the most significant group is older people who become too frail to live independently without help with care. We saw above that more people are living to greater ages; their numbers are increasing, and so is their proportion of the population. Looking at this group therefore summarizes the overall pattern of services within which a social care practice must operate. Moreover, since UK community care provision for frail elderly people is similar to many systems, in Europe, for example, it indicates a direction for social care practice more widely than in the UK.

Le Bihan and Martin's (2006) comparative study of six European care systems provides useful comparisons of the elements of a care system. In most countries studied, the following were available: nursing care, personal care, housekeeping help, technical assistance with home care, accommodation centres, nursing homes, day care centres, geriatric hospitals and psychiatric institutions for temporary or permanent help. These are all elements of the package that UK social care practitioners are involved with. All systems used a case management system that relied on the individual assessment of elderly people and focused on providing domiciliary help as a priority. In most countries, as in the UK, assessment for monetary benefits is separate from assessment for care services. Medical treatment is also often provided separately from care packages, although it interacts with them. A common basic package is domiciliary care together with respite and/or day care. This is true also of the UK. Generally, in the UK, the number of hours of domiciliary care provided increases with the level of dependence.

In most European countries studied by Le Bihan and Martin (2006), financial contributions to the cost of the care package were made by the state, the elderly person themselves and the elderly person's family. There was also a balance between the contribution made by the state care package and the informal care of the elder's family. Within this pattern of service and payment for it, social care practice has to implement the idea of caring.

Conclusion

I argued in this chapter that social care implements caring ideas of continuity, development and receptivity by trying to normalize caring so that it connects with the social contexts within which people live, by valuing their identity and the place from which that identity develops. Social care cannot be receptive and developmental unless it tries to achieve this. Normalization means to connect service provision with widely accepted social values. Consequently, practitioners need to develop and maintain an awareness of general social factors, community and the cultural values of users and carers that they work with.

Social care is long-term care, and to maintain receptiveness, connectedness and development over a long period, social care has developed a model of practice that contains five elements. The first element is avoiding residential care and the other four elements are part of that reaction. They emphasize the management of risk and protection in the community rather than through caring in institutions. To do this, social care promotes day care, particularly where this assists in maintaining the social division between work and education on one hand and family and leisure life on the other. It emphasizes care in the family, in people's own homes and by supporting informal carers and it emphasizes the development of independent living for people whose care might make them dependent on others.

In Chapter 1, I examined how we may understand caring. In this chapter, I have suggested that to implement that understanding in caring services, a model of social care service provision has emerged. In Chapter

3, I examine the implications for practice of the organizational context of this model of social care.

main points

- Social care seeks to normalize care in the context of the places where people live.
- It connects the care services people receive with the values of their family and community.
- Practitioners therefore need awareness of the social, family and cultural contexts of users and carers.
- Social care has developed a model of practice that involves a reaction against residential care.
- Its consequent focus is on managing risk and protection in the community, through providing day care, home, family and carer support and the development of independent living.

stop and think

- Consider how 'place' is important to your identity and how dependence on care may change the way we organize our ordinary daily life.
- List your usual day, evening and night-time activities. If you were ill and unable to care for yourself, would these activities and their location change?
- Think about some aspect of life in which you are self-caring, then imagine an accident or illness that makes this impossible. Who would care for you? How? And in what setting?

taking it further

- Day, G. (2006) *Community and Everyday Life*. Abingdon: Routledge. A useful and recent book on ideas about community.
- Trevillion, S. (1999) *Networking and Community Partnership*. (2nd edn) Aldershot: Ashgate.

Good recent texts on residential care are:
- Ward, A. (2006) *Working in Group Care: Social Work and Social Care in Residential and Day Care Settings*. (2nd edn) Bristol: Policy Press.
- Clough, R. (2000) *The Practice of Residential Work*. Basingstoke: Palgrave Macmillan.

Useful organizations and websites
Statistics websites: UK: http://www.statistics.gov.uk/
European Union: http://epp.eurostat.ec.europa.eu/
USA: http://www.census.gov/compendia/statab/

3 The state and the individual

Social care service agencies and policy

Some argue that social care is at the centre of the relationship between the state and the citizen (Antonnen et al., 2003), because they are at the heart of an unstated contract for an exchange between the citizen's contributions to society and the responsibility of the collective for the citizen. How should that responsibility be balanced against personal, family and community responsibilities? This is an issue, since nearly everyone is self-caring to some degree and many people are self-caring for most or all their lives. We are all also carers for others within our social relationships. So, self-caring and caring within family and community social relationships are the norm. When and how does caring by formal services fit in with that? How does a formal service become part of the caring arena for someone who needs care?

In Chapter 1, we saw that care is carried out in personal relationships, it often involves intimate bodily contact and that this has important emotional implications for the people involved. This chapter addresses a crucial question for social policy and public administration, therefore: how is it possible to provide this intimate personal relationship as part of a public service? The difficulty is that public policy is made in public debate to achieve collective goals. These goals are directed and perhaps constrained by public finances. Officials employed by or on behalf of public agencies provide the services and do not necessarily have a personal relationship with the people cared for. Formal social care also reflects ideological and cultural assumptions that may not accord with the values of service users.

Social care is always carried out in the context of an agency, an organization established to pursue public policy, but this cannot always be consistent with connected care, and emotionally engaged relationships. However, there are some advantages in the collectivist nature of public provision, since people may perceive it as a mutual and equal engagement, in which citizens have rights that connect with the family commitments they take on. This may mean that people will not see social care workers in for-profit agencies as offering this mutuality. On the other hand, a different kind of mutuality is offered by the market relationship, and since most care is publicly funded, if not publicly provided, many people may not think the difference important.

Therefore, all social care practitioners need to understand and tackle making use of their agency's resources for users and how the agency and policy affects them. In this chapter, I start from the connections that users within their community have with the agencies that provide services for them, by examining structures for service delivery. I then move on to how practitioners may explore and keep up to date with the policies and legal bases of their practice.

Understanding social care agencies

Users have two connections with an agency. The first is the political relationship that they have as citizens with a service provided by public funding and political mandate. A private agency is usually part of a publicly funded service. Even if users are paying the whole cost, the availability and organization of services are matters of public policy and any organization needs to make provision for people with an interest to be able to complain and comment about the service. As citizens and voters, or as consumers of a service available to the public, therefore, they are part of a collective relationship with an agency. The second user relationship with the agency is a service-providing relationship. Users interact with social care workers who provide their services. Much of that relationship is about day-to-day care, but this reflects care policies and agency decisions. For example, are users free to make their own decisions about smoking, drinking alcohol or taking drugs such as cannabis? There might be controls on such decisions because of the law, fire regulations, safety arrangements, the agency's responsibility for good health, the agency's reputation or the attitudes of staff.

For example, the neighbours of a supported group home for people with learning disabilities (but it could easily be any other user group) complained about excessive noise from music played late at night by residents. The neighbours had vehemently protested to the planning authority about the home being set up, so one thing to be disentangled in this situation was the extent to which this complaint reflected their residual anger about losing this protest and their stigmatization of the user group. Their political relationship with the public authority in the area may have connected with their personal relationship with the service users. However, their protest was also a useful learning tool in educating the service users about appropriate behaviour in community relationships; maintaining good relationships with neighbours involves compromising personal preferences with their needs and wishes.

Management structures

All agencies have management structures designed to deal with these two kinds of relationships with users. Figure 3.1 shows an outline structure, organized in an unfamiliar way, giving priority to the users' connections and to inter-agency connections; I shall look at more conventional line management structures later.

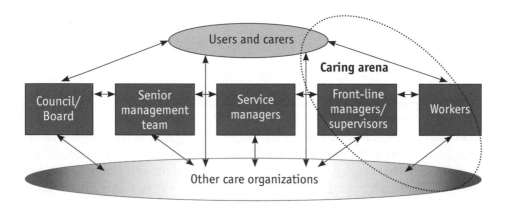

Figure 3.1 Inter-agency management structure, showing users' relationships

The caring arena (see also Figure 2.1) is where practitioners interact with service users, through a continuing relationship, as the users make them aware of their needs, and they work with the users/carers meeting those needs. The workers are responsible to front-line managers, sometimes called supervisors or team leaders, who also sometimes interact with users and carers. They are responsible in turn to service or 'middle' managers, who are organizers, appointing staff, determining priorities and managing budgets and facilities. They are responsible to senior mangers, working on policy, strategy, planning, and financing the organization. Mostly these managers do not have very much direct contact with users and carers, but their work and decisions influence the service provided.

These managers in turn are responsible to a council or board. This consists of people who are not employed to run the organization, as managers are, but who take overall responsibility for its direction, setting its values and policy and being its public face. In public authorities, this may be the local council. In voluntary organizations it may be called a board of trustees, since in charity law, the members of a charity board are charity trustees holding the objectives of the charity in trust for the future. Alternative names are council of management, management committee or, as a private company might call it, a board of directors.

Users have a political connection with the council or board. In a public authority, they may have elected the council, while in a voluntary or private sector organization they may influence it through representations or campaigning. Whatever the exact nature of this relationship, there is always a mechanism for users collectively to have some influence on the policy and strategy of the organizations through its council or board of management. The right to have this influence and the value their experience can offer to agencies and to other people who share similar problems are important reasons for encouraging users to work collectively, through organizations that represent their interests or through advocacy schemes.

Figure 3.1 focuses on the relationship between users and carers and a single care organization, but it also shows wider inter-agency relationships. Users, carers and workers at different levels in an organization have links with many other groups in the community. Adult social care or children and families teams in LAs have relationships at different levels with other LA departments, particularly housing, or with local NHS organizations. Users and carers will also interact with other departments, and have their political relationship with those departments through the council. All will have contacts with many community and official agencies. Sometimes these will be cooperative, shared working relationships, sometimes they will be commissioning relationships, and again at other times there may be conflictual, adversarial or advocacy relationships. Since social care brings together many different agencies to provide care, practitioners need to understand and work within the links between these organizations and users and carers.

There are different ways of understanding the relationships between groups of staff and users in an organization. Discussing this, above, I used the phrase 'responsible to', meaning that the connections between these employees are about accountability. Most organizations have structures that require employees to take responsibility for complying with the aims, policy and practices of the organization and for their actions on behalf of the organization. They are accountable to the users and carers they help, as well as to their management structure (or formal accountability) relationships within the agency.

Relationships within organizations are both formal and informal. Figure 3.2 shows a management structure within an organization, referring to the same staff groups as Figure 3.1. The chief executive and three assistants form a senior management team. The senior managers are accountable to the chief executive and the lines connecting them represent that duty to account, and the chief executive's right to give them instructions on behalf of the organization. Similarly, team members are accountable to team leaders and, through middle managers, to senior managers. In any organization, the line of responsibility from the most junior person to the most senior can be traced in this way; it is called a line management system. The advantage of seeing an organization in this way is that

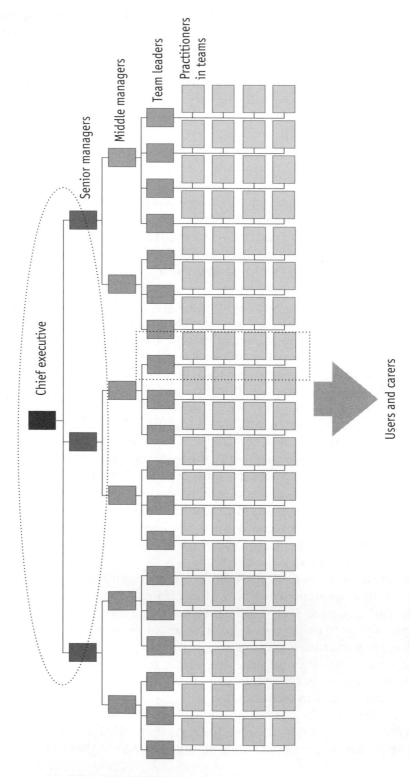

Figure 3.2 Line management structure

it makes clear where accountability lies, and clarifies administrative divisions within the organization. However, one of the disadvantages of this kind of diagram of responsibilities is that it does not make clear the relationships outside the organization, particularly users and carers, and does not mark responsibilities to them.

However, most people work in groups, and are therefore influenced by and responsible to their colleagues. We can see this in Figure 3.2, since the pecked lines show two groups, the senior management team and a team of practitioners and their leader among many others. Managers, for example each senior manager, are members of both the senior management team and the team of workers responsible to them. They form the link between them, and are called a 'link pin' (Likert, 1961).

Looking at the groups within the organization alongside the line management structure creates a systems view of relationships within the organization. People work within groups, putting most of their resources of time, skill and work into that group, to which they therefore have loyalties. However, it is also useful to understand relationships between the different groups. For example, Figure 3.3 represents a disabilities team in a local authority, within the circle. There is a group of care managers, with its team manager, and a separate group of administrative workers, responsible to a director for administration. The arrows represent lines of responsibility outside the team. The pecked lines represent the two groupings. Identifying groupings using diagrams like this helps to see relationships between groups.

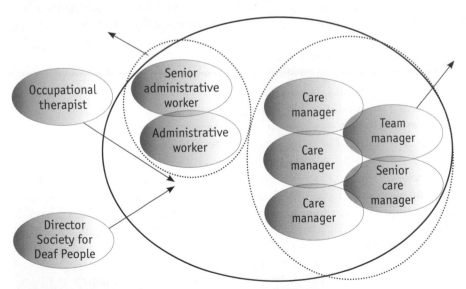

Figure 3.3 Systems diagram of a core and periphery team

Everyone has some responsibility for how relationships work, although individuals may have specific roles. The team manager and senior administrative worker sit on the boundaries of the team. Their memberships elsewhere give them an important communication role. An occupational therapist, part of a specialist team working jointly with a local primary care trust (PCT), and the director of the local voluntary society for deaf people both work closely with the team of care managers and occasionally attend joint meetings with them. The diagram also shows these links and raises the question of how well liaison works. This shows a 'core and periphery' team (Miller et al., 2001); some people are part of the main team, others are less important, less regular, or less formal members of the team. Again, what does this mean for relationships?

As well as hierarchical accountabilities through the line management structure in the organization, responsibilities may be identified to:

■ Professional expectations and requirements, such as those contained in the Codes of Practice published by UK social care councils
■ Groups of colleagues
■ Other parts of the organization
■ Outside organizations, for example where organizations have contracts to supply services or where users receive services from both and therefore form a connection between organizations.

Groups do not have relationships with one another, individuals do. A systems view of organizations shows how individuals form links between groups of people. So, as with the families and communities (see Chapter 2), workers in agencies also form social networks. Practitioners are points of contact and responsibility within agencies, and have links throughout the organization, allied agencies and the community. Contacts might be grouped as follows:

■ Public, private and voluntary/third sector
■ Areas of users' personal welfare, such as education, employment, healthcare, housing, social security
■ Significant professions: education, housing, medicine, nursing
■ Geographical areas or communities
■ Significant resources, such as day, residential or community facilities.

Contacts will overlap across these. For example, residential care exists in each sector of the economy, concerned with different areas of welfare, involving different professionals and covering different areas. Individuals can map their own contacts and team projects to do this can also be useful.

Social care is part of a wider system of care, involving agencies with a focus outside the 'social', in particular education, healthcare and housing. To be caring, and therefore seamless, social care structures in different sectors work in partnership, the official term for inter-agency cooperation, and practitioners from different services collaborate, the term for working together as a practical part of services (Whittington, 2003). The practice required for this is dealt with in Chapter 5.

Public, private and third or voluntary sectors

The previous section points to differences in structure and relationships with users between public authorities, private companies and voluntary sector organizations. A practitioner in multi-sectoral social care needs to understand these. This section looks at organizational distinctions between these different sectors. Many organizations are hybrids, with some element of public, private and voluntary within them. The term 'sector' refers to sectors of the economy. The term 'third sector' refers to the voluntary sector, a 'not-for-profit' alternative to the public and private sectors. Table 3.1 sets out the distinctions.

Table 3.1 Distinctions between public, private and third sector organizations

Areas of difference	Public sector	Private sector	Voluntary/third/not-for-profit sector
Funding	Taxation, loans, charges for services, surpluses	Stock market, bank loans, charges for services, retained profits	Donations/ fund-raising/grants, loans, charges for services, surpluses
Mandate	Permissive and mandatory legislation	Memorandum and articles of association	Governing instrument/ constitution
Ultimate authority	Elected authority, appointed authority, agency	Board of directors	Trustees, management committee, board of directors
Appointment of authority	Election, appointment	Election by annual general meeting, appointment	Election by annual general meeting, appointment
Board membership	Allowances, elected councillors, co-option	Fee-earning, executive and non-executive directors	Unpaid, no executives

The first row of the table examines funding. Public organizations are the only sector that is funded from taxation. National public organizations are funded from national taxation, mainly income tax and revenues from goods and services, such as customs charges and value added tax. Local government is funded by a locally raised property tax, the 'council tax' and by revenue grant from national government. Private and voluntary organizations benefit from taxation through charging for services provided to public organizations and grants from public bodies benefiting the public sector. Only private sector organizations make profits, and this is an important reason for their existence. Public and voluntary organizations may achieve surpluses, where income is greater than costs. All sectors make some charges for their services. These make people aware of the value of services, and enable people to contribute to or completely pay the costs of the services they receive.

The second row refers to the organization's mandate; where the right or duty to provide services comes from. Public organizations in the UK may only do something if an Act of Parliament allows (permissive legislation) or requires them (mandatory) to provide some service. Other organizations have documents setting them up and stating their objectives. Private sector companies and voluntary organizations that are companies have a 'memorandum and articles of association'. All these are phrased in very open ways, usually permitting wide discretion.

Understanding organizations' roles requires knowing about their structure and the policy context of their work. One structural issue about private sector organizations is that increasingly they are international and their strategy involves seeking profit in particular kinds of markets, rather than being concerned with client needs (Holden, 2002). LAs may be driven by the needs of particular populations and localities, and a third-sector organization by its views on how services should be run or the needs of the population group that it seeks to benefit. An example of a structural issue is that recent UK government neoliberal economic policies mean that market systems of provision are preferred to achieve service and cost efficiencies, and therefore public provision is discouraged, even where it may be a good way of providing particular services (Player and Pollock, 2001). For example, Scourfield (2006) argues, in relation to domiciliary care for older people, that stable integration with healthcare and housing services suggests that public sector provision would be the most effective place to develop new services, but the reliance on the market to stimulate efficiencies makes this politically untenable.

The third row of the table sets out differences in the body with the ultimate authority to determine policy and practice in the organization. This is usually done in a very general way. The fourth row shows how these bodies are appointed. For companies and voluntary organizations, election at annual general meetings is not the main focus for finding members, since usually people are found by existing board members or the executives of the organization, their appointments being confirmed at the AGM; competitive election is rare. This may be the picture also in local government, since the shortage of people prepared to be local councillors may concentrate power in the hands of a few leading members of the party in power. Payment of board members, set out in the fifth row, is a significant difference. By charity law, trustees may not receive money for their participation, and local authority members usually only receive an allowance for expenses, although recently there has been provision for salaries for leading members. Also, only private sector organizations may include paid executive staff in their decision-making boards.

Regulators

Regulators in care services are agencies that make sure that services are managed or controlled according to the laws, policies and requirements of governments. Those relevant to social care, set out in Table 3.2, are a

Table 3.2 Regulators relevant to social care

Regulator	Type of regulator	Role	Legislation
Audit Commission; Audit Scotland; Northern Ireland Audit Office; Wales Audit Office	National	To improve public service by investigating and reporting on how public money is spent	Audit Commission Act 1998; Public Audit (Wales) Act 2004; Scotland Act 1998
National Audit Office	National	Scrutinizes public spending on behalf of Parliament	Government Resources and Accounts Act 2000; National Audit Act 1983; older legislation
Commission for Social Care Inspection	Service	To improve social care by inspecting and reporting on commissioners and providers of social care	Health and Social Care (Community Health and Standards) Act 2003
Healthcare Commission; Healthcare Inspectorate Wales	Service	Inspect the quality and value for money of healthcare and public health	Health and Social Care (Community Health and Standards) Act 2003
Health Service Commissioner (Ombudsman)	Complaints	Investigates complaints about the NHS in England	Health Service Commissioners Act 1993
Local Government Commissioner (Ombudsman)	Complaints	Investigates complaints about local government services	Local Government Act 1974
Office for Standards in Education, Children's Services and Skills	Complaints	Inspects children, families and education services	Children Act 2004
Quality Assurance Agency for Higher Education	Service	Sets standards for and inspects higher education institutions	
Northern Ireland Ombudsman; Public Services Ombudsman for Wales; Scottish Public Services Ombudsman	National	To investigate complaints about public services (includes NHS)	Various legislation relevant to the country
General Social Care Council; Care Council for Wales; Northern Ireland Social Care Council; Scottish Social Services Council	Professional, Education	Social care workers, initially social workers and their education in England	Care Standards Act 2000; Health and Personal Social Services Act (Northern Ireland) 2001; Regulation of Care (Scotland) Act 2001

SOURCES: Internet (accessed: 26th May 2007): http://www.ombudsman.org.uk/contact_us/if_we_cannot_help.html, http://www.nao.org.uk/about/faqs.htm, http://www.gscc.org.uk/About+us/Our+partners/, http://www.ofsted.gov.uk/assets/3765.doc, http://www.qaa.ac.uk/aboutus/

mechanism for accountability outside line management responsibilities. Regulations are the rules that set out the detailed way that law and policy should be implemented. For government services, regulation comes from the original laws setting up or governing services. Regulation is increasingly required for several reasons:

■ Greater concern for consumer and service user rights has led to external supervision of government and private sector activity.

■ Greater use of private sector providers of government services means that conflicts of interest arise. For example, government departments or agencies might compete with similar private sector providers, and so cannot act as regulators, or government agencies plan or commission services, and have contracts with providers, and cannot then be regulators independent of the providers.

■ Society is less deferential towards government and professionals, and so independent assurance of their standards of service is increasingly required.

However, greater regulation raises questions. Independent regulatory bodies allow governments to avoid direct accountability for service quality. Also, since government continues to provide most of the finance, it cannot completely evade responsibility, but regulation is a negative way to achieve accountability. Tilbury (2007) argues that if, in a pluralist, democratic society, government promotes a variety of provision, it must also accept responsibility for developing and supporting the range and quality of the provision in a positive way, and for training initiatives. This is one of the roles of commissioners and various support services for residential and home care.

At the time of writing, there are moves to merge or connect CSCI with the Healthcare Commission, which regulates healthcare organizations. By doing this, the government is trying to reduce the burden on organizations of involvement by different regulators, reduce the costs of regulation and make regulation 'joined-up'.

Social care policy and legislation

Policy can just mean a consistent practice by a group of people or an organization, as on the occasions when we say: 'It is our policy to do it this way.' However, it usually refers to a process that takes place between a number of interests to form an agreed way of responding to social issues and needs. Jenkins (1978; Chapter 1) describes a process in which inputs of demands, support and dissent for particular ideas and resources go through a political process of decision-making. Policy is formulated in statements and documents and occasionally in law, regulations and guidance aimed at managing public expectations and behaviour and at the way people implement the policy. As policy is implemented, outcomes are achieved that affect services and people such as service users and practitioners. Policy statements and documents contain elements of political philosophy, pragmatic response to events and practical management requirements. Social care practice is policy implementing the products of political processes and broader assumptions and policies from professional groups, managers and practitioners about how they might achieve desirable results. Political policy and the assumptions, training and management of the practitioners set elements of what is seen as desirable.

Practitioners need to understand the main elements of policy and where they come from. This changes all the time, so the main focus of this chapter is in understanding the general structures of services, which change only slowly, and how to examine the present position of social care by exploring current policy. I then look at some examples of structures through which the government implements policy that affects practitioners and service users. Readers can build on this beginning by studying social policy more extensively. However, my main objective here is to draw attention to the following points:

- Social care policy is not well developed and is often created in the margins of government initiatives in related areas. It plays a part in individualizing broad social and political objectives for public services but is not a strong focus of political attention.
- It is useful to look for, understand and be critical about mechanisms government uses to influence practice. Government does this through policy statements particularly about principles and values, through legislation, guidance and formal regulations, and through administrative machinery such as regulatory bodies and practice development initiatives.

Policy about social care

Policy about social care reflects its dependence on education, healthcare, housing and social security policy, and also reflects the political philosophy of the ruling party. Three broad political philosophies are conservative, neoliberal ideas, which give priority to wealth-creation through economic markets. Such views favour social provision that ensures social stability that, in turn, supports stable markets. Socialist philosophies value social solidarity and planning achieved by collective provision and action. Social democratic policies try to combine elements of the market and collective action and a combination of planned services with incentives provided by the market. At any time, a consensus about the strategic direction of political policy exists. This is both because democratic political parties compete for policy positions that engage support from a wide range of public opinion, which changes only slowly, and because a limited range of ideas drawn from the political philosophies constantly circulates, renewed by insights into changing attitudes and preferences. Therefore, social care does not have a policy and legal existence. Its policy and legislation rely on policy priorities in related areas.

The main legislation using the term is the Health and Social Care Act 2001, most of which is concerned with healthcare. Its main relevance to social care is that it makes provision for partnership arrangements between PCTs and their related LA. The 2001 Act also makes a clear legal distinction between social care and healthcare by prohibiting LAs from providing or paying for nursing as part of residential care. The absence of a social care act of Parliament or UK legislation referring solely to social care is an example of the elision of social care with healthcare serving primarily the interests of healthcare services.

There is no government ministry of social care. The main government department concerned with social care is the Department of Health, which at the time of writing has a 'minister for care services' who has a wider remit than social care. The Department for Children, Schools and Families is responsible for the social care aspect of the 'Every Child Matters' policy. Similar social care ministries may be found in the governments of the other UK nations (see websites at the end of the chapter). Practitioners might usefully, perhaps as a team project, keep in touch with changes to this pattern.

In many European countries, in contrast, there are ministers for social affairs, ministries for social welfare, and major roles for social services of various kinds. Social care in the UK might be seen as marginalized: however, in most countries, social care is integral to other aspects of wider social provision. In some Nordic countries, for example, social care services are part of social security rather than healthcare, as in the UK. A group of Nordic writers saw social care as at the centre of the Nordic welfare state, mainly because provision for substitute child care permitted women to go to work (Sipilä, 1997); this is not how the UK would understand social care. My overall assessment is that social care is always integrated in people's minds and in policy with other aspects of public provision. Rather than worrying about the status of social care and kicking against this, it is more helpful to practitioners to understand and pursue relationships that are appropriate to incorporating social care effectively into each national system of social provision. If they do that, they will be making a social care perspective integral to other services.

Legislation on social care

The main legislation on social care practice is in two areas: care for children and families, and community care provision for adults with long-term handicaps or conditions. Table 3.3 sets out some examples of this division, which are the main legislative bases for social care. Other legislation builds on or connects to these primary acts and regulations and government circulars come from the legislation, which generally sets out the broad directions for practice. In addition to these pieces of legislation about social care, there is other legislation relevant to social care practitioners. This includes:

■ Law about social care workers, generally based on the Care Standards Act 2000, the basis for the regulation of social care

- Law about social work responsibilities and legal duties, which comes from the same legislation
- Law about general rights and responsibilities affecting everyone, but which practitioners take special account of, including the Human Rights Act 1998 and discrimination legislation
- Legislation providing for the needs of groups, such as people with learning disabilities, and people who are deaf or blind
- Legislation that deals with particular protective procedures, such as the Mental Capacity Act 2005, and the safeguarding and protection of children and vulnerable adults (Brammer, 2007).

Legislation is the formal expression of government policy in law, added to by regulations and guidance from ministers, which often virtually have the force of law.

Table 3.3 Main social care legislation

Children and families		Adults	
Act	Comments	Act	Comments
Children Act 1989	Main source of children's care: Part III requires LAs to provide services for children in need	National Assistance Act 1948	Main source of adult care: Part III provides for LAs to care for people
Care Standards Act 2000	Arrangements for the provision of private, voluntary and registered children's homes	Health Services and Public Health Act 1968	Source of the power for LAs to provide services in older people's homes
Adoption and Children Act 2002	Provision for adoption of children	Chronically Sick and Disabled Persons Act 1970	Requires LAs to find and register disabled people and provide services
Children Act 2004	Promotes coordination of services between education, health and social care services: source of the 'Every Child Matters' policy	National Health Service Act 1977	Source of the duty to provide home care
		Mental Health Act 1983	Main source of the duty to provide services for mentally ill people
		National Health Service and Community Care Act 1990	Main source of the system for assessment and care management for adult community care services
		Mental Health Act 2007	Renewed mental health legislation

Social care, children's services and healthcare

Since social care is mainly about children's services and healthcare, prac-titioners need to understand how its policy and law connect to policy and law in those areas. The National Health Service (NHS) provides healthcare as an agency of national government departments. In England, as discussed above, these are the Department of Health and the Depart-ment for Children, Schools and Families; in Northern Ireland, the Depart-ment of Health, Social Services and Public Safety; in Scotland, the Cabinet Secretary for health and well-being; in Wales, the Department of Health and Social Care. Policy is differently implemented in each of the four countries of the UK, whose governments are not necessarily led by the same political party, so that, although the NHS is a national service, provi-sion and policy are different in each of the four countries. Education and children's work also vary in their roles and policy. Information may be found on the relevant government website: see the end of the chapter.

Social care is provided by LAs; independent political and legal entities, coordinated with and largely funded by central government through the Department for Communities and Local Government and the local government departments in each country. On social care matters, advice and guidance are issued by the relevant specialist department: thus funding and the local structure for social care are separated from policy responsibility. Table 3.4 summarizes the organizational consequences of this in healthcare for England, as an example of the divisions, which vary slightly in the other UK countries.

Table 3.4 Local–central relationships

	Healthcare (England)	Social care (England)
Central government department	Department of Health	Department for Communities and Local Government
Agency	NHS	
Funding	To PCTs and Foundation Hospital Trusts	Through local community charge and central government distribution of the business rate and revenue support grant
Central government advice and guidance	Department of Health	Department for Children, Schools and Families and the Department of Health

Historically, NHS and social care provision separated in 1948, at the break-up of the Poor Law, with aspects of Poor Law provision designated as health-care mostly becoming the NHS, while public health provision and welfare services went under different legislation to LAs. Crucially, NHS services are provided free, while LAs are authorized, and increasingly required, to charge for services. Reorganizations in the 1970s emphasized this distinction creating SSDs in LAs, and merging all welfare, social services functions and some health service functions, mainly home help and mental health community care. Attempts to create coterminous LA and NHS boundaries to facilitate coordination have faded in various boundary reorganizations since then. Also, since this period, there have been attempts to promote local coordination and joint provision through funding and policy initiatives.

Since the 1970s, NHS provision for long-term care has transferred to social services, and this of course means transferring free services to charge-making LAs, with the NHS increasingly becoming an acute services provider. These transfers particularly affected mental health, learning disabilities and older people's services, with large NHS hospitals closed in favour of smaller-scale, local, mainly social services provision. There is general public and professional support for these changes, because they provide more flexible and responsive provision for these groups of service users.

However, social security changes in the 1980s concealed the financial consequences of this move from most people. These changes led to the development of a private sector in care home provision, funded initially by social security payments. When this was found to provide a 'perverse financial incentive' to fund institutional provision contrary to community care policy, a new community care policy was established in the NHS and Community Care Act 1990. This separated *commissioning* and planning services, seen as a public function, from *providing* them, contracted out to private or voluntary sector providers, although public authorities continued to make some provision. Thus, an organizational structure developed to make arrangements for a public service 'commissioner' assessing need and then choosing between different service providers and coordinating a 'care package' including services from a variety of sectors of the economy. This associates assessment of need closely with decisions about financing users' services but has succeeded in halting rapid increases in long-term care costs.

In this new structure, the traditional distinction was maintained between community provision by PCTs in healthcare (currently called 'continuing NHS care') being free and provision seen as social care ('community care') being charged for. The definition of healthcare is dominated by the decision about whether it requires medical oversight and nursing input. The decision about this has financial consequences for families, since if care needs are long term, community care users have to pay a considerable proportion of their income and wealth, and may be financially supported by their families, while 'continuing care' remains free. Continuing care is called this because it substitutes residential, nursing home or home care for care that would otherwise have to be provided by the NHS in a hospital. A series of court cases and determinations by the health service ombudsman (for example Health Service Ombudsman, 2003, 2004) placed increasing pressure on the Department of Health and local PCTs as they have tried to maintain flexibility in determining need and constraining cost increases.

The overall distinctions in the pathway to social care and healthcare services, and payment for them, are set out in Table 3.5. There are different routes to gain access to services, leading to complexities in the relationships between health and social care, which are hard for users, carers and practitioners to understand. Changes in central government organization in 2004 followed from the implementation of the Care Standards Act 2000 and the Health and Social Care Act 2001 and various children acts. This has led to the dismemberment of social services, with children and families work being transferred to education departments, and adults work being maintained in newly renamed 'adult social services departments'. Although possibly leading to improved coordination with education and healthcare, the primary objective of government policy, it negates the advantages of the SSDs created in the 1970s, which was to coordinate social care services to a family. For example, I dealt recently with a woman receiving health and social care services, whose child had emotional and behavioural disorders. This meant extra difficulties for a very sick mother, for which the children's social worker took no responsibility, while in generic SSD structures, she would have been responsible for both sets of issues. Every structure is a politically driven choice between discontinuities in provision; every organizational change both resolves and creates coordination problems.

Table 3.5 Pathways to service

	Healthcare	Social care
Family or individual	Registers with GP (usually independent contractor to NHS)	Applies for services to local authority of residence
Referrals	To district general hospital (DGH) or other secondary provider	To children and families division of the education department or adult social services department
Joint arrangements	Some local joint care trusts, particularly in mental health and children's services	
Specialist provision	From DGH or GP to specialist provider (for example hospice)	Funding arrangements for out-of-area services
Commissioning	PCT commissions healthcare services based on GP's surgery address	LA commissions social care services based on service user's address
Funding of community services	Through NHS continuing care finance	Through community care provisions of NHS and Community Care Act 1990

Recent government policy documents on health and social care emphasize the further development of social care and social work as enabling and assisting service users to manage 'direct payments' or 'independent budgets' as a 'co-funding' arrangement, in which both public funding for care arrangements and individual and family financial support are combined. The policy focus is on 'personalization' of provision, with the implication that individuals and families will take stronger responsibility for managing their own care within the clear financial and service constraints. At the time of writing, the final policy determination is still to be published, but such a pattern is likely to be acceptable to both main political parties, so it may be a politically sustainable arrangement. I take this point up again in Chapter 8.

The next sections discuss briefly two important areas of policy: community care policy for adults and care for children who are looked after.

Community care and child care policy

Chapter 2 noted that social care policy for both community care and also children and families has been influenced by the shift from institutional care and service developments that react to that shift. Community care as a formal policy for health and social care has been widely accepted in the UK since at least the 1950s. In children's policy, the interaction of concern about deprivation with worries about young people's offending has swung between more and less offence-focused approaches, but where the issue has been neglect, abuse or poor care, child care policy has shifted decisively towards care approaches from the mid-20th century.

There have been five phases in the development of community care and children's policy, set out in Table 3.6.

Table 3.6 Phases in the development of community care and child care policy

Period	Community care phase	Child care phase	Comment
To the end of the 19th century	Institutional	Rescue children from neglect, abandonment and criminality	Main response to social need is to 'incarcerate' people in institutions
To 1950s	Commitment	Increase in family-based solutions for children in care	Increasingly committed development of positive and community responses to social need
1960s and 1970s	Community/ collective	Focus on deprivation not delinquency; treatment and care priority over incarceration	Ideological commitment to 'community' and care in response to social need
1980s and 1990s	Individual	Assessment for specialized care for children with disorders, emphasis on permanence for care solutions	Shift from 'community' to emphasis on responding to individualized definitions of need

1990s onwards	Market	Specialist care for children with severe difficulties; otherwise, increasing emphasis on family support and education solutions	Development of active solutions in care provision, using a quasi-market of care providers and care management

SOURCE: Developed from Payne (1995).

The long-term shift towards increasingly large residential care as part of controlling social disorder and containing social risks forms the starting point of current policy (see Chapter 2). Major turning points in the institutional period are as follows:

■ Locally managed, centrally coordinated workhouses in a crucial development became the centre for care for most children, older and disabled people during the 19th century. They were the foundation of a health and welfare workforce, of many innovations in care, and of buildings. All these transferred into the welfare state services after 1948 and were the basis of NHS and local authority welfare provision.

■ The development of large public sector 'asylums' for mentally ill people and 'colonies' for people with learning disabilities became the basis for hospitals and care from the 1940s.

■ Concern about 'mental defectives', at its height with the influence of the eugenics movement in the early part of the 20th century, led to a duty to 'ascertain', 'certify' and often institutionalize people with learning disabilities under the Mental Deficiency Act 1913 (Walmsley and Rolph, 2001).

■ The religiously based charities seeking to rescue, in particular, destitute children and prostitutes from the streets developed large institutions for their care in the urban centres of the mid to late 19th century (Young and Ashton, 1956).

The commitment phase developed from many of these initiatives:

■ Experience of guardianship and supervision under the Mental Deficiency Act 1913, although patchy, led to the Mental Deficiency Act 1927, which made it a duty of local authorities to provide training for 'mental defectives'. This led to the development of occupation and industrial centres, the forerunners of adult training and social education centres and community care provision more generally (Walmsley and Rolph, 2001).

■ The development of social work within the voluntary sector, and the role of medical and psychiatric social workers during the 1920s and '30s offered an occupational base for people to be employed in community services (Payne, 2005).

■ Experiments with 'boarding out' children and young people from Poor Law institutions in foster care, and family group homes in place of large institutions led to more flexible provision for children (Packman,

1981). This developed into a movement, influencing the Children Act 1948 and leading to an LA social work agency – the children's departments – independent of healthcare.

■ Ideas changed in the 1950s about institutions providing long-term care in several fields, raising the possibility of institutions having the capacity to be non-custodial, therapeutic and beneficial to their inmates. It also made possible confidence in non-medical treatment outside hospital. Realization of poor standards of institutionalized care for elderly people followed Townsend's *The Last Refuge* (1962) and scandals about institutional care arose in long-stay mental illness and mental handicap hospitals. Old 19th-century buildings were ending their useful life and became expensive to run.

■ Distaste for the dehumanizing and unpleasant environments offered by, particularly, mental hospitals emerged. Theoretical work by Goffman (1961) on total institutions (that is, those where all or most aspects of life were provided for within the institution) and Barton (1959) on the adverse effects of institutions on their inmates leading to 'institutional neurosis' strengthened these ideas.

■ The Percy Commission (1957) examined the mental health services, popularized the term 'community care' and proposed a new LA social work service for mentally ill and handicapped people. This aimed to avoid unnecessary incarceration in mental hospitals, offering alternatives outside, and providing care after discharge. The Mental Health Act 1959 implemented community care policies in new LA mental welfare departments.

The community phase was the high point of commitment to community responses to care needs:

■ The implementation of the Seebohm Report (1968) created SSDs, and led to a community base in local area offices, for social work services and support for community work.

■ The Children and Young Persons Act 1969 derived from a policy that child delinquency should be seen as a product of deprivation, particularly in poor communities. Much of it was not implemented, but approved (in Scotland, 'List D') schools were incorporated into the child care system emphasizing care rather than incarceration, and 'intermediate treatment' was created to promote personal development and community involvement for deprived and delinquent young people.

■ Adoption was reformed, in accordance with the Houghton Report (1972), by the Children Act 1975, which began a movement towards focusing on permanency in LA child care services.

■ Community consultation over local and strategic plans for physical development of local authority areas encouraged participation in planning.

■ The Chronically Sick and Disabled Persons Act 1970 encouraged provision of home care, equipment and other supports for physically disabled people, and eventually people with learning disabilities and mental illnesses, to remain in their homes as healthcare treatment policies made care at home more viable.

- The idea of 'community social work', an important forerunner of social care (see Chapter 5), aimed to debureaucratize social work by focusing on local areas and bringing together social workers with home care staff.
- Moves to close long-stay hospitals and focus healthcare provision on acute and curative services requiring medical and nursing intervention shifted care for long-term conditions into LA responsibility. Funding mechanisms were set up to ease this transition, including joint finance and joint care planning in the 1960s and '70s.

The individualistic phase was the first stage of moves by the Conservative government of the 1980s and '90s to create a market through a policy based on neoliberal public choice theory. This is the idea that the responsibility of government is to enable people to make choices in a quasi-market, rather than to focus on the provision of a range of services by public authorities. The main features of the individualistic phase were:

- Funding, provided for the first time through social security allowances, enabled people to choose to pay for residential care; previously, most residential care was provided as a managed service by local authorities. This provided a source of finance for private sector residential homes, although this outcome of the social security changes had not been foreseen.
- The run-down of long-stay hospitals, particularly those for mentally ill people and people with learning disabilities, provided a workforce interested and skilled in long-term care, particularly for older people, and also people with learning disabilities and mental illnesses.
- Children's services increasingly focused on specialist care for children with 'emotional and behavioural disorders', replacing the offending-oriented care homes with education on the premises, while children's homes were increasingly phased out in favour of more individualized and family-oriented foster care and adoption. Professional foster care, in which foster carers provided for increasingly disabled and difficult children, and adoption for children with emotional and other difficulties became more commonplace.
- Growth in property prices enabled small-scale care homes businesses to start, secure in the knowledge that a capital gain could be achieved by buying and adapting property, even if the care home was unsuccessful as an enterprise.
- Finance for local authority home care and for developing further residential care and supported housing was constrained. This meant that there was no competition for care homes.
- Consequently, a 'perverse incentive' (Audit Commission, 1986) was

created to build up residential care, even though the government's policy was to promote community care.

- Growing social security costs led to reform of the community care system through the NHS and Community Care Act 1990, following the recommendations of the Griffiths Report (1988).

These developments led the way towards a more market-oriented provision of care services, in which all sectors of the economy provided services commissioned by public sector authorities.

Community care entered a quasi-market. LAs worked with other sectors of the economy to construct a community care plan for the services in the locality. Care managers assessed people's long-term care needs and put together a package of social care services to meet them from the services commissioned and contracted for as part of the plan.

Work with 'children in need' moved social work increasingly towards a child protection rather than child welfare and social care role, and provision of care within children's services shifted towards family support.

The organization of healthcare provision has changed over time, responding to government initiatives, but has also settled into a pattern of a quasi-market, in which competition by providers within a planned market is designed to increase patients' choice, and cost effectiveness is encouraged through market disciplines.

Community care services where service users are means-tested, contributing financially to the costs of the service, interact with NHS continuing care, where patients who are assessed as having a 'primary health need' receive full funding of their care through the NHS.

From the 1990s onwards, new Labour policies focused on family support as an important aspect of provision for children (Home Office, 1998). Better parenting and greater support to families were an important way of responding to instabilities in society; for example, courts were enabled to make parenting orders in the Crime and Disorder Act 1998. Research on LA child protection work identified the weaknesses of an investigatory approach to section 17 of the Children Act 1989, which therefore failed to encourage child welfare. Instead, there was to be a 'refocusing' on family support services. There was criticism that this ignored the resource implications of such a move in an under-resourced area of work. There were also doubts about the cost-effectiveness of the child protection system and its capacity to deliver positive services. Partly this arises from the difficulty of social workers shifting their attention from risky situations, where failings might later be criticized (Platt, 2006). Implementation of the Children Act 2004 may offer new organizational structures for inter-agency delivery of services to families and children through community facilities associated with schools. This might enable effective preventive and restorative work to be undertaken, for example through parenting training (Bell, 2007).

Practice impact of policy and finance for community social care

There is a long history in the UK of services for the user groups served by social care being inadequate in various ways. Generations of practitioners, concerned people and politicians have tried to get improvements – responding to the problems, needs and views of each generation. Some occasions when these needs were highlighted are:

- There was a battle in the 1950s to get civil servants to accept that government should have responsibility for providing support services for elderly people in their own home (Means and Smith, 1998). This was a legacy of less-eligibility attitudes engendered by the longstanding Poor Law, because otherwise good services would be an incentive for people to use them and would cost too much money.
- The concern in the 1960s about very low standards in residential care for older people (Fowles and Jones, 1984).
- The development of community care policy in the 1960s for, first, mentally ill and, then, other groups of people requiring long-term care.
- The decision to give priority to long-term care in health and social services funding in the 1960s.
- Programmes to coordinate health and social services funding in the 1970s, after the clear separation of NHS and LA social services financing and administration.
- The increasing funding of private sector residential care in the 1980s, leading to a shift in the assumption that LAs would provide most social care.
- The use of market disciplines to drive down health and social care costs, and the requirement on social care service users for contributions towards the costs of services have become increasingly controversial. This is because the proportion of people with long-term care needs receiving free NHS care has declined as long-term care has moved out from residential institutions, while care provision that incurs contributions has become more important.
- As the proportion of older people in the population has grown, there has been increasing controversy about the contributions to the cost of care. The majority report of the Sutherland Commission (1999) on long-term care recommended that personal care be funded by the taxpayer, but this has not been accepted in England. While long-term care is funded from taxation in Scotland, it is not clear that this will be economically possible in the long term, as the proportion of older people in the population continues to grow over the next three decades.

Social care practitioners are concerned with how policy and finance develop for the groups of people they are responsible for, because this affects their role and work. In a useful comparative survey, Glendinning

(2002: 311) looks at the factors that make for differences in national systems:

- How the responsibilities of the individual, their family and the state interact at national and local levels
- Shifts in the boundaries between health and social care services
- How health and social care services are coordinated
- The rights and entitlements of service users as citizens.

How these factors interact develops all the time, as central and local government agencies make policy and people react to it. Practitioners, their representative organizations, their values education and their knowledge base and skill-set are part of that reaction. One important question for practitioners is what to do when they disagree with policy. The resources may not be enough, the standards of practice or organization are not good enough, or policy, guidance and instructions from agencies go against providing what they think is a good, or a reasonable, or the best service. As well as practitioners' involvements in the care system for particular users, carers and families, understanding and responding to opportunities within agency systems to influence change are always possible. Government policy initiatives often provide opportunities for consultation, influence and innovation to practitioners, if they choose to take them.

Policy initiatives

All governments establish systems for implementing their policies. It is important to be aware of these as they develop, to influence them and raise problems. For example, during 2007, after rising concern about how NHS continuing care had been operating for several years, a new national framework and 'decision tools' were introduced. There were several consultations on these during the year, and some pilot efforts to try them out. When they were introduced, consortia of PCTs in my area got together with LAs to create their own forms and procedures. In all these processes, practitioners could have useful influence, because they had practical experience of how things worked. The best way of having influence in myriad similar situations is by keeping up to date through reading the journals and websites suggested at the end of this chapter.

National service frameworks

As examples of this sort of policy initiative, I discuss here the national service frameworks (NSFs), which are processes for establishing practice policies, and quality and dignity initiatives reflecting issues of political importance relevant to social care.

NSFs are the current way, launched by the new Labour government in 1998, in which the government sets and promotes a strategy for meeting the needs of a particular group of service users (DH, 2007b). Most are about health conditions, such as coronary heart disease or renal conditions. Social care services are often part of a multiagency and multiprofessional effort to help people with such a condition. Looking at the standards they set might be useful if practitioners join such efforts, either occasionally or as part of a continuing team. NSFs provide a clue to the sorts of standards aspired to.

A number of NSFs are particularly relevant to social care, because they cover a large group of people whose non-medical needs are important, and include:

■ Mental health
■ Older people
■ Long-term conditions
■ Children.

These NSFs particularly focus on links between health, social care and, in the last case, education.

Quality and dignity: social care policy from 2004

A government initiative started in 2004 arose from the Gershon review (Gershon, 2004) of public sector efficiency. As a political initiative of the Treasury, this was designed to head off rising criticism of increasing Labour spending after 2000 for investment in public services. Gershon's aim was to move staffing and their resources to support front-line services, rather than policymaking or administration. A minor offshoot of this led to the Care Services Efficiency Delivery (CSED) project to try to improve the effectiveness of commissioning of services.

From 2005 onwards, government social care policy moved forwards. The title of the first Green Paper, *Independence, Well-being and Choice* (DH, 2005a) indicates the public choice policy thinking behind the document. Respondents to the consultation (DH, 2005b) supported the vision of increasing the independence of service users, but had reservations about many practicalities. An important practical proposal was to increase the use of direct payments and individual budgets that users controlled themselves to pay for their own carers. Experiments on extending these through independent budgeting pilot schemes are in progress at the time of writing. Direct payments (see Chapter 6) have been used particularly with people with long-term physical disabilities, but there were doubts that these could be extended to frail elderly people or people with learning disabilities, who might have less capacity and energy. A greater difficulty may well be the long-standing division in British welfare that money payments are made through the social security system, while local government social care mainly provides caring services. This tradition means that systems for payment and management of cash sums are not well established in LAs. The Green Paper also made proposals for a wide range of service developments, mainly concerned with multiagency working and shared commissioning of services to improve coordination with healthcare (see Chapter 5). It also raised the balance between protecting people from risk and enabling them greater freedom of choice about how to live their lives (see Chapter 6).

At the same time, the Department of Health conducted a consultation about healthcare, through a 'public engagement exercise'. This focused particularly on receiving feedback from excluded groups whose views are not often heard (Warburton, 2006). The outcomes of this were combined with those coming from the social care Green Paper and led to the publication of the White Paper on health and social care, *Our Health, Our Care, Our Say* (DH, 2006a). Many of the proposals are mainly about healthcare. The overall focus aims to move services from hospitals, so that people mainly receive care in their own homes. Improving local multiagency cooperation also features strongly. Management proposals emphasize users having a choice of service providers, and strong local commissioning. The document places partnership between services in achieving health and social care objectives alongside other social objectives for children's services and for the 'respect agenda', which seeks to deal with antisocial behaviour among, particularly, young people.

Proposed outcomes for social care services, which were strongly supported in public and professional consultation, were:

- Improved health and emotional well-being
- Improved quality of life
- Making a positive contribution
- Choice and control
- Freedom from discrimination
- Economic well-being
- Personal dignity (DH, 2006a: para. 2.63).

It is not surprising that these achieved wide support. These statements are 'motherhood and apple pie' values; many people can agree with them but would not necessarily agree about how to implement them. Drawing attention to the fact that social care is not a universal service, the White Paper (see Chapter 4) emphasizes the importance of good access to services and continues with the Green Paper's proposal of direct payments and individual budgets for providing social care. It suggests piloting these, however, in view of doubts about how useful they will be for some user groups. For people with long-term needs, the main proposals are better multiagency and multiprofessional help for people with very complex needs, and greater support for carers.

Another political initiative in 2006 was the Dignity in Care project (Lewis, 2006), launched with another series of 'listening events', which was designed to promote dignity particularly for older people receiving health and social care services. The Report of the public survey (DH, 2006b) identified ten major issues about dignity:

- Clarifying what dignity is
- Making the complaints system more accessible and easy-to-use
- Being treated as an individual by finding out their needs and preferences, not talking to them as a child, not assuming that they need help with everything, and being patient in allowing them time, for example to finish meals and activities
- Ensuring privacy
- Giving help with eating meals
- Ensuring that people have the right help to use the toilet
- Being addressed by staff appropriately, for example not using demeaning terms such as 'poppet' or 'love', which treats older people as children
- Helping people maintain a respectable appearance
- Providing activities that are stimulating and offer a sense of purpose
- Ensuring that advocacy is available to speak on behalf of people when making complaints.

Minor issues were language barriers between staff and users and mixed-sex facilities. SCIE published a research-based practice guide for social care workers to promoting dignity in care as part of the project (Cass, 2006).

Conclusion

In this chapter, I have examined ways in which practitioners in social care can explore the structures and policy that form their practice. National policy on social care is underdeveloped. Nevertheless, there are extensive structures through which professional practice in social care is developed nationally and within care organizations. This means that social care practitioners have a complex task of understanding the structures within which they operate and which they have to make work for the users and carers that they serve. However, this is a crucial task because caring in social care requires engagement with social institutions, making them work for users and carers, particularly as connectedness between services and users' and carers' values is the only way of ensuring that they are fit to provide a receptive, developmental caring.

- Practitioners need to understand how social care agencies interweave their work with the family and community lives of service users and carers.

- Users and carers interact individually with practitioners in the caring arena and politically as citizens.

- Social care policy and organization is integrated with education and healthcare and a strong policy and legislative framework has not yet developed.

- Community care and children's social care policy has shifted from institutional to integrated community services for major groups of people with care needs.

stop and think

- In your organization, how do managers' and workers' responsibilities to each other and their connections with service users work? What mechanisms are there for user and carer involvement and influence?
- Draw a diagram showing more complex relationships and interactions both within and outside team boundaries. How might you enhance organized connections with users and carers?
- Identify a user group that is important to you and seek websites relevant to their interests, comparing their views with what government websites say.

taking it further

Good general texts on social services policy and organization are the edited volumes:

- Hudson, B. (ed.) (1999) *The Changing Role of Social Care*. London: Jessica Kingsley.
- Hill, M. (2000) *Local Authority Social Services: An Introduction*. Oxford: Blackwell.
  These provide a good analysis of social care as part of the social services, but do not give a comprehensive picture of present systems.

Good general texts on community care and child care policy are:

- Means, R., Richards, S. and Smith, R. (2003) *Community Care: Policy and Practice*. (3rd edn) Basingstoke: Palgrave Macmillan.
- Fox Harding, L. (1997) *Perspectives in Child Care Policy*. Harlow: Longman.

- Cass, E. (2006) *Dignity in Care*. (Adults' Services Practice Guide 9) London: Social Care Institute for Excellence.
  This excellent guide contains ideas for practice projects, guidance on appropriate behaviour and a summary of the evidence base of the guide. It is a good guide to present government approaches to the practice of social care and is available on the internet: http://www.scie.org.uk/publications/practiceguides/practiceguide09/files/pg09.pdf

Websites

- UK Parliament website http://www.parliament.uk/index.cfm
  The UK Parliament website gives you access to Parliamentary debates (click 'Hansard') and research reports for MPs on all sorts of relevant topics. You can search Parliamentary debates for relevant topics; if you look at 'advanced search' and click 'select category' you receive a list of topics, of which 'health, well-being and care' is the most relevant: within this 'care' enables you to get at most of the topics relevant to this book.

Relevant government departments

- The most relevant ones are the Department of Health 'social care' website: http://www.dh.gov.uk/en/Policyandguidance/Healthandsocialcaretopics/Socialcare/index.htm and the Department for Education and Skills 'Every Child Matters' website: http://www.everychildmatters.gov.uk. There is also a social work careers website: http://www.socialworkandcare.co.uk/. This provides useful information about a range of social care roles.
- The Northern Ireland government website that covers social care is the Department of health, social services and public safety: http://www.dhsspsni.gov.uk/ . The Scottish government website gives access to information about Scottish policy on 'health and community care' and 'people and society' (for issues about social inclusion and the third sector): http://www.scotland.gov.uk/Home. The Welsh government website on health and social care is: http://new.wales.gov.uk/topics/health/?lang=en

4 Engaging and assessing in social care

Engagement: taking on a social care identity

This chapter, in which we look at engaging with and assessing service users and carers and their social situation, begins the sequence of chapters (4–7) that explore social care practice. Engagement is a process by which practitioners and service users become enmeshed in working together on social care issues faced by the user. It creates a connection between workers, their agencies and users and carers so that the social care services become part of the connectedness that generates a feeling of caring in people's lives. It leads to assessment, which involves practitioners in examining the range of factors affecting an individual, group or social situation in order to prepare, plan and take action to meet social care or other service objectives. Engaging and assessing means that practitioners face starkly the tension, explored in Chapter 2, that caring means receptiveness and aiming at personal development for users and carers, but social care requires intrusion of the official on private space. This means dealing with users' apprehensiveness about the profound change of identity from being self-caring to being dependent implied by being considered for social care.

Social care practitioners bring the potential power of public service, law and control of decisions directly into contact with the personal needs and wishes of individuals. For example Miller and Corby's (2006) study of parents' responses to the children's assessment framework, introduced in 2001, showed that many parents found its official and intrusive style unhelpful, since it raised questions about their parenting, rather than seeking to resolve difficulties helpfully. Many users are also aware of policy debates around costs and charges, so they know that practitioners have a duty to assess and perhaps to ration and refuse the care that users prefer. Many of the issues that arise for a worker as they engage and make relationships with users thus go back to tensions inherent in the individualizing and privatizing assumptions of Western society. Western societies, and present political policies, emphasize individual choice and personal responsibility while also providing for social cohesion and collective responsibility; these two elements of social care sit uneasily together and social care practice has daily to reconcile them.

In social work and social care, developing a professional relationship that has the style of a personal engagement is designed to enable service users to have a sense of security and safety that comes from the caring receptiveness of an interpersonal relationship. This interpersonal engagement allows practitioners to deal with difficult issues that arise around care and care services, and to make appropriate assessments of risk and need; without it the job cannot be done.

Some engagement techniques, by personalizing the interaction partly aim to disguise the public intrusion. For example, reducing the prominence of official documents and ticklists – by stressing the personal aspect of an assessment interview – hides to some extent the degree of official involvement and classifying of a human being. Dissembling through personal relationship skills is in tension with practitioners' social and personal commitment to openness that is integral to caring, and is the only effective way of tackling social difficulties. Therefore, practitioners face an ethical issue in using interpersonal engagement techniques to achieve the semblance of personal caring. There are two responses to the ethical problem:

- Genuineness in being caring
- Transparency about assessment responsibilities.

Maintaining an appropriate response to this ethical tension in all engagement with users and carers requires a self-awareness of the ways in which the engagement is an intrusion in the privatized family life of carers, and a genuine caring response to their predicament.

The social construction view of what is going on in engagements between workers and users provides understanding that helps meet this ethical responsibility. It is neither cynical about the motives of the participants nor exploitative of users and carers. Social construction analysis suggests that service users seek to construct a picture of themselves in the practitioner as an 'appropriate client', while practitioners seek to construct a picture of themselves with users as competent people (Taylor and White, 2000); in this way, they give each other confidence about themselves and allow the work to go ahead as a partnership. Users demonstrate their credibility as a truthful exponent of their situation by various conversational techniques. For example, they might try to show that they are appropriately involved in the situation, that they behaved morally and reasonably; describing the situation in convincing detail and showing how it is exceptional and therefore requires action. A man being referred for admission to residential care might emphasize the difficulties that he has been having, in spite of having tried to cope without extra help. Alternatively, users who are trying to defend themselves from involvement might minimize their responsibility for crucial events. A young person entering care, for example, might say that everything that has led to her admission is not her fault, or that it occurred in the past, but she is back to normal now. The picture that people try to create comes from their assumptions about what is appropriate, and they may be mistaken about this.

practice example

I recently visited a man who, presenting himself as a moral and reasonable person, told me that he did not want to take painkillers too readily in case they made him dependent on drugs. Therefore, he waited until he was really in pain before taking them. The picture was of someone trying to manage his illness by his own efforts, and not misusing the resources provided. In fact, he was accepting unnecessary suffering, since the painkillers are most effective when they are taken regularly to prevent pain, and in this situation do not create dependency. To deal with this, it is important to make transparent the message underlying the misunderstanding. I explained the medical information to him, and said that I appreciated how he might want to save public money and remain in control of his condition; in this case, the best treatment was to take the drugs regularly.

Often, practitioners use the picture that users try to create to gain insight into the personality and attitudes of the user. Using a social construction view, we do not have to be critical of users and carers presenting themselves in the best light; their doing so helps us to understand and work with how they see both themselves and also practitioners and their roles.

On the other side, workers often construct a picture of competence by allying themselves with the identity of their agency, using jargon and procedures. Morrison (2001) describes a team project in a social services department in the 1990s to reduce jargon in needs assessments written for service users. They started by trying to replace negative jargon about what users could not do with positive words, but found that this was full of jargon too. It required a lot of effort and constant self-criticism to achieve jargon-free needs assessments.

Engagement practice

A practitioner's responsibility to engage with the service user arises because any assessment or action in social care can only develop from the participation of both parties, and also of other relevant people, especially carers or potential carers; failure to engage must mean no further action. Miller and Corby (2006) found, in users' and carers' responses to a new children's assessment framework, that gaining trust was enhanced by listening to and validating participants' concerns, sharing concerns and creating an open interpersonal relationship. Involving parents was also necessary so that they felt they genuinely had influence and the practitioner was confident that they would try to make a contribution to improvements in their children's care. In this research, we can see how the positive developmental aspect of caring depended on achieving the receptiveness aspect through engagement. Engagement is the practitioner's responsibility because achieving social care objectives depends on it, but since it is a two-sided process, users and carers must also play their part and if they cannot or do not do so, practitioners need to help them engage. Engagement means that everyone present is clear that there is a connection between them that aims to provide social care and also clear about who is involved and why they are involved.

Receptive caring environments

Receptive caring means that simply by being there practitioners embody the availability of a service and a service system that offers caring. Avoiding a 'doing' mentality, and, conversely, building an emphasis on this place, space and period being open to caring are important. Many settings have multiple purposes that are unhelpful to caring tasks. For example, I have seen noisy and distracting children's home settings, with poor furnishings worn out and damaged by the residents' undisciplined liveliness. These need reorganizing with greater respect for the residents, with areas where privacy is possible. Old people's homes are sometimes laid out formally, with everyone sitting in chairs against the wall gazing at a constantly-on television screen; alternatively, fastidiously informal groupings can be just as limiting.

Practitioners can usefully think through how to shape environments to benefit caring. Settings may hinder a shared 'presence', in which users and carers together with practitioners can create a potentially helping social care space. Interview rooms can be made warm, clean, private, free from interruption and the people present comfortable; or they may be otherwise. In a home visit, practitioners need to negotiate to control interruptions and distractions, and try to organize the people involved so that everyone is comfortable. I recently visited a home with a comfortable sofa for two people sharing a room with a large kitchen chair and a plastic garden chair for sitting at a table. If the user, a disabled man, sat together with his wife on the sofa, the visiting professionals towered over them in the kitchen and plastic chairs. The man did not like people he saw as guests in his home sitting on uncomfortable chairs, but it did not help the interview for us all to sit on a row on the sofa. It was hard to find somewhere that was inclusive and put the people present on a level of equality and comfort.

The environment of a home visit and day or residential care settings need to provide for many different elements of living. Some interactions are shared; some require privacy. However, the purpose of day and residential care is to invoke at least some shared experiences. Therefore, people's comfort requires careful decisions about what is shared and the times at which sharing is relevant, and places and times when privacy is required for engagement. When I have been a visiting practitioner, it has sometimes been assumed that it is reasonable for me to catch the resident or attender in a public space to do private interviews. Many day and residential care conversations are routine engagements about daily living. This makes it harder to have serious conversations about life-changing matters when necessary. Taking people aside to a private place may come to feel demeaning or create apprehension. Also, sometimes the only private place is the administrative office, and that also brings expectations and sometimes an environment that is not appropriate for relationship-building.

Receptive caring in a caring environment generates a context for engagement. Research into family resilience suggests that, for children, family organization and emotional climate will strengthen vulnerable children's resilience in the face of adversities (Walsh, 2006). Walsh characterizes the requirements as warmth, affection and emotional support in the caring relationships and a clear-cut, reasonable structure and limits; this fits with the research reviewed in Research Boxes 2.2 and 2.3. Such an approach extends to everyone who needs care. Thinking about the requirements of caring relationships in general helps to decide how to be warm and responsive, kind and sympathetic and to organize the environment in a way that people can see is sensible.

The three rules of engagement follow from the need for receptive caring at the outset with a genuinely caring attitude:

- Practitioners' attitudes should be warm and welcome contact. A smile, an invitation to sit down, eye contact and a focus on the user are important, even if practitioners are doing something else. People in a hurry don't have to appear hurried. When I am in our hospice, I try to walk around slowly, make eye contact with the people I pass and say 'hello' or at least nod. This gives patients and colleagues a chance to stop me to say something, and if they do, I take the time to make an initial response.
- On first introduction, practitioners need to say their name, spell it if it is unusual or might be spelled in different ways, give their agency's name and some brief explanation of its main task with this user. If possible, I offer a visiting card, even if the user is blind, so that they have a record of who I am and can show it to a relative, another visitor or their carer. I also do this, personalized with a date and 'given to Mrs Edna Jones', when visiting people's rooms or bedsides in our hospice or in hospital.
- Explain in normal, jargon-free language the practitioner's role.

Another aspect of receptive caring is to make it clear that practitioners are paying attention and focusing on the right issues and people. Demonstrating caring means having eye contact with the people involved. Concentration on their concerns means observing and picking up small things as well as large things, non-material and material things. Practitioners, therefore, should start out by concentrating on being, rather than doing and saying things.

Developmental caring

Concentration then means responding to what is seen, said and done by moving on from being receptive to taking up the active, developmental aspect of caring. Starting to 'do' comes from receptive caring, because caring is the central aspect of social care, so having been caring begins the process of building confidence and making a relationship with users and carers that will facilitate the assessment and later intervention.

Critical incident, narrative, pathway and trajectory

Practitioners build on the referral or request they have received through receptiveness to users' and carers' concerns. Starting an assessment or admission to social care, practitioners are often presented with one or both of two things:

- A referral by another agency or a request for a service that comes from a critical incident that seems to demand social care
- A story or history of how the user has arrived at the point of needing the service.

The referral or request for service communicates a problem or need, as either the referrer or the user has identified it. However, the user and carer represent themselves according to their assumptions about what the practitioner is doing. This in turn affects the nature of the problem and how it is presented. Their presentation aims to get to the point where the practitioner's agency provides the service. Therefore, the presentation is constructed to achieve credibility for the problem as an entitlement to service. Users and carers may differ about what is credible as a problem that might lead to a service being provided. They may also be prepared to disclose only part of the situation, keeping back information that they think might be discreditable or displeasing. Therefore, it is useful to disentangle the variety of narratives that might exist within the stories told.

Thus, the description of the critical incident that has led to the referral reflects the possibly different perceptions that users and carers might have of what will achieve service. The story is formed into a narrative, an organized account of what has taken place, which comes from the family. Within the narrative, there is a trajectory, a description of the development of problems to the point where the social care intervention is sought to deal with them. This pattern is represented in Figure 4.1. This shows that the family's pathway in life continues, independently of any service interventions, although probably affected by interaction with services. As a problem arises, it begins to have significance for the family outside its normal pathway, so its rising trajectory as a problem takes it outside the family until a critical incident stimulates a request for service or referral. At this point, the family's narrative about their life pathway and a collection of narratives about the problem and its trajectory begin the service's engagement with the problem and the family. Observing how matters are presented helps the practitioner find out what is important and difficult to users and carers in the situation. The trajectory may be unusual or typical, and may gain veracity for the practitioner accordingly, and the narrative usually reflects a variety of struggles to deal independently with the issue that users are facing.

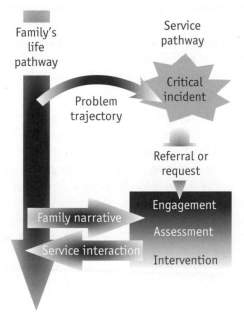

Figure 4.1 Pathway to service

case example

Joan, an elderly woman, had a flood. Some days previously, her main carer, a daughter who lived in another town, had visited and suggested she should apply for a home help to meet her increasing practical needs. Joan was familiar with this service because her mother had had a home help, but her mother's home help, twenty years previously, had performed mainly domestic tasks, and she was not aware that requirements for being provided with a home help were now more stringent or more connected with personal care than in the past. She telephoned the adult SSD and asked for help, but was told that this could not be provided without an assessment for social care, which would take several weeks. My guess is that at that time in the progress of her disability, she would not have been eligible for social care because her condition was not 'critical' enough, in the 'fair access to services' guidance that allows LAs to set funding priorities (DH, 2003). Joan sorted out her own flood, but her daughter found that she was resistant to further applications for social care, because 'if they can't help in an emergency, what's the point'. To Joan, an emergency was just when help was needed, while to the SSD duty officer a more comprehensive view of need was required.

Later, Joan's condition deteriorated, but to get her to agree to referral for social care took a lot of persuasion and a referral from Joan's GP some years later, when she was very much more disabled. This is an example where lack of responsiveness and a clear-cut system for dealing with people who are ineligible but in difficulties made things worse later. Joan would produce the story of the flood as a reason for not calling on social care services; this was partly a way of saying that she did not want to become dependent on outsiders. Her daughter felt that it was also connected to an argument that her daughter should move back to her home town. Different people involved would have a different story about what was important about the events of that critical incident.

When the referral finally bore fruit and an assessment led to regular visits from carers to help Joan get up in the morning and go to bed in the evening, she began to develop a relationship with the care manager and care workers. In the end, Joan formed a very good relationship with her two or three carers as she became more disabled and isolated. She received social care help with meals, disability aids and, again by referral from the GP, district nurse assistance with bathing and medical dressings. The story of her relationships with social care at the end of her life was very positive, and two of her carers took time off to attend her funeral.

A trajectory is the path followed, for example, by a bullet from the gun to the target. In healthcare, trajectory refers to how illnesses or conditions develop and change over time. In both cases, there is a typical pattern of how a bullet travels or how a condition develops, and looking at the service user in comparison with the typical path helps to understand whether problems have arisen quickly and in a complicated way, or more slowly. This concept also helps to see how far along a trajectory of a disability or problem the user has progressed. Trajectory helps to compare observations with formal knowledge about a disability social problem. Difficulties users experience can be compared with similar histories.

There are two uses of the term 'pathway' in social care. The more general meaning of pathway is the route by which people come to the service (Payne, 1992; see Figure 4.1). In Joan's case, above, the start of the route had been when her daughter had made some suggestions. Often, people are impelled along a pathway by a need and try several different places for help. Their experiences at each one affect how they deal with that agency, and how they tell their story when they move on to the next agency. Joan was in her own home, but if she had been in council or social housing, she might have gone to the housing authority or housing association for help, received it and not seen the importance of social care. Housing and healthcare organizations are the starting points of a pathway to social care for many people, being more universal services than social care. For children, education or the criminal justice system may often be the starting point; which route children take will affect how they are dealt with by a social care agency.

Joan's flood was a 'critical incident' in her life. A critical incident is an event that makes a 'significant' contribution, either positively or negatively, to the general aim of an activity (Flanagan, 1954: 338). In this case, a warm receptive expression of concern from the SSD duty officer and a redirection to an emergency plumbing service might have achieved a different outcome in Joan's pathway through the services later on. We can look at particular incidents in people's lives to see what significance they had for them and for the services' responses to them. Often the event that led to a referral or approach to a social care service is not the critical incident, but something that made that event appear significant to the people involved. So at a later stage of Joan's pathway, she had a fall, a neighbour found out, a police officer had to break in and call an ambulance, and she was taken to the accident and emergency unit of the local hospital. This alerted the GP to the need for referral for social care and was another critical incident on the pathway.

The more specific meaning of pathway in social care is the concept of a *service pathway*, a route through the available services that users with a particular medical diagnosis or assessed need follow. Sometimes these are 'integrated pathways' or 'integrated care pathways' that specifically define connections between services in different sectors of the economy or offered by different providers. In many areas, creating a pathway for different aspects of service is a way of increasing collaboration between different service providers (see Chapter 5).

Assessment

Most engagement takes place in the context of assessment of various kinds. Assessment in social work theory is itself an intervention because it helps to clarify the issues that users and carers face and focus attention on the alternatives. In turn, this helps them begin to respond to their problems.

Types of assessment

Assessment means examining the range of factors affecting an individual, group or social situation in order to prepare, plan and take action to meet objectives. Those objectives may be previously established, proposed by referrers or drawn from the assessment. The social work assessment role has a long history, from the work of the charity organization societies of the 19th century, and their church-based forerunners. They saw that collecting and organizing knowledge about applicants for services allowed them to allocate resources fairly and rationally. This is still why we do social care assessments. For example, doing assessments in adult social services care management assumes that detailed collection of information will enable practitioners to make decisions about the user's level of need, risk and therefore entitlement to services.

Social care assessment focuses on the social and on care. Therefore, it examines social factors, relationships and institutions relevant to the objective of providing care. This is different from many healthcare assessments, which as a starting point for treatment look at the base level of particular symptoms or problems that a patient is experiencing and then in later assessments check the change from that level.

Among assessment models that have influenced social care, the following represent different priorities and approaches:

- *Assessment in children's residential care* – this often involves extensive individual behavioural, family and community history and pathway analysis, identifying how various issues have arisen, because it is assumed that treating or repairing difficulties in the child's past life will be based on this.
- *Individual programme planning (IPP)* – this model, deriving from work with people with learning disabilities (McGrath, 1991; and see Chapter 5), focuses on ensuring that different professional perspectives, for example education, social care and psychology, are included in a comprehensive plan for delivering services.
- *Assessment as part of care management in community care* – this model examines factors that enable plans for a package of services from different providers to be assembled in adult social care.
- *Assessment on admission to residential care, or other specialist services* – this model seeks an overall understanding of a resident to establish their needs and wishes in residential life, or their needs for a particular specialist service, such as physiotherapy, occupational therapy, or speech and language therapy. It also seeks to ensure that the particular residential care or other setting can meet these needs.
- *Person-centred planning (PCP)* – this American model, deriving from work with people with physical and learning disabilities, focuses on bringing together all family members and carers as part of the assessment and planning process (LeRoy et al., 2007). It influenced the Department of Health policy on 'valuing people' in learning disability services (DH, 2001). Experience of this model of practice suggests that it leads to an organizational, and possibly legal, shift towards focusing

on users' requirements for services, through participation and direct payments (Dowling et al., 2006).

Drawing a clear distinction between these types of assessment is not entirely valid, since all have influenced each other. However, this list of assessment models draws attention to some of the tensions inherent in social care assessment. One tension exists between individual judgement and discretion and participation by different potential interests. Major interests are professionals, commissioners, providers, users and carers and family and community members, so some of the models aim to ensure getting all the relevant people involved. Sometimes the assessment is done by one of them, to plan access to services, and this usually means that specialists, such as a physiotherapist or the manager of a care home where admission is proposed, will need to carry out a separate assessment for their services at a later date. Person-centred and individual programme planning are attempts to increase the influence of user and carer interests on preparing the plan. The existence of these models recognizes and tries to limit the power of commissioners and providers and the impact of limitations of finance and availability of services. Instead they try to focus on the needs and wishes of service users and carers: IPP engages a range of professional views independently of service provision; PCP focuses on involving users and their social networks.

The assessment process

Social care assessment incorporates a cycle in which assessment is continuous, or at least regularly reviewed and amended. This is because it derives from the social work assumption that assessment is continuous, since information is only revealed over time, as engagement succeeds in achieving trust between worker, user and carer. Also, as social relationships achieve behaviour or social change, the practitioner's view of the situation changes. This assumption is less true with other professional assessment in healthcare and psychology that focuses on particular symptoms or behaviour.

The model of care management assessment adjusted from the DHSS guidance on care management is a fairly comprehensive example of social care assessment, and is set out in Figure 4.2. The assessment cycle can be seen here in the circle from assessment, through care planning and service provision (see Chapter 6) and evaluation and monitoring (see Chapter 7), returning to assessment again as a result of the review.

Prior to this cycle, there is a process called 'screening'. This has a number of different meanings. In UK community care practice, it means deciding on the complexity of assessment required, excluding people whose circumstances are not yet serious enough to benefit from a full assessment. A similar approach informs the Common Assessment Framework (CAF) for children and young people. If a young person does not require complex services, the individual professional provides for identified needs. In the USA, case management ideas, from which care management is derived, propose population screening to identify everyone who might need services and prioritize their needs. This sense has unfortunately been lost in the UK, so that care management has taken on a rationing approach rather than seeking to manage priorities after a full assessment of needs in a particular community.

Figure 4.2 contains two other elements, which have been introduced into care management assessment after its original formulation. One is provision for carers' assessments, brought about by the legislation summarized in Table 5.2. The other is the provision for direct payments or independent budgets to users for organizing their own services rather than having them organized by the care manager (see Chapter 6).

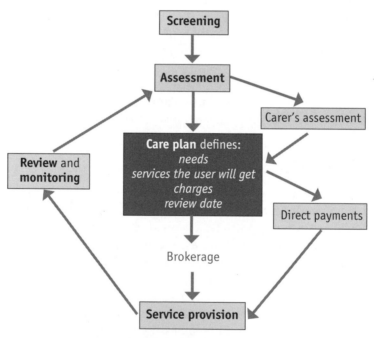

Figure 4.2 Community care assessment pathway

A further interpolation in Figure 4.2 is the stage of 'brokerage'; here, this refers to a way of organizing care management. It is not universal, and is therefore in lighter type in the figure. Where brokerage exists, the care manager assesses and plans the care, but a separate practitioner or department of the LA commissions the services from a range of agencies that the LA has contracts with.

Carrying out assessments requires practitioners to gather information. However, as with referral and requesting a service, this process also has social aims. Its most basic aim is to present a case for entitlement, so therefore the worker selects, organizes and describes the facts to present the best possible case for the service, or, alternatively, for not providing it. The assessment needs to present the practitioner as a competent and credible presenter of entitlement to service, and align the worker's behaviour and judgement with the behaviour and assumptions of other similar workers. Otherwise, questions might be raised about the validity of the worker's judgement.

Forms – tick infestation

One of the criticisms of social care assessment is the focus on completing the tick boxes on forms, or 'tick infestation', a light-hearted analogy I have borrowed from Gurid Aga Askeland and Mel Gray. The criticism is that it adds to impersonality in social care, because it involves completing many forms, rather than concentrating on the human beings that the forms are about. 'Ticking the boxes' also implies doing the job in a routine way to get approval, rather than looking at the human beings involved in a more complex way. Box-ticking on forms seems to make social care about boring paperwork, rather than human contact. It also makes users feel that they are objects of procedures, not subjects making decisions and plans about their own lives.

Not every practitioner is the same. One of my early social work learning experiences was to sit on a working party designing new forms for an SSD. Following my anti-tickbox views, I argued for lots of 'white space' for people to write what they wanted in a structure that was right for their material. We did a survey about two forms, one with boxes and one with space, and the response was virtually 50/50. Many respondents felt that they would not know where to start with lots of space, fearing that they might miss something important. People who preferred space to boxes, however, accepted missing out irrelevant boxes. We decided on making both boxes and space available. The study in Warwickshire mentioned above (Morrison, 2001) showed how an adult services team in a local authority adapted their 'open white space' community care assessments for users with some agreed phrases to improve consistency and make the assessments easier to write.

There are three answers to the tick infestation criticism:
■ Forms are fair; they improve justice and equality in decisions about allocating resources by collecting the same information about users in similar ways
■ Forms help to give the full picture
■ Forms can be adapted in a personal way; but practitioners need to work to avoid twisting people's needs to meet the form.

Admission to residential care is a useful guide to the processes we need to think through in all kinds of engagements. The residential care experience of Brearley et al. (1980) on children's admission to care is a useful summary of areas to focus on in assessment.

- What knowledge will they and the people around them need to make a decision about what they want, what they need?
- In turn, what do we need to know?
- How might they prepare for this change in their lives?
- What will be the personal implications of the change?
- How will the transition take place?
- How might they best feel integrated in the new situation?
- How will they recover from the change?
- What elements of the process will feel forced upon them, and compulsory?
- What losses and gains will they experience?
- What will help them adapt?
- In the new situation, what is the balance between freedom and independence, and between risk and safety?

Users and carers need to know from practitioners what the various options are and what it will feel like to take them up. What is a residential home or day centre like? Does the worker know it? Can they visit to see it? Can the worker say something about the experience of having a carer in their home? What are the practicalities? How will the job of the paid carer be negotiated with family members? If they are leaving their home, what will they need to pack? If someone is coming to their home, how will they make a plan for what the carer needs to do? What do they need to do to be ready for them? And so on.

I discussed above how engagement and assessment build the assessor's and applicant's veracity. Assessment systems ask for information to be presented in a way that allows managers or external observers to evaluate the practitioner's judgements. This leads agencies to increase the length and complexity of assessments over time, and reduce creativity and flexibility for practitioners to respond to issues. Assessments may be increased in credibility by confirming sources of evidence and comparing different sources, for example by comparing users' and carers' views with practitioners' observations. Finally, there is often a process of interrogation by independent observers. 'Assessment panels' allow senior staff to ask assessors interpersonally about their judgements. Assessors may find that the depth of information and the degree of personal as opposed to impersonal information that they can retell at such events support their credibility as competent practitioners. An early study of such a panel (Donald and Brown, 2003) found that it assisted by identifying cases where additional specialist assessment was required, and a number of cases where, with a period of intermediate care, a lower level of care provided at home could be achieved.

An assessment is, however, not wholly undertaken by the practitioner and received by service providers, users and carers. It is also used to manage resources and services, so that commissioners and providers extract information from it to make service provision decisions. Users and carers use it to present their case for services, so that they may limit or direct information to get it to move in the direction that they want. They may also be unaware of the options available to them. An example is direct payments, where there is evidence that workers downplay the opportunity to receive direct payments where they do not perceive the user as an appropriate candidate (Ellis, 2007; and see Chapter 6). This points to the reality that assessment is sometimes not a process that is open to all alternatives, since practitioner, agency, user or carer may close options off for their own reasons. However, openness about the alternatives available, and engaging in a negotiation about them, is an important way of strengthening users' and carers' security and confidence in the assessment and service provision. Most users and carers would prefer to be aware of the issues that practitioners consider, although it is also inappropriate to subject them to the anxiety of detailed information about negotiations and inter-agency discussions when they are powerless to affect such interactions. The best course is probably to discuss with them how much they want to be involved in the detail of such matters.

Needs assessment

The assumption behind much assessment, and the explicit requirement of community care assessment and assessment of children 'in need', is that assessments are of need. Bradshaw's (1972) study distinguished between four different kinds of need:
- Felt need, experienced by a user
- Expressed need, where the user informs others of a need
- Comparative need, where need is assessed by comparing users with similar people
- Normative need, where a need meets a defined requirement.

This approach identifies the way in which needing something is a psychological response to a personal or social experience that leads people to seek to remedy it. This is converted by administrative processes into something that demands the allocation of resources of services or expertise. This usage of 'need' is in tension with the management of resources, since the care deficit means that there are not necessarily resources available to remedy needs that are felt, expressed or normatively or comparatively assessed. Social care assessments are, therefore, a process in which several things happen:
- Potential service users come to understand that a need exists and accept that entering social care processes is a way of responding to that need, and meeting it, partially or fully.
- Felt need is expressed and understood by practitioners, who enable users and carers to be secure in the knowledge that their felt need is understood.

- Understood need is expressed as applications for resource allocation.
- The commissioners of public services decide the extent to which and the ways in which the need will be met by public resources.

Assessment may offer help because there are many alternatives at each stage of this process. For example, the user's trajectory may have forced them to apply for services, without fully understanding or accepting the need that exists. Their pathway may have led them to social care when an alternative pathway or their preferences might have led them somewhere else – to a housing service for example. During the assessment, they may find that they want to meet the need partially through their own or community efforts, rather than formal social care.

At the second stage, users and carers may not have the experience or communication skills to either feel or express their need adequately and practitioners may not be able to understand it or express their understanding well enough. At the third stage, the application may not express the need in the administrative terms required to achieve an allocation of resources, or to satisfy the user and carer that it has been satisfactorily expressed in ways that they find acceptable; they may object to being classified as 'disabled' or 'with dementia'. At the fourth stage, there are many different ways in which applications are dealt with. Practitioners may be able to commission some services, and make available their own time and efforts. However, mostly they may have to apply to a manager or through an assessment panel, which helps administer decisions consistently.

Carers' assessments

Since legislation (see Table 5.2) requiring assessment of carers of adults separately from users, a carer's assessment may, as Figure 4.1 indicated, be a requirement of many care management assessments in the community care system. One of the difficulties of doing this is the focus on users' needs, by both practitioners and carers themselves.

Nicholas (2003) reported an early study of the implementation of carers' assessments, which recommended that these assessments focus on outcomes. These included outcomes in:
- Quality of life for care-receivers
- Quality of life for the carer
- Managing carers' roles, including helping them to be well-informed, prepared, equipped and if necessary trained for their task
- Consequences for the organization of services, for example giving the carer a say in how the services are provided, to support their morale and sense of control in their own home.

This generated a process which moved between assessing and reviewing carers' needs and explicit gathering of carers' responses to the exploration and assessment at each stage, so that there were clear opportunities for feedback and a clear requirement to include the carers' views in final assessments. Assessments needed to define intended outcomes for carers and users and test the achievement of those outcomes at the review stage.

Thus, practitioners can usefully integrate carers' assessments in their assessment, care planning and interventions, rather than treating the carer's assessment as a separate entity. However, it may also be useful to be clear that a carer's assessment is being done and what are its outcomes, because this enhances carers' sense of partnership with practitioners. Of course, each different group has particular needs. For example, in a study of assessments of carers of people with learning disabilities, Robinson and Williams (2002) found that careful preparation for the first interview, reading the file, being prepared to explore the full needs of the carers and users and having a private meeting with the carer were all crucial to identifying carers' needs adequately. This needed to be allied to detailed life planning for the user and carers together, since occasional help for carers unconnected with careful planning for the user was inappropriate.

Government initiatives on assessment

There are two main government initiatives on assessment: the Single Assessment Process (SAP) for older people and the Common Assessment Framework (CAF) for children and families. These initiatives attempt to use assessment to achieve fairness between potential service users with disparate and complex problems and to manage potential costs. At the same time, these common assessment processes address the policy issue of making the service response seamless so that different services can start from the same initial assessment.

CAF is being rolled out from 2006, when guidance was issued (DfES, 2006a, b). It is connected with the intention to have a single 'Contact-Point' for professionals involved with children to see if others are already involved. This proposal is controversial because some argue that comprehensive records of children may be intrusive and label children as difficult in several services, when their problems have only actually affected one or two settings. The aim, as discussed above, is that most children without 'additional needs' will be dealt with through ordinary service provision. Children with additional needs, for example where there are parental problems, offending or special educational needs, will be assessed by an individual professional involved with them. If others need to be involved, a multiprofessional assessment will then be undertaken. Children with complex needs, such as those who are subject to a child protection plan, who are looked after, leaving care or where adoption is planned, will have a full multiprofessional assessment. The aim is to ensure that cooperation between services is achieved in working towards shared objectives.

People in social care responsible for children may find that a child comes into their service with a plan, or will be part of creating one. So a child who comes into residential care may have had an assessment if work in the community has been going on for some time, while if it is an admission after a court hearing or in an emergency, an assessment may be done in the early stages of their care.

SAP was introduced as part of the national service framework (NSF) for older people in 2002, mainly to coordinate health and social care services (DH, 2002). Local collaboration projects involving both health and social care agencies produce an agreed format in which they collect and share information. Mostly this should have been done by 2004, but the system constantly advances. It is supposed to apply to all services for older people, but in reality is mainly used for the most commonplace community care services for older people; specialist services that older people also use, particularly in healthcare (for example renal, cardiovascular or palliative care), are much less well provided for in most areas. The health and social care agencies also agree on consistent assessment tools. Available tools and documents can be seen on the websites listed at the end of the chapter. Local assessment systems are being progressively aligned to the local SAP.

Financial assessment

LAs make charges for care to parents for looked-after children, under Para. 22, Part III, Children Act 1989, and for all other services, under the National Assistance Act 1948. Therefore, the user or a relative is assessed by the LA to decide the extent to which the user or carer has a duty to make payments and is able to do so. There are complex procedures. Care practitioners often complete the forms for the assessment alongside an assessment of need or other work of engagement, although sometimes separate staff do this. Financial assessment therefore faces practitioners and users with the fact that service providers use their assessments to manage resources. This may be in tension with the aim to secure for the user and carer a sense that they have control or influence over the processes that they are entering. Moreover, a family's financial circumstances are part of the private arena. Some people may not have realized that applying for or accepting social care implied disclosure of their financial circumstances. The traditional stance of social work to try to get the best for users is inconsistent with their assessment and rationing role in community care. This has led to a feeling among social workers that they cannot act as advocates, which I argue in Chapter 5 is still an appropriate role. A similar view, but pursuing a different outcome, leads to the Green Paper on social care (DH, 2005a) proposal that an important role of social workers should be supporting users in operating independent budgets or direct payments.

One of the problems of financial assessment is that charging for social care is controversial. Among the reasons for charging are:

- Demonstrating in monetary terms the value of services offered
- Reducing the burden or service provision on the public purse
- Indicating and retaining personal responsibility for self-care
- Equity between those who can afford to pay and those who cannot.

However, in conflict with these is the concept of citizens' rights to services as an exchange with the state. In return for working, paying taxes and participating in society in other ways, users may feel they have contributed to society and are entitled to receive services if they need them. Users' felt need may not accord with normative definitions of need used by the state to manage resources.

Two particular areas of difficulty for practitioners are child care payments and payments for residential care for older people. Parents of 'looked-after' children often lose parental responsibility without choice, and resent having to pay for their children's care. Older people have often saved, had a struggle to buy a house, and, by paying care costs, face losing these savings or cannot pass an inheritance to others. Family members may also be aggrieved at the loss of an expected inheritance. A general response to users and carers raising such issues is that financial participation demonstrates continued commitment and acceptance of responsibility for being self-caring. It also buys entitlement to involvement and participation in decisions, and leverage for arguing for participation.

Among the responses to older people raising such issues is that buying a house is a financial transaction and life choice, entered into earlier in life, at least partly to save for later difficulties. The time of difficulty has now arrived. Also, the general social exchange requiring self-caring continues, and the state should not pay for people who are able to do so. Some complain that this user saved whereas others were irresponsible, but often the reality is that others could not afford to save to the same extent as this user. An older person and their family may feel greater self-respect by making a contribution.

There are two elements that make this sort of argument difficult. One is the general perception of poor standards in community social and residential care. One of the points made by the Sutherland Commission on long-term care (1999: chapter 8) was the need for good quality supportive services and a better balance between home and residential care, which would avoid the need for more expensive care services. Users and carers fear 'serial' carers, that is, having a different paid carer for each 'care event' only working for a few minutes before leaving for the next task with the next user. The argument of this book is that organizing services in this way is not an adequate standard of social care, since a continuing relationship and caring presence is required for effective social care. The other issue is the shift from NHS to social care for long-term conditions (see Chapters 2 and 3). Many people see the overlap between nursing and personal care and find it hard to understand and accept the narrow administrative distinction between health and social care responsibilities. While only a political change will resolve this issue, practitioners doing an assessment can enable people to express their feelings about this and help them make applications for available help. Being receptive to their feelings and acting on people's rights is part of the process of helping them adjust to the role of social care receiver. In the next chapter, I argue that practitioners make a positive contribution to dealing with these feelings and rights by working with other agencies and colleagues on behalf of users and carers.

Conclusion

In this chapter, I focused on the starting point of social care provision, the practitioner's engagement with a potential service user and informal carers and the assessment process. A crucial aspect of the engagement and assessment process is that it confirms a potential shift in personal and social identity for users and carers from being self-caring to being social care service users, in which an official service crosses the boundary into their private domain. Financial assessment and government initiatives to ensure equity and financial and management control of decision-making about social care emphasize the official intrusion.

The aim of engagement and assessment is to create a relationship that enables users and carers to feel secure that the practitioner will be able to provide a continuing service that will meet their felt and identified needs well. Moreover, because of apprehension about the consequences of the potential identity shift, the engagement and assessment needs to demonstrate users' and carers' continued involvement in making the decisions and control of their lives, in spite of losing the status of being self-caring.

An initial assessment takes place early in social care provision, undertaken by the practitioner on behalf of care agencies, involving users and carers. The introduction of financial assessment in the initial stage to permit charging for services may raise questions about the security of service supply in the minds of users and carers, and is therefore also in tension with the main objectives of assessment. This chapter, therefore, presents the case for practitioners' implementing engagement and assessment in a way that establishes, at the outset of care provision, that social care will involve a practice relationship that offers a caring presence in the new caring arena of the engagement of user with caring services. One of the failings of UK social care is that its processes do not ensure that caring continuity. In this chapter, I have suggested that how practitioners engage and assess care makes a difference at the beginning. In Chapter 5, I propose that effective work with colleagues and other agencies will enhance continuity, and in Chapter 6, that how they develop intervention and service provision can also help to deal with these difficult issues.

main points

- Social care engagement practice aims to help users and carers feel secure and in control as they exchange a self-caring identity for an identity of social care dependence and state intrusion.

- A social construction view of assessment suggests practitioners, users and carers will seek to construct a credible picture of themselves.

- Assessment involves exploring the user's narrative of how a critical incident in the trajectory of their problems has impelled them on a service pathway.

- Assessment involves tensions between individual judgement and discretion and the need for services to be accessed and provided fairly.

- Users and carers need to be involved in the preparation of assessments, so that they can present their felt needs and feel secure that the assessment will meet them.

- Financial assessment for social care services may raise concerns about security of service provision for users if payment is difficult, either emotionally or practically.

stop and think

- When you have encountered users and carers, what would have improved the environment and how could you have secured that improvement?
- Think about the jargon or complex words (see the Glossary) you might use doing an assessment or case review, and devise some normal alternatives.
- In the case of a person who might have to come into residential care, what will they, their carers and you need to know? How might you help them with preparation and feelings about the move?
- How would you respond to a parent who objects to paying charges for a looked-after child or to an older person entering residential care unwillingly?

■ Milner, J. and O'Byrne, P. (2002) *Assessment in Social Work*. (2nd edn) Basingstoke: Palgrave.
A good general book on assessment.

■ Holland, S. (2004) *Child and Family Assessment in Social Work Practice*. London: Sage.
Useful specialized book on child and family assessment.

■ Dowling, S., Manthorpe, J. and Cowley, S. with King, S., Raymond, V., Perez, W. and Weinstein, P. (2006) *Person-centred Planning in Social Care: A Scoping Review*. York: Joseph Rowntree Memorial Trust.
Useful summary and research review of person-centred planning and associated developments.

Websites

Useful websites on the Common Assessment Framework (for children and families) and the Single Assessment Process (for older people) are available on the relevant government websites:

■ Common Assessment Framework: http://www.everychildmatters.gov.uk/deliveringservices/caf/

■ Single Assessment Process: http://www.dh.gov.uk/en/Policyandguidance/Healthandsocialcaretopics/Socialcare/Singleassessmentprocess/index.htm

■ For SAP, the resource website at the Centre for Policy on Ageing is also very useful (and a bit more user-friendly than the DH website): http://www.cpa.org.uk/sap/sap_home.html

5 Partnership with agencies and colleagues

Partnership to provide continuity

Caring requires continuity because the receptive element of caring derives from connectedness between a user, their personal networks and formal care networks and the developmental element of caring requires a holistic focus on the development of the service user as a person, that is, on the whole person, including their social relationships. However, social care comprises a 'range' of services, as the definitions in Chapter 1 put it, part of wider services in education and healthcare. Somehow that range must be brought together to provide a holistic, continuous service. Focusing on social and cultural issues in social care requires a concern for the networks of relationships in which users live their lives and the social institutions involved in providing care. Practitioners also need to interact with colleagues within their own and other agencies. Negotiation, liaison and advocacy are crucial skills. Skilful work in all these areas enables good practice.

Many concepts in this area of practice, such as partnership and teamwork, are aspirational. That is, simply using these terms expresses the hope, wish or intention that ways of working should improve. However, aspirational talk sometimes conceals difficulties in achieving practical results. This is because the hoped-for outcomes are unclear or contradictory, or because it is not easy to move from the present to desired outcomes. Partnership ideas are expressed as political or managerial aims, but rely for their achievement on interpersonal professional practice. Organizational structure and management cannot achieve many partnership objectives. Instead, partnership comes from practitioners finding it useful and possible to achieve the necessary relationships.

Several concepts lie behind ideas of partnership, as follows:

- Holism, the assumption that services can and should deal comprehensively with an issue or with a user's or carer's problems and needs.
- Participation, the assumption that by participating in decisions or actions people will gain power to pursue their interests.

- Boundaries and barriers, the conception that interests of different parties in social care may be shared or may conflict. Differences of power, influence and status therefore create barriers and boundaries in the relationships between the parties in social care. Teamwork, partnership and collaboration are all practices that try to deal with those issues in social care.

This chapter therefore reviews some issues about boundaries, and then the various ways in which social care services seek to deal with boundaries, to create partnerships that provide holistic services.

Boundaries

Boundaries are the perception of lines marking an edge or limit that separates two connected aspects of life. Many of the most important boundaries are between different social groups and their social identities. Social inequalities, and particularly economic inequalities, are reproduced in barriers between users and carers of social care services and other social groups who do not have to use such services.

These social boundaries are accentuated by structural barriers in social care and related services (see Chapter 3). Charnley's (2001) analysis suggests several barriers that get in the way of partnership working in social care and in other public services:
- Structural issues, such as differing geographical boundaries and management systems
- Procedural issues, where workers have different lines of accountability or degrees of discretion
- Professional issues, where different professional groups have different values and cultures
- Financial issues, where budgets are constrained
- Policy issues, where there are different priorities, and conflicts, gaps or overlaps in service.

Partnership focuses on perceiving, crossing and maintaining boundaries. Everyone has different roles in their lives: in their work and families, as volunteers and as professionals. Usually, people try to control interactions between different parts of their lives by building or maintaining boundaries and by managing connections. The aim of doing this is to manage expectations of and demands on us. Delights or troubles in one part of our life should not make us unduly optimistic or worried over other things. The same is true of agencies and individual practitioners: they try to manage demands and interactions by establishing boundaries. Such boundaries follow the same boundaries between social groups as economic and social inequalities. Thus, boundary divisions between services connect with socio-economic divisions – making them relevant in social care as well as in other social interactions – and in doing so make them worse.

A boundary can mean different things. Some boundaries are markers, the white lines on a cricket or football pitch: we may step over them, but recognize a change in our status or role as we do so. Other boundaries are like walls; they prevent us from seeing what is on the other side, or require an effort to get over them. Some boundaries are like an ocean; we need a boat to get over them. Sometimes it is not easy to see where a boundary is. Is a sea's boundary at the top of the cliff or the rocks at the bottom? Is it as far as we can walk out to sea, or is it where the waves break on the sand? Is it high tide or low tide? It is also like this with human beings and organizations.

We decide boundaries to our behaviour by looking at the aims of our task or job. To have an effect on users and carers in their lives, we have to have a relationship with them and mean something to them. We help best by concentrating on their needs and wishes at a time of difficulty in their lives. Our focus on helping to care builds a connection across the boundary between their interests and ours; this means not seeking anything for our organization or for ourselves from the people we help. We therefore keep our boundaries by focusing on our role to provide care for users and carers and on their needs.

Negotiation

Because social care is about relationships between social institutions, ways of making arrangements between organizations are an important task for practitioners. Negotiation, mediating or bargaining are important skills to develop in achieving this. Activities involving negotiation, mediation or bargaining are practices undertaken by individuals on behalf of organizations. Often the aim of such practice is not to change the policy of the organization, which is cause advocacy (see below), but to achieve exceptions or accommodations within the policy.

All negotiation involves bringing together parties that have interaction with each other where there is potential for achieving changes towards greater agreement in actions, decisions or direction. A process takes place in which they move towards each other; to do this, the parties must understand that they have an interest in the outcome. If not, they cannot be engaged in the negotiation process.

Three ways of viewing a negotiation process are as follows:
1. A process whereby each side makes 'bids' to move towards a final agreement somewhere between their starting points. This view seems to place the parties in opposition to one another, and create a 'game' of guessing what the opponent's view will be and making bids to achieve a mid-point between them. It also assumes a 'zero-sum game', that is, that if one party loses something in the negotiation, that is a

gain for the other party. Many management texts on negotiation and studies of international conflict resolution understand negotiation in this way (for example Fisher et al., 2003).

2. A process of exploration, in which the parties investigate a territory unknown to both, and finally achieve a shared understanding through a process of mutual understanding. This is a less clear process than a bidding negotiation, but it can better represent complex negotiations, and allow both parties to gain from the process, rather than assuming that each will 'win some-lose some'. Raiffa (2007), for example, describes 'negotiation analysis' as a way in which groups of people might make joint, collaborative decisions.

3. A process of persuasion in which one party gets the other to understand and accept their point of view. This may be a way to see advocacy on behalf of user or carer, but it represents an extreme form of the zero-sum game. It is particularly inappropriate to use persuasion with a user or carer, because it interferes with their right to make decisions for themselves.

Mediation occurs when an outsider helps two parties come to shared understanding and agreement, and generally uses similar processes, with the benefit that an independent outsider can make the process more equal and open.

case example

Mrs Crawshaw, an increasingly frail older woman, was admitted for a trial period to a care home. This happened when her son, Joel, who lived nearby, found her one day having burned food onto two saucepans on her stove, because she had forgotten that she was preparing lunch. He worried about the risk of an accident and, in spite of having increased his support for her over the years, that she needed more care than he and other family members could give. Joel met with his two sisters, who lived further away and were prepared to agree to this, at least partly because they were unable to offer much practical support. Through his mother's GP, Joel referred her for a community care assessment. Under the 'fair access to care services' criteria various factors led her to be assessed as critically at risk and she was eventually admitted to a care home. She had really been persuaded of this in the crisis by Joel's strong personality, and by a congenial care manager who, however, had used a 'bidding' style of negotiation, which persuaded her that she was not finally giving up her home, but having a rest and 'trying out' residential care.

Towards the end of the trial period, Joel, the GP and the care manager successively tried to persuade her that she would like to stay permanently. Mrs Crawshaw's bids in this process referred to the promise that this would be temporary, but crucially she referred to the 'heartbreaking' loss of her own home. 'It's my home,' she said, with an emphasis on the 'my' and the 'home' in various of her statements. The opponents equally had bids in the negotiation: the doctor and care manager had professional assessments that she was at risk and, together with Joel, that they would be unable to provide the necessary support at home. Finally a favoured daughter agreed to take her mother out to try to persuade her, also without success: her mother chose the most expensive dish on the menu, complained about the cooking in the luxury restaurant, and firmly resisted all blandishments, complaining that Joel did not care.

As the care manager, perhaps you would hope not to have been put in the opponents' camp. I have often been in the situation where others have called upon me to persuade someone to do something they did not want to, so as to avoid risk. I have found it is nearly always counterproductive in the long term, since the user either dies (sometimes the case with assertively arranged admission to care for older people) or is then much more difficult to work with in the future. A further night at risk is only a further night in the same situation as before, and has been chosen by the user.

Looking at this situation as a mediator, I would go where the emotion is. I would want to explore with Mrs Crawshaw this 'heartbreaking' choice. Rather than persuading her what is necessary, in the eyes of others, I would want to spend as much time as possible exploring how it feels to her. I would ask her to assess the risks herself, to sit down with a list and count up all the advantages of each course. I would ask her to work out what she could do to help herself, to assess realistically what others might do.

Mrs Crawshaw has real power here, and she probably knows it. If she refuses, nobody else can stop her going home, nobody can lock her in residential care. If nothing else, the efforts of everyone to exert persuasion will be evidence to her that she can prevail. She is not yet at the stage where she has lost the capacity according to the Mental Capacity Act 2005 to make decisions for herself. Therefore, compulsory action is unlikely to be possible. If she goes home, the services will have to do what they can. It will not perhaps make her safe, but it would improve the situation. Eventually, therefore, it may be necessary to agree to a care package at home, and then sit down with Mrs Crawshaw to assess how safe it feels to her.

Mrs Crawshaw's case, therefore, is an example of the value of a 'let us explore together' approach to negotiation, and of the need for effective engagement and relationship-building in social care rather than persuasion and assertion. It also reflects an approach that values the user's own decisions and may reflect a social justice approach, since assertive persuasion is often used against people who do not have choices because they do not have the money to pay for their choices.

Community social work

Community social work is an important forerunner of social care for two reasons:

- It emphasized place as a basis for service provision with its emphasis on service being based in very local 'patches' or communities
- It incorporated home care as a major aspect of social work services for the first time.

Thus, community social work sought to promote continuity by focusing on the meaning of boundaries to particular localities, and locate service users within that boundary connecting them to that locality as a priority. It also tried to break down boundaries between social work practice and home care, giving greater priority than previously to services delivered in the home. It was an important feature of the community phase (see Chapter 3) of social care development because of its localism. When created in 1971, SSDs had taken over home help and mobile meals services from LA health departments. By integrating them into its thinking, community social work was the first innovation to see that social care services required a wider focus than social work.

It started out from local experiments in area social services offices during the mid-1970s. Then, it gained more influence when the majority recommendations of the Barclay Report (1982) on the role and tasks of social workers proposed it as an effective SSD organization. Social workers became engaged with it because it was a way of making progress with social change alongside the delivery of effective services and as part of a generic social work. Several SSDs used it as the basis of reorganizations to make services more responsive to local needs and interests. This became controversial, because it was the ultimate form of generic social work with responsibility for all the social work and care needs of a family being dealt with by one worker, without specialized training or responsibilities. The task seemed unlimited, and it made relationships with specialist services more difficult. In particular, generic social workers did not gain the confidence of users and carers involved with specialized child care or of healthcare professionals, who were used to practitioners focused on their specific conditions or problems. This affected mental health and physical and learning disability services. Research was an important contributor to the development of community social work, and there were a number of important studies of different aspects of it (Research Box 5.1). They showed that it improved their local understanding, but did not necessarily improve practice and service users did not experience any strong benefits or understand the innovation and how it was supposed to benefit them. Eventually, it lost its influence because the social services legislation of 1989–90 and the growing role of child protection required separate child protection and community care teams in SSDs.

Community social work

Why these studies were undertaken – To demonstrate the 1970s' ideal of the effectiveness of localized social services incorporating community development and home care service provision.
Methods – Case studies of local service development.
Results:
Going Local – collected accounts by staff involved in local experiments introducing community social work schemes. Documents current developments (Hadley and McGrath, 1980).

When Social Services are Local – comparison of two neighbouring and similar area social services teams, one using community social work, to show increased knowledge of local support provision among staff and greater integration of home care services with social work (Hadley and McGrath, 1984).

Creating a Responsive Public Service – case study of the reorganization of a social services department along community social work lines, demonstrating a more effective response to local issues (Hadley and Young, 1990).

Whose Welfare? – case study in the same local authority from the point of view of service users, demonstrating little understanding or involvement in the reorganization (Beresford and Croft, 1986).

Practising Community Care – case study of community social work in a local area social services team, showing that increased local knowledge resulted, but little responsiveness to local need (Bayley et al., 1987).

However, in its focus on continuity and connection with local commitment in delivering services in the community, community social work practice (Hadley et al., 1987) usefully contributes to social care practice.

Social care and wider care services

As social care has developed after the home-care focus of community social work, a range of types of care have emerged, connected together; these are set out in Table 5.1. The assumption of this view of care is individualistic, that is, most people look after themselves, and so are self-caring within their families and ordinary social networks. Many different forms of care are potentially available, and one of the roles of social care is to link with these, to help in forming a seamless whole, which de-emphasizes the boundaries that exist.

Table 5.1 Types of care provision

Care type	Location	Description
Education	Schools, colleges, day care, education centres, youth centres	Personal development through enhancing understanding and skills in dealing with life and fulfilling personal objectives
Primary care	GP surgery	First point of contact between citizen and the healthcare system, providing assessment and most treatment
Creative arts	Education, health and social care agencies, community provision	Using creative and artistic activities to achieve personal fulfilment and express emotional and cultural ideas
Social work	Social work agencies, and other welfare, education and health settings	Using social and psychological understanding interpersonally to influence social change, especially with people from deprived and excluded social groups, empowering them to act effectively, reduce social and personal risk, enhance social cohesion, provide welfare services and attain fulfilling lives
Psychological care	Education, health and social care agencies, private practice	Counselling, psychotherapy and arts therapies designed to assist people deal with psychological and emotional problems
Supported housing	Housing schemes/ community	Schemes that provide intensive support to people with care needs in housing built or adapted to meet their needs
Community care	Community/care, homes	Policy of providing health and social care in non-institutional, normalized settings
Social care	Community/care, homes	Personal care to meet non-healthcare needs
Residential care	Care homes, care homes with nursing	Social work, social care and education provided in settings where people live in groups with others
Secondary healthcare	General hospital, including psychiatric units	Accident and emergency services in large centres and base for assessment and treatment on referral from GPs
Intermediate healthcare	Hospital/ community	Care to assess and rehabilitate to return home patients who have had extended or complex treatment in secondary or tertiary care
Tertiary healthcare	Specialist hospital or healthcare establishment	Advanced treatment for unusual or complex illnesses or conditions, including psychiatry, and palliative care for people who are dying and their families
(NHS) Continuing care	Community/care, homes	Care to meet a primary healthcare need that would otherwise require hospital treatment

SOURCE: Developed from Stevenson and Spencer (2002).

The first part of Table 5.1 therefore starts from three general types of service – education, primary healthcare and creative arts – that are part of everyone's lives, provide resources for personal resilience and social cohesion and often contribute to aspects of care. The second part of Table 5.1 covers social work and psychological care, which also make contributions to many different agencies with their different ways of dealing with personal problems, and social integration. Being less universal, although widely available, their focus is to respond to difficulties that people have in personal and social integration into a cohesive society. The third part of Table 5.1 lists a range of care services, growing in complexity and the extent to which they intervene in people's private lives. This table does not represent an integrated system. Two important elements are community care and NHS continuing care (see Chapter 3), which in different ways finance health and social care services in people's homes and the cost of residential care. These are connected outside the table on the left. The three main elements of NHS healthcare, primary, secondary and tertiary healthcare, form a system of increasing specialization and are linked on the right of the table. Many other elements of care services are linked into NHS healthcare.

Forms of service partnership

Partnership

Partnership working is an important aspect of government policy in health and social care and in other aspects of social policy, for example in dealing with community issues, urban regeneration, probation and offender management and housing. Partnership is an aspiration to create cooperative relationships between personnel in different services so that they pursue similar objectives in coordinated ways. Therefore, promoting partnership implies focusing on relationships between personnel, their aims and the way they work together. Partnership can mean working together between:

■ Central and local government
■ Private, public and voluntary sector organizations
■ Community organizations and official agencies
■ Commissioners and service providers
■ Service users and carers and health and social care or education agencies
■ Service providers and educators
■ Service providers and researchers.

Policy, both of government and within the organizations concerned, seeks to support structural arrangements for partnership and agreed aims, which in turn support partnership practice. Systems of joint funding or organization particularly between health and social services organizations have developed over many years; there have been constant changes to try to improve cooperation and collaboration through funding and management mechanisms.

For example, at the time of writing, developments in local commissioning are being planned, reflecting shifts in focus on local, regional and national coordination. An example of structural arrangements for partnership is the legal and structural provision for 'flexibilities' in the Health Act 1999 section 31, renewed in the National Health Service Act 2006, section 75, which is an attempt by national policy to enable local coordination in practice. The flexibilities provide for:

- Lead commissioning, in which a local PCT or SSD would take the lead in commissioning services on behalf of both for particular aspects of provision
- Jointly commissioned services, in which managers in separate state organizations work together planning the pattern of services in their area
- Integrated provision, in which they would merge parts of all their services
- Pooled budgets, in which they would agree one budget for services in some or all parts of their provision.
- Care trusts, where the whole service is combined to create single-purpose legal entities to deliver care services in an integrated way.

Many partnership structures are, like this, examples of aspiration: they depend on how practitioners are enabled to use them in everyday practice. Also, coordination objectives through organizational integration of this kind are unlikely to achieve improvements in services because there has been no commensurate transfer of resources from healthcare to social care (Glendinning and Means, 2004).

However, useful developments may come from practitioners and managers finding ways of working together. An example of joint commissioning is the learning disabilities commissioners for health and social care in one of the authorities that I work with, who meet regularly and plan commissioning together. They approached my hospice to plan end-of-life care for people with learning disabilities. They joined meetings with us about the plans and advised on how they would fit with other elements of the service. However, because this coordinated practice involves new resources it does not come up strongly against barriers between existing services. Everyone can agree that it is an improvement, and shares interests in supporting it and making it work, as in this example of end-of-life care for people with learning disabilities. Nearby, the services for mentally ill people are part of a care trust in which the local authority has delegated its elements of service to an organization managed as part of the health service. This has required a much more extensive realignment of resources and clashes with different professional and disciplinary interests, so it has been much more difficult and expensive to organize.

A variety of possible structures might be used, therefore, depending on the pattern of services in any particular area. Most areas have not taken full advantage of the potential flexibilities, because of differences in aims, practices, financing and responsibilities. It usually requires considerable management, policy and political drive to deal with all the complexities and structural changes required to advance partnership to deal with inter-personal and organizational barriers. One way of responding to these barriers is to provide support and leadership in making the changes, for example through demonstration projects, either taking research from an existing project, or building upon an existing initiative. A recent example is work to pilot the user involvement initiatives on individual budgets and self-directed care (see Chapter 6) coming from the social care Green Paper (DH, 2005a) and the NHS White Paper (DH, 2006a) and undertaken by the Care Services Improvement Partnership (CSIP, 2007). A number of pilot sites for trying out the policy were established, and the website contains interim reports on outcomes, documents used by various projects, queries by practitioners working in the projects and official replies and connections to partner agencies representing users. All this enables a more immediate involvement by a wide professional constituency in development projects compared with previous generations of development. However, it also requires practitioners to keep in touch with the relevant websites (see the website list at the end of the chapter).

Participation with carers

An important aspect of continuity is maintaining relationships with carers in the service users' social networks, since carers will be at the centre of care for many users. They may be coordinators, although often users coordinate their own care, or influence that coordination. Practitioners therefore need to think about their partnership with carers, and policy since the 1990s suggests that this partnership should facilitate carers' participation in deciding on and delivering care. Previously, health and social care professionals decided what would be provided. Services had developed in quantity and sophistication for some decades and the political impetus had been constant improvement. During the Conservative governments of the 1980s, political assumptions shifted to reducing state responsibility for informal care, at the same time that a carers' movement developed collective action. The focus became support to carers rather than substituting for them. The Griffiths Report (1988: 5), which laid the foundation for the community care system, solidified the shift, stating: 'Families, friends, neighbours and other local people provide the majority of care in response to needs which they are uniquely placed to identify and respond to.' Research also supported this move (Twigg et al., 1990).

These moves culminated in legislation to institutionalize the role of carers within services. Table 5.2 sets out the steady progression of carers' rights. Alongside this was an equivalent development in the role of foster carers and adoptive parents in child care practice. All these developments represent a political shift towards the recognition of rights to involvement in decision-making, which parallels users' greater rights to involvement in decision-making, for example the now common process of involving parents in decision-making about looked-after children, and physically and learning-disabled children. The primary right affecting social care is the duty to carry out a separate assessment of carers' needs as part of the community care assessment process (see Chapter 4). Although initially enacted in the mid-1990s, this right has been continually reinforced by legislation, most notably the Carers (Equal Opportunities) Act 2004. The reason for this has been that practitioners have not readily taken this responsibility on, at least in part because there are few resources to provide any services. Also, healthcare professionals mainly focus on patients' needs, and do not refer carers for assessment. In my experience, many healthcare professionals are not aware of the right to separate assessment, although part of the reason for lack of referral may also be a sense that resources are not adequate to provide the necessary services.

Table 5.2 Legislation on carers

Legislation	Main points	Comments
Carers (Recognition and Services) Act 1995	Introduced carers' assessments	First statutory recognition of carers separately from users. Ineffective because it required carers to request assessments
Carers and Disabled Children Act 2000	Rights to services, direct payments and respite care vouchers; charges for services to carers	Responded to evidence of neglect of disabled children
Employment Act 2002	Rights for parents of disabled children to ask for flexible working arrangements and unpaid time off in emergencies	Beginnings of the process of making employment flexible for carers
Carers (Equal Opportunities) Act 2004	Duty to promote social inclusion, provide assessments and meet education and work needs of carers	Reinforced the 1995 Act and requires a more positive approach by local authorities
Work and Families Act 2006	Rights of employees to ask for flexible working for caring responsibilities	

SOURCE: CSCI (2006).

Recognition of the role of carers is important, but there are complexities in the relationship between carers and formal services:

- Conflict of interest between users and carers
- Distinctions between support and empowerment. Carers in their caring relationship with users may wish or need to be enabled to take on more responsibility for directing services, whereas providers, perhaps to constrain costs, seek to be in control
- The role of costs and charges connects with providers' need to be in control. In Chapter 4, I suggested that financial assessment is a major issue for carers in care management decisions in adult services
- The poor resources available for work with carers, and the need, felt by both carers and practitioners, to give priority to users' needs.

Because most people are self-caring in most things for most of the time, receiving care services implies dependence, and receiving carers' services also implies dependence for carers. Service providers may overgeneralize about self-caring being the norm and take it for granted that users are self-caring, when they are not and carers are doing a lot for them that goes unrecognized. Alternatively, providers may assume self-caring to be desirable and stigmatize carers who are not cooperative about providing care. Receptive caring means that practitioners need to examine the extent to which and how carers might be able to take or retain control of their family lives and caring tasks. Developmental caring means looking at how people may be enabled to take or retain control. Being self-caring means being self-sustaining as a carer, and it may not occur to many carers to be an issue over which they can have control and for which they can actively seek to get help to achieve. Barnes's (2006) study of carers' biographies (Research Box 5.2) makes clear how their life histories have placed them in positions that limit their capacity for control over their lives. This is because the kinds of social negotiations identified in Research Box 2.1 have left them with few choices other than to make decisions to accept burdensome caring responsibilities. The lack of choice significantly connects to gender inequalities, since, as suggested above, inequalities in caring services connect with wider social inequalities.

Legislation and financial support for caring provides opportunities for help to carers. The Employment Rights Act 1966 gives carers the rights to reasonable, but unpaid, time off and parental leave to meet caring responsibilities particularly for the child care responsibilities of parents. The Work and Families Act 2006 gives further rights where people are caring for other dependent relatives, including flexible working and part-time work. Many employers are more generous in their provision than the legislation requires, because this allows them to support social cohesion and maintain their workforce. Social security provision includes the carer's allowance for carers themselves and disability living or attendance allowances for the user, which can help to pay for care costs. Government policy moves towards direct payments or independent budgets (Chapter 6) can also provide for carers' costs.

Barnes's carers' life histories

Why this study was undertaken – To identify, by examining carers' accounts of their lives, how a present caring relationship interweaves past history and future hopes for the people involved.

Methods – Extended interviews with twelve selected carers: five mothers with disabled children, one son and three daughters caring for parents, three older people caring for partners because of long-term disability or dementia.

Results – Caring tasks are important, but carers generally saw caring as situated within sets of relationships, in many cases in gendered roles; giving and receiving caring was part of long standing connections between people. Care givers and receivers saw caring as part of political relationships and human relationships: caring was a right in a shared human relationship and an expression of citizenship that should be offered to and received by people as part of society.

Source: Barnes (2006).

Issues with user participation

Participation has been a crucial element in policy development in attempts to deal with inequalities. Giving people a voice in service development aims to redress inequalities that lead to injustice in care provision: movements for carers' participation in planning and delivery of services to users are part of this. However, there is a critique, deriving from such participation in social development and planning, of a universal allegiance to participation as an ideal of service provision. It has been described as a new 'orthodoxy' (Stirrat, 1997) and 'tyranny' (Cooke and Kothari, 2001). Some of this critique applies equally to social care. There are a number of reasons for concern about participation:

■ The user or carer's internal knowledge and understanding may be limited; external input and analysis may be helpful to achieve successful outcomes.

■ Populism may result from participation; that is, pandering to the assumed wishes of the majority, who may not have been fully consulted, on the basis of well-publicized views that have, for whatever reason, gained credence in an organization. Minority ethnic groups and disabled people particularly resent practitioners making global assumptions about what 'they' want.

■ Weaknesses in representation may weaken the value of participation. It is important not to see this as an argument that because there have not been formal elections or other structures for nomination of representatives, participation is not valuable. It is more that people may not be able or may not wish to represent a range of views in the face of significant problems that they face as individuals. For example, I sometimes meet carers in representative capacities whose stage of thinking about services reflects only their personal experience; in effect they repeatedly 'tell their story'. While this is sometimes helpful, it does not contribute well to planning or research projects. If this is so, we might not abandon attempts to achieve something because participation is absent, but need also to examine how we might organize participation so that it enables or trains users and carers to achieve it. They are not achieving participation if they are irritating everybody.

- There may be a myth of a community of interest between a group of local residents, or the people who live in a care home; sometimes their interests conflict.
- Related to the previous point, there may be a plurality of views among participants, and this may make it difficult to make decisions or resolve disagreement.
- Manipulation of participants may take place. This is not necessarily intentional. Often, for example, uninformed, unconfident or inexperienced users and carers may accept the views of respected professionals. It is sometimes said that too much credence is given to doctors, because of the respect engendered by their high social status and good education. Similarly, what an official says may be accepted uncomplainingly, even if people have doubts about it. This may be particularly true with social groups such as people with learning disabilities or children who have not been able to form their views, or have insufficient experience of or competence in expressing them.
- The agency sets parameters of participation inappropriately by its objectives. For example, agencies often ask users questions that interest them, but do not listen to points users make that do not fit in with agency concerns.

These points are not an argument against participation. They are an argument for careful implementation of and preparation for participation, and careful consideration of opinions that result. Therefore, practitioners should be realistic about the capacity and resource for carers to become engaged in participative endeavours. Carers give priority first to their caring, and want to see direct results from participation in improvement for the person that they care for (Rogers and Barnes, 2002).

It is also important to examine the needs of different social groups for support in the caring that they provide. For example, a variety of studies have examined the experience of minority ethic groups. Hatfield et al.'s (1996) survey of Asian families experiencing mental health problems found that Asian patients and families did not reject mainstream services in favour of help from their families or communities. However, they needed help to make use of medical and other help, and past experience of language difficulties and racism made them apprehensive in approaching services. Practitioners need to be aware of these possibilities and compensate for them. Hatton et al.'s (1998) study of Asian people with learning disabilities and their families and carers found that in spite of a high need, carers and users had little awareness of services, which were not targeted at those with the greatest need. Social care workers could help by getting information from and consulting with people in Asian communities, compensating for variations in service provision and responding to the fact that local service histories had a strong influence on what was available.

Coordination between services

Collaboration

Since organizations cannot participate, only people can, organizational partnerships operate through people and their collaborations, which may take the form of:

- Strategic collaboration, with the aim of aligning policies and management structures
- Collaboration or joint service management
- Joint service delivery, including multiprofessional work
- Case management structures; collaboration in responding to the needs of particular cases.

Higher levels of this list of inter-agency structures may provide the context for practitioners' collaboration in providing services or working with service users, but collaboration at the practitioner level is not completely dependent on structures. However, there is evidence that conflict over resources between managers may limit the effectiveness of practitioner cooperation over cases (McGrath, 1991). Therefore, caring services are better provided in a strategic and management partnership, but the main focus of collaboration is likely to be between managers and practitioners at the lower levels of organization, in their everyday work.

Teamwork

Teamwork is often proposed as a way of promoting collaboration. Teamwork arises in social care in various ways:

- Teamwork between users, carers and practitioners. This is another way of understanding users' and carers' participation in planning their own services, helping people feel that they are equal members of a team working together.
- Teamwork with colleagues doing the same work in the same agency.

Most agencies organize staff in groups, which may be developed to make progress in improving the service.

■ Teamwork between colleagues doing similar work in different agencies – multi-agency teamwork.

■ Teamwork involving people drawn from different knowledge and skill backgrounds (multidisciplinary) or from different professional backgrounds (multiprofessional). Multidisciplinary teamwork deals with differences in approach from different intellectual backgrounds. For example, doctors and nurses are trained in biomedical sciences, social workers and psychologists in the social sciences. Multiprofessional teamwork deals with differences that come from different training and socialization. For example, doctors, nurses and psychologists often have an individualistic focus, on the specific patient or client, while social workers focus more widely on families, social networks and community needs.

■ As a form of collaboration, a variety of ways have grown up for developing teamwork; this is usually called teambuilding. Table 5.3 identifies four different types of teambuilding.

Table 5.3 Approaches to teambuilding

Approach	Strategy	Critique
Organization development	Plan an organizational structure including teams that meet organizational objectives	Top-down, prioritizes organizational not team aims; excludes users and carers
Group development	Improve interpersonal and group relations	Focuses on team relationships, encouraging 'navel-gazing'; excludes users and carers
Contingency or situational teambuilding	Identify team members' preferences, types of work done and organizational imperatives and develop teamwork accordingly	Responds to needs and wishes of team members and their work; focuses on tasks rather than people; focuses on team rather than users and carers
Everyday teambuilding	Identify and tackle team issues continuously in every aspect of work; use team projects to develop team resources	Practical and relevant to everyday tasks; more difficult meeting strategic and change objectives; may involve users and carers

SOURCE: Developed from Payne and Oliviere (2008).

Organization development as an approach to teambuilding connects with strategic forms of partnership discussed above. It largely excludes practitioners, users and carers, and therefore is unlikely to achieve participation. Group development teamwork focuses on group relationships, trying to create a cohesive group of people and is an important approach to social care teamwork. It aims to build cooperative relationships and shared decision-making in the group. Activities to achieve this include team meetings, social events, 'awaydays' and projects. However, this approach to teamwork is based on psychological theory that groups take on a life of their own because they need to create a shared identity and purposes, which may differ from the preferences and concerns of team members. Agencies also place expectations on the group to reflect the organization's agreed or approved identity and give people team roles that also cause them to behave differently from how they would behave in a natural human group. Thus, people often find that teamwork creates tensions between personal aims and hopes and ways in which they are expected to behave in the group. Teamwork makes this worse because of the additional tensions imposed by organizational aims. Team-building in a group relations perspective assumes that these tensions and conflicts may sometimes need to be exposed in order to be made clear and dealt with. This worries people because they fear that it may lead to relation-ship difficulties in the team. It may also raise emotions and interpersonal conflicts that are hard to deal with. Therefore group relations teambuilding that goes beyond improving interpersonal relations among workers is often difficult to achieve and resisted by the people involved.

Situational teambuilding is knowledge-based. It sees members of the team as bringing their personal skills and knowledge into the group. The purpose of teamwork in this approach is to facilitate people to contribute to the team's work, enabling the team to learn together to develop their work jointly. Wenger (1998) discusses how effective work groups become communities of practice, in which by working together they can contrib-ute to developing a shared approach to practice. Opie's (2003) study of a range of teams in social services organizations is an example of this approach in action (Research Box 5.3). One important outcome is the guidance to team leaders to facilitate contributions of their expertise by team members, rather than simply keeping relationships happy.

research box 5.3

Opie's knowledge-based teamwork

Why this study was undertaken – To explore how organizational context affected teamwork, by examining how knowledge was used in effective teams, rather than focusing on the quality of interaction between team members.

Methods – The researcher studied six New Zealand teams deal-ing with long-term illness and disability in in-patient and community settings by observing and tape recording succes-sive meetings, case conferences and other events where most team members came together to do significant joint work. Tapes were transcribed, themes analysed, and teams' narratives of themselves in the organization and how they made their work effective were identified.

Results – Rich data about how the teams worked is available, which I do not summarize fully here. In health and social care organizations, the body and person of service users are fragmented, and different professionals' involvements are brought together in the team. Teams create knowledge about the user and their social setting drawing from the work of different members. In this study, effective teams helped team members express their assessments and roles with users, and brought these together in a joint plan, which also accepted and integrated different professionals' conceptions of their role and tasks. Effective teamwork skills did not lie in interpersonal or interprofessional interactions, but enabled the expression of knowledge from different disciplines and enabled a discourse to take place, which integrated that knowledge into an overall conception of the user, their circumstances and the 'case', accepting however that there remained different points of view and different roles to perform.
Source: Opie (2003).

This has been achieved most clearly in mental health work. Onyett (2003), reviewing research and practice literature on mental health teams, identifies a range of interventions that provide support to staff, including:

- Promoting role clarity
- Creating manageable workloads
- Minimizing paperwork
- Maintaining physical safety
- Promoting interpersonal contact between team members
- Sensitivity to gender issues
- Autonomy to control work and exercise professional discretion
- Promoting effective leadership
- Helping people achieve a personal focus for their work
- Organizing peer consultation to share expertise
- Making team meetings work well.

Another important distinction is between:

- *Organizational teams*, where teamwork is used to build relationships to meet organizational aims. Examples are regular liaison meetings to deal with issues that affect two or more organizations or local commissioning groups.
- *Service teams*, where teamwork is used to improve integration in a range of services or in a particular community. Examples are community health or learning disabilities teams, or assessment teams for older people or people with dementia.
- *Case teams*, where a group of people work together on a particular case plan and coordinate their work.

Team members may have different views of the team. People who are often excluded from lists of members are managers and administrative staff. This raises questions about their different roles and interests: to what extent and in what ways is a manager a member of or separated from a team? A network diagram of regular connections may draw attention to some with which team members have not taken care to build up relationships (see Figure 3.3 for an example). Similarly, a network map dealing with the connections in a complex case, shared with others, can draw attention to different ways in which you deal with a case.

case example

A care manager discovered that a care home resident had, for reasons of past domestic violence, been given an injunction against her husband, who was not supposed to contact her. When she entered the care home, he had taken over some practical responsibilities, and needed to contact her. Also, she wanted him to visit her, needing his emotional support at this time. This reflects the ambivalence that people often feel in conflict situations. The home manager was concerned about possible risk to her staff, but the experience of the husband's visits had been favourable and she was prepared to let them continue, since the patient had the right to vary the order. However, the husband asked for a letter about how successful the visits had been to take to the court in a further hearing. The care manager felt that the husband might have been treating the situation as an opportunity to influence the court hearing. Also, as it was the care home staff who had contacted the police about the terms of the order, she did not have sufficient information about the detail of the events that had led to the injunction to be able to make a decision about arrangements and support for the resident on discharge.

This case draws attention to the need for clarity on an everyday basis about who does what and why in particular cases. In this case, the care home manager was focused on concern for her staff, while the care manager had the responsibility for ensuring that the ambivalence of the service user did not lead to her being unsafe. It also draws attention to the importance of gaining a range of views about conflict situations, where different views of events may be relevant.

case example

A care manager was arranging services for a patient being discharged from a psychiatric unit after very difficult behaviour. Visiting the user's parents' home, he asked about the behaviour of the user at home, to discover a history of violence against them by the user when he failed to take his medication. The discharge was likely to place them at considerable risk. However, the staff at the hospital had accepted the user's accounts of what had taken place, in which his behaviour had seemed fairly innocuous. Enquiring further, it seems that the user saw the parents as over-restrictive, and had been encouraged by staff at the hospital to be more assertive with them about his needs for freedom. This seemed likely to encourage and validate further violence against them.

This case illustrates again also how carers (the parents) and users may have very different assessments of the situation. Those whom Twigg and Atkin (1994) called superseded carers may be in a complex situation. This is where the carers may wish to be protective, but developing the independence of the user may entail a certain degree of risk.

These examples lead me to the fourth type of teambuilding in Table 5.3: everyday teambuilding. This arises when team members agree to take a responsibility for developing teamwork as they go along in every task, and connects with case teamwork. The following process can help to decide on involvements, and incorporates users and carers in the team, even if they are not formally in the organization's team:

- Identify, using a genogram or family tree, the user's kin networks
- Identify, using social network analysis, formal and informal connections in the user's life
- Looking at the care plan, identify agencies and the workers in them that have to be kept in contact with the situation
- Consider whether a family meeting, or agency case conference is needed as part of developing the care plan
- Consider what regular mechanisms are needed to keep in touch in order to provide suitable support mechanisms that make you and the services accessible and available
- Consider timescales and the places in which contacts will be regularly maintained.

By planning everyday teamwork carefully in each individual case, practitioners can helpfully improve the response of the network of agencies and people involved with meeting a particular user's needs. By looking periodically at the regular contacts generated among agencies by doing everyday teamwork, practitioners can work on developing teamwork across agencies and professions, without needing formal teambuilding activities that can produce angst and take up time. Moreover, everyday teambuilding connects the team directly with users' and carers' needs, involving them more actively in the team's thinking with greater equality, improving how formal and informal networks interweave.

Advocacy

The general meaning of advocacy is to speak on behalf of someone in favour of their interests. It is most commonly associated with the professional role of lawyers, particularly in their work in courts on behalf of their clients. Social care incorporates two types of advocacy:

- *Cause advocacy*, called macro social work in the USA. This practice identifies and works to remove or modify political and social issues that form barriers to achieving users' and carers' aspirations.

- *Case advocacy*, the process of representing the interests of individual users and carers or groups within agencies or service systems.

Practitioners have an everyday role in case advocacy for the needs of the users and carers. Social workers routinely do this by referring users to other agencies. They also, through assessment and other processes, present the case for particular users and carers to receive services. As we saw in Chapter 4, this is a crucial element of their role of finding, selecting and presenting evidence.

Practitioners have a less clearly defined cause advocacy role within their services. They have an ethical requirement to make clear to service managements when resources or management arrangements are not adequate to meet the needs of users; in social care codes of practice, employers of social care workers have a duty to provide adequate resources and a responsibility to their users and carers.

This is unenforceable in reality, since finances may not permit a reasonable level of service provision, and practitioners nevertheless have a responsibility to provide the best service they can. However, involvement in professional and political activity, using social work expertise and experience, and in service development over the long term can help practitioners contribute stepwise to improvements. Also, it is important to be clear when resources are so inadequate that risk to users and carers arises, and at least record this. The Public Interest Disclosure Act 1998 protects public employees from dismissal when they raise issues of malpractice in the public domain; however, this is not likely most of the time to be relevant to disputes about users' and carers' needs.

Advocacy services may empower service users and carers to make their own cases for resources and services. Citizen advocacy aims to train volunteers to assist people with presenting their needs, for example people with learning disabilities. Self-advocacy seeks to train users and carers to present their own needs, where this is possible. Group advocacy brings people together to provide collective support in doing so. Such movements emerged during the 1980s and '90s among user groups, particularly with learning disabilities and with mental illness. Support mechanisms were thought useful, since these groups might not have had the capacity to represent their own needs (Brandon et al., 1995).

Practitioners and services have a responsibility to develop a 'culture of advocacy' (Dalrymple et al., 1995), in which the provision of advocacy services for users and carers is accepted and integrated into the arrangements for services provision.

Carers and users may want to be involved with developing services; see Chapter 4 on carer participation. Many agencies value this, and many government and research processes now seek to incorporate users in formal policy development and review processes. Particularly with frail people and people who do not have a mental capacity, this may be difficult. However it is not impossible. For example, Monroe and Oliviere (2003) have shown that even dying people may be involved in participating in service improvements and providing feedback on their care, provided this is carefully planned to meet their needs. Taylor (2006) carried out an audit of the training needs of ten old people's forums to see if they could be engaged in policy participation. They needed training to become effective in researching and analysing policy information, support for carrying out research locally, and information to guide useful targets of local research.

Brandon and Brandon (2001) analyse stages of advocacy, which I have adapted to offer practical guidance useful in any advocacy situation, set out in Table 5.4.

Table 5.4 Advocacy practice

The Brandons' stages of advocacy	Practice issues
Explain the advocacy process	Users need to understand what is involved before they can participate
Listen to the user's situation	Receptiveness to users' views
Explain the relevant systems	Users need to choose between different available procedures
Take instructions	In advocacy, users' control of decisions is crucial
Seek additional information	From users, carers, other agencies – to identify issues for other interests that may affect the advocacy process
Feed back this information, exploring the consequences	Information may reveal the limits of what is possible, or other options
Take revised instructions	Even though the course of action may be unwise, users still direct the process
With permission, negotiate with influential people	Permission may involve limiting practitioners' freedom to negotiate
Further feedback, exploring the consequences	
Prepare formal appeal, complaint or legal actions	This may involve deciding whether to instruct a solicitor or other specialist advocate; if not, collect evidence carefully, constructing arguments, including answers to points against the user's case
Evaluate the whole process to learn lessons	Going through what happened may help users and carers to understand their position more clearly; it may also help later cases

SOURCE: Adapted from Brandon and Brandon (2001).

This draws attention to an important aspect of advocacy; that it comes from the point of view of the user or carer and not from the agency.

'Giving instructions' can seem inappropriate to workers accustomed to responding to the needs of users and carers that they work with rather than to their wishes and feelings.

case example

A young person used a professional child advocacy scheme to represent her view to a case conference that she would like to return home to her parents, even though her father had been sexually abusing her. In the case conference, the very experienced social worker responsible for the child's care was publicly critical of the advocate for putting this point of view, when clearly it was impossible to do this in the child's best interests. The advocate was forced to point out the requirement in the Children Act 1989 also to consider the child's wishes and feelings, and that it was her role to present these effectively, while it was the conference's role, not hers, to make the decision balancing the two elements.

This is an example of what Dalrymple et al. (1995) mean when they refer to a 'culture of advocacy'. For professional advocacy to be effective, the agency and its staff need to accept the validity of this approach to representation of views. It is another way in which users' and carers' views can be incorporated into decision-making, but it does not negate the responsibility to make decisions.

Conclusion

Starting from the continuity requirement for caring practice, this chapter examined the role of social care to make connections between various aspects of 'the social'. These include the social institutions that form the system of social care, the partnerships between various agencies to commission and provide services nationally and locally throughout all sectors of the economy. The other aspect of the social is the social networks of users and carers and their caring relationship. Government and professional policy seeks to organize these partnerships to develop holistic responses to individuals and their social networks, and yet professional, financial and policy constraints make this difficult. I have argued here that important skills in understanding boundaries and negotiating enable practitioners to make a contribution. Various structures have attempted to make this possible. The 1980s' innovation of community social work was an important forerunner to the combination of social work practice and home care that eventually became social care. A wide range of services have emerged, with many connections. Practitioners need to look for and grasp these connections in partnership practice that incorporates users' and carers' contributions. However, social and gender inequalities are difficult to balance with support through social care services, in spite of legislative requirements to interweave formal services with carers' networks. Teamwork and advocacy are ways for services to achieve holistic provision and respond to need and inequality.

main points

- Caring requires continuity and thus coordination across a range of social care services.
- Partnership is the expressed aspiration to promote holism in provision, wide participation in planning and delivery of services.
- Partnership is achieved though cooperative relationships between colleagues in service provision, covering a range of connections.
- Users and carers should be engaged as important partners in providing and planning formal services in social care.

stop and think

- List the members of your work team, or another team you have been a member of.
- Draw a network diagram with you at the centre, and connections to the people you regularly contact on behalf of users.
- Select a fairly complex case, and draw a similar map of people you contacted in that case.
- If you can, compare your lists with other similar people. Discuss similarities and differences.

taking it further

- Stalker, K. (ed.) (2003) *Reconceptualising Work with 'Carers': New Directions for Policy and Practice*. London: Jessica Kingsley.
  A good summary of recent research on carers.
- Barnes, M. (2005) *Caring and Social Justice*. Basingstoke: Palgrave Macmillan.
  Contains a useful account of policy development on carers.

Relevant books on partnership and teamwork are as follows:

- Quinney, A. (2006) *Collaborative Social Work Practice*. Exeter: Learning Matters.
  Covers a broad field of social work, focusing particularly on official and legal roles in different settings.
- Balloch, S., and Taylor, M. (eds) (2001) *Partnership Working: Policy and Practice*. Bristol: Policy Press.
  Usefully connects policy and practice in a range of fields.

- Weinstein, J., Whittington, C. and Leiba, T. (eds)(2003) *Collaboration in Social Work Practice*. London: Jessica Kingsley.
  Another worthwhile collection of practical and conceptual articles.
- Hadley, R., Cooper, M., Dale, P. and Stacy, G. (1987) *A Community Social Worker's Handbook*. London: Tavistock.
  A useful guide to community social work techniques.

Websites

- The Care Services Improvement Project is a useful organization concerned with a range of care developments, and well worth keeping in touch with, since it provides an update on many active development projects in the field of social and health care: http://www.csip.org.uk/
- A part of CSIP, the National Institute for Mental Health in England, provides useful resources on projects aimed at improving mental health services: http://www.nimhe.csip.org.uk/
- The website of CAIPE, the leading UK organization in interprofessional education: http://www.caipe.org.uk/index.php

6 Personal and social intervention

The objectives of social care practice interventions

Individualism is sovereign in the current political understanding of care. Late 20th-century Western governments gained the political insight that people want greater control of their personal lives. This comes partly from cultural shifts in favour of individual material consumption. Care is no exception. We have seen that social care requires intrusion on users and carers, although its caring is both receptive to and developmental of users' personal fulfilment. How can practitioners convert intrusion across individual boundaries into successful *intervention* to benefit users?

The developing government prescription for this is *personalization*. This means, in general, to change something so that it suits someone or is connected with them. In information technology, it has a recently developed meaning of adapting a standard format such as a letter, email or website so that it is addressed to or shown as coming from a particular person. In social care, building on this, it means to adapt services to the needs of a particular service user, by giving the user increased control over assessment, planning and management of the budget for the care provided. A Demos report on the future of social work in Scotland describes it as:

> people as active participants in shaping, creating and delivering their care, in conjunction with their paid and unpaid carers, so that it meets their distinctive needs and hopes for themselves ... Whether people want to self-manage and live independently or if they are heavily dependent upon services they should feel in control of their lives. (Leadbeater and Lownsborough, 2005: 4)

The report concludes that this should include having housing, health and other services that prevent people becoming dependent on care services, but where more intervention is needed, social work should foster participation and control. Further, where users are very dependent on services, these should fit in with their lifestyle, not the other way round. Personalization policy aims to shift the role of social care away from rationing resources, and practice away from gatekeeping scarce resources and being risk-averse in a way that restricts independence. We may identify a similar sort of approach in plans to get GP surgeries to open at times convenient for patients rather than times that suit the staff.

The conceptualization of receptive and developmental caring describes practice actions needed to implement such a policy. However, critical comment (for example Glasby and Peck, 2005) suggests that focusing on prevention in personalization is more concerned with reducing demands on more expensive services, than fostering choice; careful management of public money means reducing the use of expensive resources. A report on services for disabled people from the Prime Minister's Strategy Unit (2005: 18), for example, emphasizes the importance of disabled people working to secure their incomes and independence, and case managers would 'help disabled people make the right choices' to achieve this. The implication is that it would not be a 'right choice' for care managers to help people not to work if they found it too stressful. Choice is inherently in tension with budgetary control: care management practice as it was developed in UK social services in the 1990s is an example of how a positive and potentially involving practice method can become misdirected to resource-control aims. Also, service and professional regulation, research and professional knowledge that should inform successful outcomes and high-quality services may be in tension with users' preferences. Another concern about personalization policy is that the duty to charge for social care for an increasing population of older people and other adult service users will inevitably mean a new settlement between the state, users and their families about the costs of care. Government documents, such as the NHS White Paper (DH, 2006a) and Prime Minister's Strategy Unit Report on disability (2005), suggest that the role of social care practitioners would be helping users and carers to identify resources that they could deploy themselves as well as offering a 'menu' of alternatives that might be available. This is not the kind of freedom of choice that disability campaigners are imagining.

Therefore, social care practice needs to focus equally on outcomes for individuals alongside their active participation in service provision. The Social Policy Research Unit at the University of York (SPRU, 2000) identified, based on a range of research on user wishes and care management practice, three different types of outcome for social care services:
- Maintenance of quality of life, for example maintaining acceptable personal comfort, safety, social contacts, meaningful activity, participation in social roles and control over daily life and routines
- Change, for example improving confidence, reducing risk, improving communication and regaining self-care capacity and skills
- Impact of the service process, for example being treated as an individual, feeling valued and respected and experiencing services as well-coordinated.

These outcomes require professional judgement and knowledge to identify what is possible and desirable, as well as user choice. Users' choices and expectations can, however, identify aims in each of these areas, and their choices can helpfully inform practitioners who make generalized assumptions about what might be desirable, instead of looking at the reality of users' and carers' lives. Both the direction of travel in personal development and the minutiae of their life as users live it are important. People do not experience services as caring unless the detail is right. Also, they cannot concentrate on development if they have to worry daily about getting dressed and fed. Some people receiving social care seem to have very little room for development: people who are very disabled or have a progressive, that is, continually deteriorating, disease. However, receptive and developmental caring emphasizes the interpersonal skills of understanding and enabling users' preferences for a good quality of life, making users feel important in defining services that meet their needs. Recently, a very disabled man whose progressive disease had left him almost completely paralysed, sent a colleague an email, using his big toe on the computer keyboard to say that his life at present was 'tickety-boo'. Part of the reason for this was that she had been organizing massage for him, a pleasing physical and social experience. Also, he was still able with his big toe to surf the internet, keep up an interest in the world and contact with friends, and my colleague had been helping his wife deal with some issues in her life. All this felt like progress in dealing with his situation, compared with a few weeks previously, before my colleague was involved. In particular, helping him find ways of keeping up social contacts was an important motivator. Quality of life in social care is about maintaining and seeing progress in the details of life; achieving 'small wins'.

However, social care services need to establish appropriate objectives, since in health and social care settings health treatment outcomes are often inappropriate. For example, users often value interpersonal relationships and social life gained through involvement in day centres and residential care, rather than any improvement in depression or anxiety that may be measured. Healthcare research has found that these cannot achieve the usual pain management and symptom control objectives of palliative care services (Goodwin et al., 2003), and therefore they have not had priority for funding. However, social objectives identified in the literature have not been tested for effectiveness (Payne, 2006).

Many social care aims are concerned with wholeness, with achieving an integration of body, mind and spirit, in the time and place users seek for themselves, allowing them self-direction and self-care within existing social networks. This chapter, therefore, focuses on how social care can build a sense of the practitioner's concern for wholeness in fulfilment for users as people in what may seem a limited and limiting situation. This is a practitioner's responsibility even where they are facilitating a direct payments form of care, for example reminding and encouraging users to take up the full opportunities available to them. However, practitioners will often be working with people who do not want or have that degree of independence. Complex situations, full of risk, can still be guided by a conception of what the user can do in a fulfilling way.

Body, mind and spirit in social care

Physical care

Physical care is essential to social care. However, because medical and nursing care focus on the physical, the social care element is sometimes neglected. The body is crucial in social care because people's bodies are an important part of their personal and social identity. Therefore, changes in our bodies affect relationships with others. People's physical abilities and disabilities define them. Users sometimes feel that disability represents them, and that others value nothing else about them. People whose bodies change because of illness or growing older often find that relationships change as a result. They may be less able to go out, lose confidence, lose sexual attractiveness. On the other hand, people can see their bodies as a project: they can improve their body image, through diet, fitness regimes or wearing fashionable clothes.

case example

A group of women in their thirties with cancer worked with volunteers from the London College of Fashion to design new clothes both to reflect their experiences in healthcare and to make themselves beautiful, in a new way. One of them, for example, designed a gown with beading on it, and repeated the beading designs on her head, bald because of her medical treatment. They took part in a fashion show and had romantic photographs taken of themselves in their designs. Another unmarried member of the group, who expected to die soon, designed the dress she would like to have been married in (Tasker, 2008).

Among the basic requirements for physical care in social care are:
- Food
- Sleep
- Cleanliness and appearance
- Toilet.

Care for all of these aspects of life involves intensely personal preferences; practitioners need to explore explicitly how users manage them, and how help might best assist them.

Cleanliness and help with going to the toilet are among the most important and most difficult of these areas, because they involve activities usually carried out in private, displaying private areas of the body to carers. Twigg's

(2000) important study of bathing as part of community raises many issues in providing physical care that apply to a range of social care settings and connects with many of the themes of this book (Research Box 6.1).

Bathing – the body and community care

Why this study was undertaken – A sociological analysis of an important area of private behaviour, connecting physical activities and the emotional response to them.

Methods – Qualitative interviews with thirty recipients of bathing help from two areas, mostly older people but including five younger physically disabled people. Thirty-four care workers and other staff were interviewed. This provides rich and complex data about people's actions and emotions, without necessarily providing explanations that apply to most people.

Results – Bathing was seen as personal care; requiring help with it marked a significant shift in people's perception of themselves as no longer self-caring. This loss was more important than loss of dignity. Bathing help involved nakedness, touch and transgressing normal boundaries of intimacy in adult life; carers unusually were able to see old bodies. Some boundaries were maintained; conventional limitations on touching breasts, genitals and anal areas were observed. Cross-gender bathing was asymmetrical: women bathed men, but men did not bath women. Intimacy generated by sharing bathing experiences was bounded by the care-work situation, and did not lead to greater personal intimacy between worker and service user.

Help with bathing involved crossing normal social boundaries, because care workers entered private areas of people's home, that visitors usually do not see. The need for help with disability re-ordered the usual arrangements of what was private and public. Help with bathing at a day centre was felt to be an intimate activity taking place in an alien space. There was temporal re-ordering: baths were usually available in the day time, not when users chose. The personal character of bathing meant that it required 'process time', flexibility in using time that allowed people to experience the bath in a way that was acceptable to them. This conflicted with the work timetables of care workers and the perception that care workers were younger people who would normally be quick with bathing, while older people might prefer a more leisured approach.

Source: Twigg (2000).

In addition to these basic aspects of care of the body, physical care might include getting around, safety in the home and carrying out the tasks of daily living. One of the consequences of needing social care is the way that users become dependent on others for achieving such ordinary activities. They may also become dependent on equipment. Among the characteristics of dependence on equipment is a fear that it might fail, or break down. Also, equipment clutters up the home and makes it a less domestic environment. One very disabled man I know festooned his various hoists and medical equipment with strings of lights, to personalize, and demedicalize them.

Psychological and emotional care

As with physical care, psychological and emotional care may focus individualistically on users' reactions to problems encountered in their lives, avoiding social and cultural issues. Reactions to needing paid carers rather than family members may generate psychological responses that result from family or cultural expectations.

case example

An elderly Asian man suffered a stroke, which left him dependent on care. He received a great deal of physiotherapy help in hospital and, when discharged, this continued less comprehensively at home. The practice nurse attached to his GP, suggested referral to adult social services for social care. He rejected this, saying that his daughter, who lived with her family nearby, would provide physical care and his son, also living nearby, would do practical things such as shopping and taking him out. However, the daughter came to see the GP to explain that she had a large family, one child having learning disabilities, and was also working part-time; the family could not afford for her to give up work to care for her father. He had taken for granted that she would do this without asking, because in a traditional family from their ethnic background it would have been conventional. Similarly, her brother was unable to do as much as her father expected because his family needed him to do long hours of overtime at work. While they felt guilty about this, and felt that they were unable to repay the caring they had received as children, their adult roles did not permit them to fulfil the traditional expectations.

Psychological and emotional responses to care needs are as important as physical changes. People's resilience derives not only from their own hardiness but also from the relationships that they are part of in their family and social networks (Walsh, 2006).

We saw in Chapter 3 that dignity in care is an important initiative of government policy. Practice requires us to try to interpret such policy concepts in ways that we can implement in practice. An example of operationalization of dignity is Chan's (2004) work. He suggests that there are four elements to treating people with dignity:

■ Behaving as though all people have equal human value, by valuing their views and wants, even if practitioners cannot follow all users' wishes

- Helping people to have self-respect, by helping them to manage as much as possible their own affairs and remain in control of decisions
- Helping people to have autonomy, by helping them to do things on their own and to make choices where possible
- Promoting a 'positive mutuality', including supporting their relationships with others, and encouraging positive attitudes to doing things with other people.

It is striking that this formulation of dignity does not rely on professional or formal systems, but on practitioners' implementation of human rights and choices.

Spiritual care

Thinking about people's spirits calls two different ideas to mind:
- Spirit as an energizing force. People are concerned with the spiritual to maximize this personal energy, through study, meditation, religion and a variety of activities, which might include enjoying beautiful art, music or nature.
- Spirit as the non-material, that is, not being concerned with achievement, money or consumption of goods. The spiritual life is one that does not give priority to such things.

In health and social care, spirituality incorporates both these senses and often also refers to responding to users' faith commitments. In this context, spirituality is about the meaning that people attach to what is happening to them (Robinson et al., 2004). As people work on current needs with practitioners, they often discuss aspects of their life, or past, in apparently idle conversation. We saw in Chapter 4 that Taylor and White (2000) analyse this kind of conversation at the assessment stage as a self-justification presenting the user as a credible exponent of their situation for the worker. Such conversation also establishes meaningful reasons for life choices, family decisions and concerns. All care needs have, because of this, a spiritual component, since the meaning of needing care to the people involved is central to their identity.

A man with lung cancer once told me it was bad luck, while his wife told me that she saw it as a result of poor diet and smoking. These are spiritual statements: accepting fatalistically what happens, or trying to connect it to behaviour. They are also about fault: 'It is not my fault,' and: 'You ate the wrong things and smoked'.

People often express spiritual issues in metaphors. Historically, these have been religious images, but may be much broader. Stanworth (2004) has examined the metaphors that people use to express, sometimes in archaic language, spiritual needs when they are dying. They include:
- Concern about time, how it passes slowly or quickly, how events connect over time
- Marginality, feeling like an outsider, or on the edge of existence

- Liminality, a concern for ways of passing through, passing between one state and another
- Control, being in charge, being dominated, letting go, hanging on
- Being heroic or unheroic
- Being loved or criticized, as by a mother or parent
- Being a stranger to their own body or to others
- Having a surplus of meaning, being confused, everything being too complex to understand.

Such metaphors give practitioners a glimpse of powerful feelings in users and carers. Picking them up and pointing out how they seem to say something important about people's feelings help practitioners to enter a more complex aspect of the caring relationship, and denote to the user or carer a high level of caring responsiveness.

> **practice example**
>
> The wife, the main carer, of a man with head injuries said to me that his accident had caused the whole family to 'slip back'. In making this liminal statement, she was expressing the meaning she attached to the family situation. Before the accident they had been making progress in income and in social standing but had recently lost the house they owned because they were unable to maintain the mortgage payments, and so had to move, 'back' as she thought of it, into rented accommodation. This is a spiritual statement, a metaphor about movement that strikingly connects with the idea of lost progress because of an accident. I had a picture of a group of mountaineers roped together to a leader hanging from a steep slope by an ice axe, as the axe begins to slip. I commented to her that the whole family had lost a lot, and she became tearful and talked about how she regretted the stress on her daughter, who had not had the support from her parents that her mother had hoped she would have.

Ecological aims: time and place

Chapter 2 points to the importance of place in social care, because it occurs in settings that emphasize changes in identity for service users as they move into residential or day care, or as care workers representing the state cross the boundaries into private space. The ideas of localism and network also emphasize human connections in space. Because much social care starts from a concern for the body, it requires thought about how people are positioned, how they hold themselves and similar issues. Also, social care needs to be concerned with where is the right place to carry out work with the body: where is it comfortable to eat? Does lighting help an older person to see? There are both positives and negatives for users and carers in thinking abut these issues. On one hand, a well-known place or our own possessions may represent security and certainty. On the other hand, time and place define and control us, so this is an area where giving people choice is a useful strategy for making social care caring (Germain, 1976, 1978).

In a study of a day centre for people with dementia, Parker (2005) shows how the arrangement of physical space in the day centre serves to hold and homogenize the users and staff, so that they are all defined as part of a service for older people. The physical environment also demarcates and creates distance between different elements of the service: there are areas for staff and users, and it permits care and control through group activities, which provide support for users and surveillance of their safety. The day centre is defined both by its space and by the activities.

<table>
<tr><td>practice example</td><td>I recently had a conversation with a man in a day centre for older people. Although he was a member, and took part in informal talk and lunch, and so was part of the day centre, he said that, as a former teacher, he did not want to take part in the creative activities, because such things had been part of his former work life. He saw them as unnecessary for him, and instead followed a programme of personal activities, outside the centre's programme. This gave him independence from the day centre, which he defined as the activities, rather than the place.</td></tr>
</table>

Time is connected with place. The next chapter draws attention to the way in which social care often raises issues for people about time. Residential care is 'God's waiting room', where time is pointlessly used up waiting for death. Day care is for structuring time to replace work that users cannot do. Often, users and carers spend their time waiting for something to happen. On the other hand, trying to speed things up can discriminate against some users. People with learning disabilities need extra time and opportunities to have information repeated and adapted to their capacity to understand. Booth et al.'s (2006) study of parents with learning disabilities in the child protection system showed they were disadvantaged both in participation and in decisions being made to their disadvantage, because of the presumption in child care that speed of decision-making is important to secure permanence and security for the child.

<table>
<tr><td>practice example</td><td>The care planning form in one of the areas that I work in has a sheet for setting out the user's seven days of the week in half-hour periods. Care managers write in times when services are needed. Although good for planning, this is restricting for users, since this form will control their daily living pattern until the next review. One practice possibility to avoid this is to start from the user's existing life choices, before going into the detail. *Is there any day of the week that is particularly important?* Perhaps a regular visit or telephone call from a relative, or seeing a favourite television programme will be a priority; services should be planned to meet with this. *What time of day is the best for you?* Some people are better in the mornings or evenings. Disabled or frail people use up their energy. Some people take an afternoon nap. Care managers might ask: *Is the timing of that especially important? How much leeway is there?*</td></tr>
</table>

Networking

Chapter 2 identified the importance of people's social networks as part of understanding social care. Trevillion (1999) proposes that intervention to develop people's networks is an important aspect of social care work. He proposes five types of intervention that may be helpful, which are set out with additional information in Table 6.1. This draws attentions to respecting and valuing users' and carers' relationships and building on them, rather than concentrating only on official or agency networks. An important aspect of networking intervention is differentiating between and understanding different kinds of network.

Table 6.1 Trevillion's networking interventions

Network domain	Objectives	Processes	Examples
Interpersonal	Restructure and develop interpersonal relationships	Develop respectfulness, reflexivity, reciprocity, connectedness	Knock before entering, greet appropriately; think how your personality comes across; encourage people to help or spend time with each other
Community	Build shared purposes and interests	Build collective identities; empower; enable mutual support	Help people to see shared interests, histories and connections; help them to learn skills, experience success; think about and practise what helps others
Relationship style	Promote flexibility and informality	Identify where formal relationships or roles hinder; interweave formal and informal links	Explain roles and job titles; use the right degree of informality for the person; interact with informal helpers valued by the user
Communication	Maximize communication possibilities	Limit closure; promote openness; manage messages; stop using information to control	Encourage people to express their preferences, ideals; make sure people receive necessary information; promote transparency of information
Action sets	Maximize connectedness between people involved	Identify and promote connections between family, agencies and informal helpers	Listen to information about people who may be involved; ask about people users or carers know; draw maps; look for inconsistencies and gaps; include everyone into case conferences

SOURCE: Developed from Trevillion (1999: 36–51).

As an example of the kind of information that might be useful in understanding and working with networks, Wenger (1994) argues that there are a variety of different types of network, which should be assessed. These are based on the:

■ Proximity of close kin
■ Proportions of family, friends and neighbours involved
■ Amount of interaction between people and their networks.

She identifies five types of network, which practitioners might find it useful to consider:

■ *Family-dependent support networks.* Their main focus is on local kin
■ *Locally integrated support networks.* Close relationships exist with local family, friends and neighbours
■ *Local self-contained support networks.* Infrequent and rather distant relationships exist with local kin and informal networks
■ *Wider community-focused support networks.* There are active relationships with distant relatives but few local contacts
■ *Private restricted support networks.* There are no local kin and minimal contact with others in the local community.

Different types of network offer different opportunities for developing informal care and call for different approaches from practitioners. Wenger (1994) proposes an instrument for assessing the type of network surrounding an older person, although her research shows that while this was easy to use, practitioners found it hard to decide what to do about the information. Looking back at Trevillion's (1999) analysis of interventions (Table 6.1), possibilities include: increasing the range of types of network an older person has, or increasing the strength or range of contacts that they have, improving communication between people involved, and building up contacts among helpers so that they can work together in planning. Some of these processes are going on in the case studies and research referred to in the following section on support.

Support

Practice providing personal support to users and carers remains crucial to social care. Sometimes focusing on this leads to criticism that it is not forward-looking (Payne, 1995: chapter 5). Such criticism derived from the social work assumption that social care should aim at therapeutic progress instead of preventing deterioration or making people feel safe and happy. Prevention, safety and happiness are, however, worthwhile achievements. Since social care is about long-term work, support may help people get through a difficult period, giving them confidence and resilience to try alternative solutions in the future. However, the critique of support suggests that practitioners need clarity about their aims. The following discussion tries to analyse what may be involved.

Support processes

Sometimes support comes from users and carers knowing that the practitioner is involved, and from *how* practitioners relate to users. Three aspects of support make a useful contribution to social care:

- *Availability* – practitioners help users feel secure in the knowledge that they will respond if necessary, for example by being clear about out of hours services
- *Substitution* – where services take over aspects of the user's life in order to help to promote independence in other areas, for example providing carers to help someone get up and dress
- *Involvement* in an important change – so that relationships that users rely on can support an important change, for example a known carer travelling with a user to a new care home.

It is also supportive to use resources and services for a user or carer, through providing information or organizing the services directly. I have previously argued (Payne, 1986: 37–41) that this form of support arises where social care temporarily takes over certain aspects of the user's life. This then leaves the user free to deal with other priorities. Interpersonal support from a practitioner may also be the glue that holds a range of services together and needs to be a planned part of a package of services. By becoming involved in detailed arrangements practitioners can demonstrate psychological availability – a preparedness to get involved and an openness to being influenced.

Family support in child care

The shift to greater efforts in family support in child care work from the late 1990s onwards (Chapter 3) has led to a renewal of activities designed to prevent and restore family functioning. Gray's (2003) study of a family support service in Tower Hamlets interviewed people from nine families and examined thirty case records. He found that a match of ethnicity between worker and family helped to develop shared aims and goals, broke through language barriers and established mutuality of feeling. Informal, non-professional styles of practice were found to be most helpful. Bringing families together and helping them to interact was an important strategy. It was also important to deal with social isolation, bullying of children and racism. A qualitative study of 23 families, including a large number of female single parents (Platt, 2006) showed that practitioners were able to overcome the restrictions of targets and government guidance on their role to undertake flexible and creative work. Detailed, specific reporting of circumstances, focusing on the events and incidents that revealed child care problems, and support from other agencies involved were important factors. Spratt (2001) studied, in 100 consecutive child welfare referrals, the factors that allowed social workers to have an orientation towards child welfare and family support, rather than child protection in their work.

Among the factors that impeded a family-support emphasis was lack of resources within the team, unless it was possible to refer a family to a specialized agency. Another factor was the perception of a critical public, emphasized by a pattern of concern about risk among the worker's immediate colleagues. A family-support orientation was assisted by having broader (rather than narrow) consultations with the other agencies involved and a supportive approach to protecting staff from the agency. This avoided an unnecessarily blaming managerial culture. Bell (2007) studied six parenting programmes based on the work of the American psychiatrist Webster Stratton, where parents are involved in videoed role play and discussion to improve skills. She found that having a shared theoretical base, shared purpose and working out of their formal agency structures facilitated effective practice. Parents benefited from a more inclusive, participative learning approach, which could develop and restore their skills.

Sheppard's useful analysis of support received and valued by depressed mothers offers ideas for supportive activities. They include:

- Emotional support, allowing users to express feelings about their situation, and demonstrating esteem and encouragement for their efforts
- Advice and information
- Direct work through befriending, building a relationship, and assessing and clarifying difficulties
- Emotional work on self-understanding, helping people to take difficult decisions
- Financial support, for example arranging welfare benefits or providing money under the Children Act 1989, section 17, which allows LAs to give money to prevent children needing to be looked after by the LA
- Encouraging and facilitating contacts with friends, clubs and offering training in social skills.

Services to carers

Services to carers build on policy development, legislation and assessments reviewed in previous chapters. Carers are not a unified group and previous chapters have identified a range of different views of the caring role. It can only be seen within the context of the long-term relationship (Ray, 2006; Payne, 1993). An extensive literature review of services to carers of mentally ill people, mainly people with dementia (Arksey et al., 2002), identified a number of services that had been researched:

- Educational interventions of different types
- Breaks from caring, including respite care replacing the carer's role
- Family interventions
- Mutual support and social activity groups
- Telephone and computer-based services
- Multidimensional approaches to caring interventions

- Counselling
- Domiciliary care services
- Changes to the physical environment to support care, by making it easier.

There were often positive outcomes, but little concrete evidence of effectiveness in changing carers' situations, except for assertive outreach to people with severe mental illnesses (see below). For example, education and information improved knowledge, but did not reduce the carer's burden. There was little evidence that any carers' services saved costs, for example in hospital admissions. North American studies showed that social work support for carers reduced the costs of other services to frail older people (Rizzo and Rowe, 2006). Chene's (2005) qualitative study of 20 carers of older people showed that stresses came not only from daily caregiving, but also from a sense of loss, sadness and resignation when the user was admitted to residential care.

Table 6.2 identifies useful interventions with carers: enabling practitioners can explore relationships, information and support from relationships with professionals that carers need.

Carers may resist long-term planning. For example, Bowrey and McGlaughlin (2007) carried out interviews with 62 carers of adults with learning disability about long-term plans for care, when they became incapacitated or died. These carers saw making future plans as unnecessary because both they and the user were still alive and they were not aware of the difficulty in securing supported housing. Lack of confidence in services, difficulties in letting go, and the present satisfying relationship with the user prevented forethought. This study illustrates the need to continue proactive information-giving and work through a process of planning for the future. Carers need to gain experience of the services that will be necessary so that their confidence in them is raised.

One of the claimed advantages of person-centred planning (see Chapter 4) is that all members of the family and carers involved with a user participate in the planning and so influence the outcomes. A difficulty is that agreement is hard to secure. However, Adams (2003) argues that focusing purely on 'care for the carer' means that practitioners do not have adequate relationships with users, especially people with dementia, and others whose disabilities make it difficult to develop relationships. The carer may come to be seen as the expert, and practitioners then do not help users to express their own wishes. The NHS 'expert patient' (DH, 2006b) and 'expert carer' (DH, 2007e) programmes emphasize how both user and carer may be more expert in the details of how problems affect individuals than practitioners with their more general understanding. Receptive caring means that even with the most disabled user, or where there is apparently little communication, practitioners need to give the time to watch and be involved with the person behind the disability and learn the small ways in which they do communicate.

Table 6.2 Areas helpful to carers

Helpful areas of work	Useful interventions
Build support networks	Help users and carers identify useful friends, neighbours, organizations, past contacts
Relationship with GP	Encourage carers to think about building (or repairing) a good relationship with a GP, as someone needing support and help, but not as a complainer or worrier; rehearse and plan assertive consultations
Relationship with social services department	Help carers ask for a carer's needs assessment; rehearse being assertive without presenting yourself as a complainer
Benefits check	Get a check on benefits and welfare rights, both for the carer and user; if no agency can help, work through a reference book
Think about the home	Help carers think through possible changes or jobs around the house that will make things easier
Get useful equipment	Local disabled living centres, occupational therapists, aids and adaptations officers, magazines, guides and the internet can all offer help. Grants to obtain equipment may also help
Combine caring with personal development	Help carers plan to take time to go on leisure or caring-related courses, or to build qualifications for the future
Education for all users, especially children with special education needs	Consider children's educational needs at each developmental stage; review needs and opportunities for all user groups – practitioners should help carers engage with these processes
Get out and about	Encourage carers to take opportunities for education, social events, visits, trips, even if the topic is new – enjoyment and stimulation will result and freshens carer/user relationships
Have fun alongside caring	Encourage carers to cultivate activities or talk that carer and user both enjoy
Be prepared	Carers should be prepared for possible medical or other emergencies (have the contact numbers to call if the user has a fall or a sudden worsening); keep them informed about possible progression of the disability or illness and be ready to cope with changes

SOURCE: Carers' Information Service (2006).

Carers' assessments

Nicholas (2003) reported an early study of the implementation of the carer's assessment, recommending an outcome focus for carers' assessments. These included outcomes in:

■ The quality of life for the person for whom carers cared
■ The quality of life for the carer
■ Managing carers' roles, including helping them to be well informed, prepared, equipped and if necessary trained for their task
■ Consequences for the organization of services, for example giving the

carer a say in how the services were provided, to support their morale and sense of control in their own home.

This generated a process that moved between assessing and reviewing carers' needs and explicit gathering of carers' responses to the exploration and assessment at each stage, so that there were clear opportunities for feedback and a clear requirement to include the carers' views in final assessments. Assessments needed to define intended outcomes for carers and users and test the achievement of those outcomes at the review stage.

Care management approaches

Care management is the overall term for a coordination approach in social care. In general, it means that a service user has one main practitioner responsible for all the aspects of care work with that person. It is based on a North American model of social work practice called 'case management' (Gursansky et al., 2003). In the UK, the term case management is used for some forms of care management, particularly with mentally ill people. The term is easily confused with care management, and the following discussion aims to draw distinctions between six forms of care management:

1. Case or care management in an in-patient healthcare setting, referring to allocating work within ward teams. I do not discuss this meaning further since it is not relevant to care management in social care.
2. Keyworking, a model of practice mainly in residential care, designating one member of residential care staff to be the main external contact point and personal carer for a resident.
3. Care management, a coordination practice in UK community care services administered by adult SSDs. It was introduced as part of the implementation of the quasi-market in health and social care through the NHS and Community Care Act 1990. This model of care management is often restricted by policy or financial necessity to people who have complex needs.
4. CPA (the care programme approach), a multi-agency coordination approach to work with severely mentally ill people, led by healthcare services, often confused with care management in community care.
5. Case management in mental health care, including strengths-based and 'assertive community treatment' (ACT), a North American model of practice, which has been introduced in varying degrees in the UK.
6. Direct payments, independent budgeting and self-directed care; these forms of care management are the basis of personalization policy.

Kanter (1989) distinguished the two basic models of case management in the USA underlying these various systems; this was picked up in UK studies by Challis (1994), as follows:

- Administrative case management is sometimes called the travel agent model, in which the case manager arranges services, but does not necessarily remain in a continuing relationship with the service user.
- Clinical case management, the travel companion model, in which the case manager provides a continuing supportive relationship as the services are used; the receptivity, continuity and connectedness requirements of social care practice obviously favour this approach.

Care management in community care services

Care management in community care services is the primary form of care management in the UK, widely used with all adult service users and carers. Its origins are as a model of social work designed to improve coordination in the fragmented US care system. It was adapted into the UK in experiments in achieving improved decision-making in LA care for older people, and in the 'care in the community programme' of the 1980s and early 1990s, aimed at discharging long-stay patients from mental hospitals (Davies and Challis, 1986; Renshaw et al., 1988). It was based on an economic model of social service provision, the 'production of welfare' approach, in which resources were put in and outcomes evaluated to understand which resources in which proportions made a difference to outcomes. It assumed a clinical case management model of a continuing, creative relationship between practitioners and service users in planning services, following the pathway of care planning, reviewing and assessment set out in Figure 4.1. This is consistent with the approach to social care practice described in this book.

However, the opportunities for flexible, thoughtful caring held out by the introduction of care management (Payne, 1995) have not been achieved. Lewis and Glennerster's (1996) study of the implementation of the reforms raised the question of the bureaucratization of social work and suggested that the focus on control of expenditure led to inadequate definition of the care management role. A succession of qualitative research studies (Simic, 1995; Postle, 2001; Jones, 2001; Carey, 2003) has shown that the introduction of care management has been primarily administrative in the UK. Ellis (1993) showed that the main function of managerialist approaches to care management has been to focus on the management of eligibility rather than opening up options. Carey's (2006) study of 23 agency care managers found a high level of mundane administrative work and rigid procedures. There was also a high level of crisis work; examples were when informal caring arrangements broke down, where a service user became unexpectedly homeless or where accusations of abuse were made against an employee in a care home. Carey argues that employing agency workers in highly unstable, particularly urban, settings connects with the deskilling and routinization of care management work. It reduced the opportunity for satisfying development of relationships, working alongside service users and carers. Weinberg et al.'s (2003) survey of care management practice showed that most care management focused on assessment and financial control, rather than review and monitoring, and services were rarely changed at review. In mental health services, care management and assessment were not specifically targeted on people with the most needs. Postle's (2002) qualitative study of care managers found that inadequate resources meant that there was a focus on assessing needs against restrictive criteria, rather than creative care planning. She also found that the need to work on financial assessments meant additional detailed work on matters that were not naturally part of clinical care planning. Time had to be allocated to using a cumbersome computer system. Managerial demands for both thoroughness and speed of processing, alongside detailed procedural guidance, seemed inconsistent to practitioners. Because of resource constraints and time pressures, most users did not receive assessment beyond initial screening, and this meant that social care workers did not fully know the risks that they faced. Assessment practice was routinized, particularly where the problem for a team was managing heavy demands. There was however considerable variation in practice, demonstrating that a good deal of front-line discretion remained (Ellis et al., 1999). Venables et al.'s (2005) survey of English LAs, drawing on data from 1998, showed that integration of health and social care services was minimal. Care managers had little freedom to commission most services, particularly if they involved services from outside the LA. Also, LAs made few distinctions in the extensiveness of assessment, although the early Department of Health guidance (SSI/SWSG, 1991) proposed six levels of complexity in assessment. This continues to be true, probably because many LAs now only provide care management services for users with extensive problems, so that simpler assessments are unnecessary, since no services are provided to people with fewer or less serious needs.

Reasons for the failure of care management in community care may be summarized:

■ The 'care deficit' (Chapter 1) means that there are not enough resources to meet the need for care, so care managers become gatekeepers for scarce resources.
■ The separation of commissioning and provider roles in the quasi-market increased administrative complexity.
■ Financial and bureaucratic accountability structures in LAs have led to rigid administrative procedures.
■ The distinction between free NHS care and paid-for social care, and the long-term shift of resources in this direction, is poorly understood and to some degree resisted by users and carers.

These factors interact. Not having enough resources means that procedures are enforced rigorously and agencies try to shift resource demands elsewhere. This pressurizes the job of care managers, because they have a stringent and rigid assessment system, a high level of dissatisfaction among users and carers and criteria that focus on high levels of current need, rather than thoughtful preparation for the care trajectory. These trends are characteristic of wider social trends. Post-Fordist economies are those where routine employment in production-line industrial processes has been replaced by low-paid service provision work, which is only economically viable for employers if there is workforce flexibility. Thus, complex implementations of care, which require flexibility and discretion, are displaced in favour of a routine division of care work into more limited care tasks.

In summary, then, while the original clinical concept of case management was a social care intervention with a continuing relationship, the implementation of care management in the UK has been primarily administrative. This has not achieved positive research outcomes in the USA (Rapp and Goscha, 2004) and has been unsuccessful in retaining a caring focus in the UK.

Will this form of industrialized care be maintained? It may be satisfactory to some service users because it is less intrusive than discretionary, clinical models of care management and more in their control. It may also be satisfactory to some care workers who may not be intellectually or professionally prepared for more discretionary roles. On the other hand, service users and informal carers may eventually demand the greater quality of service that comes from flexible discretionary caring.

The care programme approach

The care programme approach fared little better. CPA was introduced (DH, 1990), to be implemented by April 1991, supported by extensive guidance (DH, 1995). Although initially intended for use with a range of severely mentally ill people, by developing two levels of planning, it has increasingly focused on people with the most severe needs. However, there was confusion about applying it because it was introduced at the same time as care management. Carpenter et al.'s (2004) survey of users' attitudes found that they valued being given involvement in decision-making, had been told about their medication and its use and side-effects, that they mostly knew who their keyworker was, felt comfortable with them and felt treated with respect. They felt more involved where CPA was well integrated with more general care management approaches, and felt less involved where services were strongly targeted, that is, focused on the users with most needs. User satisfaction was highest where user involvement was a specific focus of the LA's approach.

Mental health case management

Much research in case management has focused on services for mentally ill people. ACT is a North American service that actively seeks out mentally ill people who are likely to lose touch with services because of chaotic or drifting lifestyles, or failure to take anti-psychotic medication. In addition to this, it includes case sharing among the team, small caseloads, a team leader who is an active team member working with users, dedicated time from a psychiatrist, 24-hour cover and services mainly in the community. Intensive case management (ICM), some forms of which particularly focus on a 'strengths' model of practice looking for good features in the users' competence to deal with life, seeks to improve users' connections with ordinary resources in the community rather than, as in administrative case management, substituting formal services for natural support networks. They are the equivalent of the normalization and independent living movements in other areas of service.

Rapp and Goscha's (2004) literature review of research on these various models summarizes markers of effectiveness in care management. They exclude administrative case management because it has no positive outcomes to offer. The main factors in effective mental health case management are as follows:

- Care managers should deliver as much of the help as possible themselves.
- Natural community resources should be the primary partners rather than formal services.
- Work is in the community, increases engagement, provides better assessment and helps in using local community strengths.
- Team care management improves continuity of care, reduces staff stress, increases people's availability and increases creativity in care planning. On the other hand individual care managers increase accountability, reduce meetings, help clarity of roles and allow one person to develop a good relationship with the user. Individual case management with team backup often seemed to maximize benefits.
- Care managers have ultimate, unshared responsibility for services. Fragmented teams who cannot directly provide services do not help integration.
- Non-specialized care managers in mental health services need supervision from a well-qualified seasoned supervisor.
- Caseload size should be small enough to allow for frequent contact, sufficient to meet the users' needs; frequency is more important than length of contact.
- Short-term care management produces effective outcomes in preventing hospitalization, stabilizing housing and sorting out money problems, but gains evaporate for more long-term supportive objectives unless there is consistent involvement over a period, with gradual transfers to new workers if required.
- Users need access to a familiar person all the time if there is a crisis.
- Care managers should foster choice.

These research outcomes suggest a model of care management that may be successful and applicable to a range of settings. However, it requires commitment to the social care practice model of receptiveness to users and carers, developing engagement in a continuous relationship, and while the present model may be managed in such a way as to achieve this, the limited resources and priority given to resource management are unlikely to achieve it. While CPA has, with some success, been widely used in healthcare settings, involving social care workers, to plan care for seriously mentally ill people in the community, it does not equate to the American model ACT, which produces a cohesive, optimistic team working collectively (Marshall and Creed, 2000). Research on intensive case management schemes in the UK shows that they do not have these characteristics. They implemented CPA with larger caseloads than in the USA and in a more disparate service setting, and have not been successful in restraining hospital admissions. The Department of Health has therefore proposed introducing 'assertive outreach teams' for users with severe mental health disorders in its Framework for Mental Health Services (DH, 1999).

For practitioners, therefore, recognizing that the care deficit is always likely to inhibit effective deployment of resources, the main focus must be to develop good social care practice with users and carers that they can achieve engagement with, and the system ensures that these will be people with priority needs. The characteristics of effective care management practice in social care settings, in addition to developing continuous supportive relationships, will be:

- Effective partnership work that delivers desired and useful services to users and carers
- Ensuring that users and carers have the highest possible degree of choice and involvement in decisions
- A focus on developing local, natural community resources.

Keyworking

Keyworking is a form of care management associated with residential care homes, and is similar to the healthcare concept of a 'primary nurse'. The aim is to strengthen the feeling of relationship security and continuity for users. It means allocating a particular worker to be the focus of links between users and the service, so that users know who is responsible for coordinating their care. This is particularly helpful when, as in residential care, a 24-hour service uses shift work, so that there is a constantly changing staff rota. Bland (1997) examined the literature on keyworking. Three models were identified; described here to be consistent with the terminology of this book:

- Setting up and monitoring care plans

- A special person with the closest relationship with the user
- A nominated social care worker who took on the integration and personal development role of a social worker within a social care setting.

Bland's research was a survey and more detailed analysis of the practice in a sample of residential care homes for older people in the three sectors. She found that keyworking was mainly used in local authority residential care with the main aim of spanning the boundary between the care setting and other services. However, although users sometimes knew their keyworkers, they were mainly unaware of their care plans and the care planning process. Regulators have since tried to raise users' awareness of care plans, as a way of empowering them to be involved in their care.

A range of other care management approaches have been tried out. Educational approaches, and information either individually or using groups have been shown to be helpful and cost-effective with frail elderly people in reducing demands on services (Rizzo and Rowe, 2006). McConkey et al.

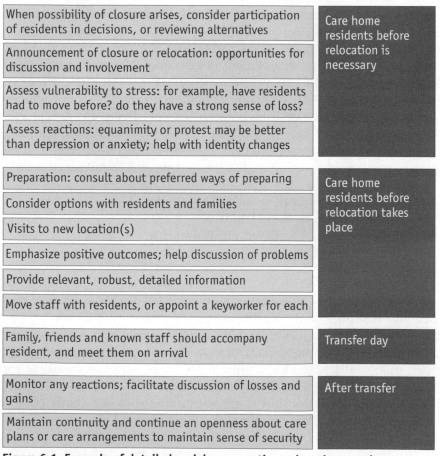

Figure 6.1 Example of detailed social care practice: relocating care homes
SOURCE: WOOLHAM (2001).

(2004) studied services available for looked-after disabled children and identified the need for local specialized respite and residential care. This was especially true for teenagers who presented behavioural and communication difficulties and were difficult to manage if you were not familiar to them. While this study covered a small group, its findings would be echoed in the needs of many other smaller groups. The balance of providing local care, familiar to the user but also able to deal with complex special needs is a constant struggle for family carers and for practitioners. Woolham's (2001) discussion of relocation arrangements for the increasing number of care home residents who need to move to another home offers a good example of the way in which effective social care practice requires careful work on the detail of people's lives. I have analysed his account as a pathway in Figure 6.1.

Care management in social care

Care management is a crucial idea in social care, but two fundamentally different models, the administrative and the clinical, have been identified. UK services have primarily implemented an administrative model in search of effective financial management, while a clinical model would accord with receptive and developmental caring but, because of resource constraints, has not been effectively implemented in the UK. While there are some benefits in coordination achieved by care management systems, the strongest benefits require social care practice to be incorporated alongside coordination objectives.

Direct payments, independent budgeting and self-directed care

'Direct payments' is the British implementation of an international shift in policy towards people arranging and paying for their own care. In the UK, it is the main focus of personalization policy. It has developed because of pressure for greater independence, particularly from the disability rights movement associated mainly with people with physical disabilities, and is also partly a reaction against the rigidity and depersonalization of administrative care management in LA community care. Instead of paid care managers organizing care packages, the level of care is assessed and a payment made to allow service users to employ their own carers in a pattern of provision that they manage and control. The idea is an extension of case management drawing on Canadian brokerage schemes (Brandon et al., 1995). Self-directed care is a USA extension of this concept, originally focused on people with or recovering from mental illnesses and alcoholism. It tries to implement ideas of self-determination in a practical way, and connects with 'direct payments'. It has four main elements:

■ Person-centred planning

- Direct payments, sometimes called individual budgeting in the USA, a terminology that is beginning to be used in the UK, for example in pilot schemes to simplify direct payments arrangements introduced by the Department of Health
- Financial management services
- Brokerage, with education and practical assistance to design and manage self-directed care plans (SAMHSA, 2005).

The structure of such provision is set out in Figure 6.2. Throughout the process, users and their family network are more involved in assessment and planning than in conventional UK care management. When care is provided, users and their family or social networks take over organizing the provision. Although the budget is theoretically negotiated, many LAs have standard lists of payments for particular care needs. Users organize services themselves. They might do this by buying their services from a selected care agency. Sometimes a user-led organization carries out the general employment and management tasks, while retaining control of how care work is organized. If one or two carers undertake this for one person, building up a better relationship than purchasing care packages from an agency, they are often called 'personal assistants'.

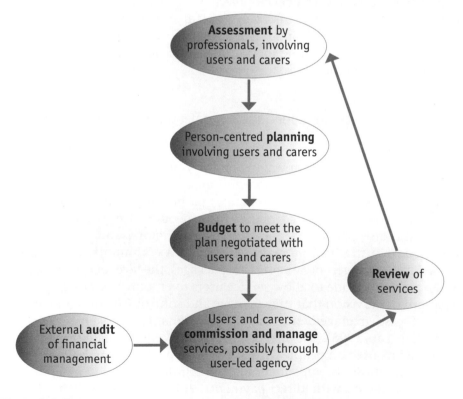

Figure 6.2 Structure of self-directed care and direct payments

The central problem with direct payments is whether individual users become responsible for the risk of things going wrong. Users having responsibility for their own care management cuts both ways. Personal freedom goes with the burden of organizing sometimes quite complex arrangements. The benefit of having an arrangement that seems comfortable for users may mean that they do not choose the best evidence-based care. Scourfield (2007) argues that there are limits to individual responsibility. Theoretical objections concern a further withdrawal from collective responsibility and service, in favour of a 'consumer' view of the citizen. Not everyone who struggles with an illness or disability is, or wants to be, an entrepreneurial, managing, risk-taking person, yet it seems that this is the only acceptable mode of being. They become not only self-managing but also the manager of public funds, with the job of keeping records and having them audited. It often means that they lose rights to service, and gain individual responsibility for providing their own. Responsibility for 'governmentality', that is, making sure that everything is well organized, is displaced from local authorities and professionals. What will happen to a commitment to equal opportunities, anti-discriminatory practice, evidence-based standards of practice? These matters are appropriately the role of public bodies, but that public responsibility is lost when individual management of care resides with users themselves. Ellis (2007) for example, found an attitude of 'it's no longer our problem' from some managers if someone receiving direct payments was at risk of physical harm, leaving practitioners feeling that they would be blamed if abuse were later found. Spandler and Vick (2005) showed that practitioners made simplified assumptions about who would be suitable, such as younger disabled people and people with a carer who would be able to handle the administration. Direct payments were also allocated mainly for services that were not routinely available, to meet special cultural requirements for someone from a minority ethnic group, for example, or to satisfy a 'difficult' service user.

Ellis's (2007) qualitative study of a number of teams in one local authority area identifies some of the practical difficulties in implementing payments, interpreted in her study as resistances to the principles. These included:

■ Uncertainties and ambiguities in the introduction of the policy from managers
■ A cumbersome approval mechanism for direct payments
■ Difficulty in dealing with users' wants as opposed to needs. This was a problem of principle, since many users with less critical needs could not gain basic levels of service, for example cleaning and laundry, and allocating direct payments to some for additions to basic provision was seen as inequitable
■ Poor monitoring of expenditure and lack of support might lead to financial abuse and an administrative burden on users
■ Information about the direct payments option was not readily available

and reinforced by workers, who were often dealing with an immediate situation rather than a planned process of development of care options

■ Direct payments were not emphasized by workers dealing with hospital and other discharges from care, where packages of care needed to be organized speedily.

There are both practical and emotional problems. Paid carers may gain loyalties to the individual user, but are low-paid, and may be unmotivated and poorly trained. As an individual serving an individual, they may adapt to that person's specific requirements, but will not have time off for training and personal development; this may exclude them from the job market later. If direct payments become widespread, voluntary organizations and companies will grow up to organize carers on behalf of users. Will these eventually be any different from the agencies that provide employees for care work already, some of which will compete aggressively for this work? They will be faced by the same problems of a mobile, low-paid workforce. If things go wrong, the service user may feel inadequate and poor at managing their affairs. A reliance on direct payments may lead to agencies withdrawing from supportive care and clinical care management, and this may lead services to lose expertise and commitment to service provision.

The answer to these issues is not to reject the advantages of direct payments for the feelings of control and self-direction. Instead, practitioners can work to develop capacity among people to manage their own social care and among the organizations that help them. A practice among practitioners who support this work that is enabling rather than blaming or controlling will be important. However, this fairly sophisticated level of interpersonal practice will be time-consuming and expensive; direct payments are not a cheap option. Service users and their carers are not a homogeneous group, so a range of choices about the way their care will be provided will need to be available.

Risk and protection

Previous chapters have identified policy and social pressures towards focusing on risk and protection as part of social care. Many people experience current life as increasingly difficult to understand and complex. This makes people feel at risk. Beck (1992) argued that people and social institutions increasingly see the world as risky to live in, and seek out safety and security. This is so, even though there have been increases in good health and security in most societies (Slovic, 1999). We can see this trend in the criticism of social workers and social care services where they are unable to protect children from abuse by their parents, or elderly people from falling and injuring themselves. Craib (1992: 179) argues that this comes from a common experience of fragmentation, in which people respond to difficult experiences in their lives by fragmenting their personality, so that they have one set of behaviours in one situation, but appear completely different in other circumstances. This general social trend has led organizations, including care agencies, to be concerned about 'health and safety' and to fear litigation against them for negligence, failures of service and for taking actions without reasonable cause. This is one of the reasons for the increase in managerialist control of social care, which limits the possibilities for using social care practice effectively.

Developing caring practice in an agency would be effective in dealing with many of these issues. Using the model proposed by this book, agencies would create a caring arena between a user's social network and the agency, facilitated by a practitioner in a continuing interpersonal relationship with users and carers. Adams (1995) argues that people deal with risk by balancing different factors that are affecting them; risk is an ordinary part of human relationships. Human beings increasingly take risks, if there are rewards for doing so. A disabled person might risk injury, for example, by trying a new treatment to increase their mobility, if they thought the improvement might be significant. However, people judge the risk they will take according to their perceptions of the extent of the danger and the likelihood of accidents. Their judgements are affected by social trust: if they are broadly trusting of the institutions that they deal with and of their society, they are more likely to take risks (Cvetkovich and Löfstedt, 1999). Reviewing relevant studies, Cvetkovich (1999) suggests that people are more likely to trust institutions whose social values they share, which they see as having similar objectives as themselves and where events that affect them seem to indicate that the institution is seeking similar objectives as themselves. People such as migrants or those using social care will take risks in relationships and personal development if they trust the culture in which they exist, if it has treated them well, and has aims and values that fit with theirs. People will take the risk of trusting a practitioner and agency if they appear similar in values and aims as themselves and where the history of their treatment suggests they have the same aims.

Taking responsibility for risk raises anxiety for practitioners and managers. A study of different approaches to risk management in a range of social care services (Research Box 6.2) suggests that the aims of risk management in a particular situation are sometimes unclear.

research box 6.2

Risk management paradigms

Why this study was undertaken – Risk management systems have become increasingly important in health and social care, but conceptual frameworks have come from a range of professions and service needs, leading to a lack of clarity.

Methods – The researcher used 19 focus groups with health and social care staff in Northern Ireland, using grounded theory to identify different approaches to risk management. Grounded theory uses ideas resulting from early cycles of research to inform later cycles, thus building results from undefined areas. Focus groups are discussion groups in which topics of interest to the researcher are focused on successively, to stimulate a range of ideas and reactions.

Results – Six different approaches to risk management emerged:

Approach	Definition	Issues
Identifying and meeting needs	Focuses on meeting the needs that users identify, including warning them of risks	Emphasizes user and carer choice, focuses on current rather than future risks; difficulties arise where users/carers want more than funding allows, or where professionals disagree about risks
Protecting users and others	Focuses on the need to challenge users who may harm others or themselves	Emphasizes the user's capacity to make decisions; extends caring role into a protecting/controlling role
Minimizing situational hazards	Focuses on the need to minimize risks in home or residential care	Unclear when risk is minimized – may lead to excessive caution; conflicts where user choice conflicts with carer's/practitioner's health and safety
Balancing benefits and harms	Risk-taking, not avoidance, is essential part of life and the job	May lead to practitioner taking a professional risk by calculating that benefits outweigh risks; common in rehabilitation and hospital discharge
Accounting for resources and priorities	Labels levels of risk as part of prioritizing and using resources effectively	Accepts rationing as a normal part of the job, in contrast to 'identifying and meeting needs' approach
Wariness of legal conflict	Concern in risky circumstances where risk-taking may lead to legal action or public concern	Conflicts arise where users/carers have citizens' rights to redress if put at risk

Source: Taylor (2006).

In addition to general issues of managing risk appropriately, social care services come into contact with four specific areas of risk concerned with protecting vulnerable people from abuse. These are the formal processes for:

1. Safeguarding children – The Children Act 2004, section 11, requires key people and bodies to work together to safeguard and protect the welfare of children. Official guidance, issued in 2005, was updated in 2007 (DfES, 2007), and is likely to be updated regularly.
2. Safeguarding adults – There is no specific legislation, although at the time of writing legislation is passing through the Scottish Parliament. However, official guidance is published by the Home Office and Department of Health (2000), supplemented by further advice from the Association of Directors of Social Services (ADSS, 2005), now the Association of Directors of Adult Social Services (ADASS).
3. Domestic violence – This includes violence in home situations, including racist violence against ethnic minorities. A national plan (Home Office, 2005) sets priorities and plans for action.
4. Multi-agency public protection arrangements (MAPPA) – These are arrangements to coordinate public protection against serious offenders, including mentally disordered offenders, under the Criminal Justice Act 2003, sections 235–7, which replaced the Criminal Justice and Court Services Act 2000, sections 66 and 67.

Although there are differences, the process of dealing with each of these situations is similar. There are local inter-agency committees with representation at a senior level, which establish a local plan and procedures for tackling difficulties and communication between agencies in general and in specific cases. For safeguarding children and adults, the LA takes a lead; in domestic violence, the police lead, although the coordination of plans is usually though the local safeguarding adults board, and MAPPA is coordinated by the local probation administration. At the time of writing organization of this service is changing again. In each case, there are arrangements for notifying the lead agency of difficulties and for coordination and training. These systems overlap and also interconnect with other systems, for example in the case of serious mentally ill people who have committed offences, with CPA.

In a study of the early implementation of the guidance on safeguarding adults, Preston-Shoot and Wigley (2002) found that workers were unclear which parts of the procedures were required (mandatory) and which permissive. Practitioners were not always challenged for taking actions according to their views of good practice rather than following the procedures, and financial and psychological abuse was less likely to be raised.

Conclusion

The policy of personalization is a new formulation of care practice, drawing on a political insight that people want greater independence and control of their own lives, rather than paternalistic services. There are many questions about how practitioners might implement it; I have argued in the chapter that receptive and developmental caring is necessary in doing so. Interpersonal caring practice helps to respond to important aspects of users' lives: physical, mental and spiritual care, place and time. A focus on networks and family support, incorporating services for carers, is also important. A range of structures for care management have developed in the past two decades and have the potential for dealing with the complex areas of practice that involve risk, or where care requires a more proactive role for practitioners than personalization proposes. However, administrative care management is ineffective and North American research suggests that assertive involvement with a caring aspect is the only effective practice.

main points

■ Social care practice policy is developing the idea of personalization, promoting participation and control of care provision by users and carers.

■ Caring practice incorporates a concern for users' and carers' body, mind and spirit and managing time and place effectively. Networking and support are also important practices.

■ Care management approaches include care management in LA community care, keyworking, the care programme approach and strengths-based case management in mental health care.

■ Direct payments, independent budgeting and self-directed care are care management approaches that form the basis of personalization policy.

■ Risk and protection is an important area of practice.

stop and think

■ How would you like your bathroom at home to be organized if you needed help with going to the toilet and bathing?

■ How would you respond to a man who says his debilitating stroke is a punishment from God?

■ At a time of difficulty in your relationship with your parent or parents, what responses from the other parent or friends and colleagues were or were not supportive?

taking it further

- Pearson, C. (ed.) (2006) *Direct Payments and the Personalistion of Care.* Edinburgh: Dunedin Academic Press.

  A useful brief collection of material on both practical and conceptual issues about personalization.
- Leadbeater, C. (2004) *Personalisation through Participation: A New Script for the Public Services.* London: Demos.
  Also brief, but a more general account of personalization ideas applied more widely than in social care.
- Rapp, C. A. and Goscha, R. J. (2005) *The Strengths Model: Case Management and People with Psychiatric Disabilities.* New York: Oxford University Press.
  A good general text on the USA approach to case management in psychiatric care.
- Kemshall, H. and Pritchard, J. (eds) (1995) *Good Practice in Risk Assessment and Risk Management.* London: Jessica Kingsley.
  An excellent and practical edited volume on risk management in various aspects of social care.

Websites

- Useful links to organizations concerned with families, parenting and child care, from the Family and Parenting Institute: http://www.familyandparenting.org/pages/page2.php?id=87 (accessed: 23 July 2007).
- The Department of Health website on personalization gives access to the burgeoning official documents on direct payments and independent budgeting: http://www.dh.gov.uk/en/Policyandguidance/SocialCare/Socialcarereform/Personalisation/DH_080573 (accessed: 30 November 2007).

7 Endings, monitoring and evaluation

Ending social care: personal and professional implications

How and where do you end social care? When a user leaves a care home or a day centre? When an older person receiving home care enters hospital or residential care? Administrative systems often treat moves like this as a 'discharge' from the service. It seems a misuse of scarce resources to continue involvement when someone in another service is primarily responsible. However, Hudson (1994) makes the point, referring to a Scottish care management project, that securing a good experience of and following up admission were an important part of good practice. Maintaining continuing connections is important to caring services, because caring is about connectedness and the direction of travel of the people, family and social network involved. My own experience of bereavement services suggests that when someone dies, that is not the end of the case because other members of the family are affected by the death. Therefore, we need to follow up the interaction of one person's experience with the effect on others.

All endings involve loss, no matter how difficult they have been. Because caring is always a personal relationship, the participants experience feelings, sometimes of loss or sometimes of relief, satisfaction, reassertion of control. Practitioners need to prepare themselves and others for those feelings; anticipating an ending may lead to anxiety, depression or conversely elation, and then possibly guilt because of relief at the ending of a burden, for a carer. Ending social care provision also has implications for the organizations involved. Again, there is loss: the loss of opportunity to provide service, to meet the agency's objectives, loss of income, loss of security for a care home or home care service that is funded to care for a user. However, agencies may also gain opportunities to reallocate or save resources. Users and carers may worry that this is their main focus. Is a service ending because of cuts in budgets? Are they denied service because inappropriately stringent priorities are in place?

A middle-aged man recently spoke to me when his elderly mother died after many years of increasing disability, leading to night-time calls and disruption of his life. He missed the regular phone calls he had made almost daily to her, and the visits in which they had explored their family history together. He also missed the opportunity to talk about his work life. Every evening after supper, he felt vaguely that something was missing, and realized that this was because his sense of routine was reminding him that he should be ringing his mother now. On the other hand, his wife found that he was talking more to her about his work life and appreciated this. They both valued the increased focus on their own needs, rather than those of an outsider to their marriage. They did not have more time with each other, but they were not distracted by other responsibilities from concentrating on each other.

This experience illustrates people's mixture of emotions and reactions as their involvement with the social care services ceases. They need to be helped to prepare for this; the service needs to be organized to plan ending in advance. Planning for ending therefore needs careful monitoring and the review of cases and services as they progress.

Practitioners also need to be aware of other issues about endings. When a child moves from parents to foster carers or into residential care for children, the parents lose a very significant aspect of their lives and family relationships. When a child leaves residential or foster care, staff, child and family members also experience losses. At the outset of many other social care involvements and in moves between home care and residential care, people do not just become dependent, they *lose* independence and relationships.

Also, when people enter the care system as older people they are beginning to face quite starkly the end of their lives. A woman recently said to me that reaching the point at which she could no longer do her own shopping and needed a carer to help her with bathing made her realize that she was not just old but was soon going to die. People may become aware of their mortality because of many events in their lives, for example a bereavement of someone close to them. When a husband or wife dies in old age, all family members may become aware that the widow or widower may also die soon. Planning of funerals, memories, and the writing of a will may become urgent. A woman in her sixties commented to me that the complexity of dealing with her husband's estate when he died intestate, that is, without having made a will, made her realize that she should write a will of her own. To do so, she consulted with her children, and this example of planning led them to think about life planning in a new way. These discussions are often spiritual in nature: people think about what contribution they have made to life and what other people have given to them; they can use them to say 'thank you', 'sorry', 'I love you' or 'goodbye'. One technique for practitioners to use with users/carers might be to plan a life review, writing a diary, or more publicly a blog, and collecting and annotating photographs. They could also collect some items about this part of their life in a memory box.

An important recent development is the Mental Capacity Act 2005. Sections 24–6 make provision for someone to make advance decisions to refuse medical treatment. This particularly affects older people who may be nearing the end of their lives, but may also affect people with disabilities, learning disabilities and mental illness. It allows anyone over 19 years of age to complete a document that considers treatments that they might be offered at a time when they do not have the capacity to decide for themselves whether they want to be treated in this way. To do this, they need to discuss circumstances that might arise and what they want healthcare staff to do. Increasingly, it is likely that health and social care staff will need to be active in getting people to think about their possible treatment and care options in advance (DCA (Department of Constitutional Affairs), 2007: chapter 9).

People who are mentally ill or have learning disabilities, or who otherwise do not have capacity to make their own decisions, may also be represented in important decisions by Independent Mental Capacity Advocates (IMCAs). This service must be provided when:

- Serious medical treatment is provided or stopped
- A person moves into long-term care
- A person moves to a different hospital or care home.

It may also be provided where a care review or a safeguarding adults strategy meeting takes place (DCA, 2007: chapter 10).

When people with impaired mental capacity are thinking through future options, they have an opportunity to explore how they think about their lives. To help the process, simplified explanations are available for people with learning disabilities, as well as fiction and books of advice for users and their families facing decisions about possible changes and endings.

Monitoring, evaluation and review

For the same reason that endings are important to social care, so are monitoring, evaluation and review. The shift away from institutional care towards community care means that to maintain users' and carers' sense of security and continuity and therefore of being cared for, ways of maintaining continuous contact become more important. People are more likely to feel isolated from decisions in their own homes, whereas a residential home is a centre of service provision. Review maintains the security of the state in taking on its caring responsibilities. However, it also leads to increasing surveillance of people receiving social care services, and therefore in the sense of intrusion by the state in private lives through social care. The research into case management in mental health care, reviewed in Chapter 6, noted that there is evidence that assertive monitoring of people's condition is more acceptable than less intensive care at least partly because the assertive involvement demonstrates concern and builds relationships with people.

Monitoring means checking consistently that care and other plans are working appropriately; evaluation means examining whether these are achieving the best outcomes for service users, their families and carers. Review looks back in an organized way at the progress of the case, and is often the foundation for future plans. These mechanisms are connected with wider audit and research discussed in the next section.

Monitoring

Monitoring involves two aspects of care; one focused on users' and carers' needs, the other on the agency's requirements. The first aspect checks that users and carers feel secure in their present situation. Deterioration or variation may occur, but security means that users and carers are able to self-manage change. The trajectory of many care situations is a slow decline in someone's capacity to manage their affairs, with occasional crises. In these situations, monitoring is supportive because it enables users and carers to feel confidence that there will be a response to crisis; practitioners can only achieve this security if users and carers are actively aware of and involved in the monitoring. Various services offer this kind of monitoring:

■ *Supported housing* so that external pressures do not create crises.
■ *Supported housing with support workers*, to provide the confidence of regular checks to identify deterioration. Continuous knowledge of the resident is important so that changes in condition can be identified.
■ *Regular visits from professionals or carers*. Where there are multiple visits and therefore probably multiple problems, it is useful to plan these visits in a programme, so that a more frequent check is possible. Also, where some of the services are from serial carers, that is a succession of carers from an agency, and different personnel visit throughout the day to perform different tasks, it is useful to intersperse these with visits from staff who have a continuous relationship with users and carers. This enables someone who knows the user to identify problems and also to integrate serial carers' contributions carefully with the care plan, through offering guidance and supervision on an everyday basis.
■ *Respite or periodic care* in a care home, intermediate care facility, hospital or hospice to enable problematic symptoms to be dealt with and to relieve carers. This can restore or increase quality of life as it is deteriorating.
■ *Day centre or drop-in provision*, so that a regular check on capacity to attend and on users' physical and psychological condition can be made. The social elements of a day centre and the opportunity to achieve personal development outcomes through artistic and educational activities (Kennett, 2000; Hartley and Payne, 2008) can increase capacity to engage in social life at home. For example, users can take home art objects to be valued by family members and have conversation about activities and relationships at the centre with other people in their social network – it gives them something to talk about.

■ *Radio and telephone call systems* that enable frail people to call for assistance if they have a sudden crisis.

For people with severe or long-term difficulties, several of these monitoring devices can be used in combination and the following case studies demonstrate a number of these forms of monitoring. While the discussion of risk in Chapter 6 focused on the formal processes of inter-agency risk management, monitoring provides an opportunity to reduce all kinds of risks faced by people with long-term care needs.

> **case example**
>
> Mr Knowles is an example of external pressures. He lived in an older person's flatlet managed by a housing association; a warden visited daily. A condition of tenancy was that no other person should live there. His son visited to stay occasionally. One day, the warden, unusually, visited early in the morning and found the son sleeping on the sofa in the living room. Enquiring about this, she found that Mr Knowles was concealing the fact the son was living there. The LA care manager found that the son was a homeless drug user and had forced Mr Knowles to accommodate him, threatening violence. A strategy meeting under the safeguarding adults procedures discussed how to protect him against pressure from his son.

> **case example**
>
> Mrs Kettering is an example of multiple contacts. She was an elderly disabled woman, with increasing dementia. Her husband provided much of the care, including careful feeding of two meals a day. Serial carers from an agency visited three times a day to help her get up, to provide a bath and to put her to bed again. A district nurse visited three times a week to perform various nursing functions, including administering medication. A volunteer neighbourhood scheme organized by the church that Mr Kettering attended arranged a sitter while he attended church and the occasional church event, and during the summer helped Mr Kettering to get his wife into the garden on sunny days. Surprisingly, one winter day when it snowed, they happened to visit, and a brief period being out in the open and handling the snow pleased Mrs Kettering. This is an example of offering a variety of opportunities within extreme restrictions that increased the quality of life of a very disabled woman and helped her carer gain respite and feel that he was doing the best he could for her.

> **case example**
>
> Mr Georgiu is an example of the value of day centre provision. A man with a long history of mental illness, he lived in supported accommodation and had meals at a local drop-in centre. His community psychiatric nurse (CPN) visited the home to check on his condition and to administer medication. There was a period when Mr Georgiu started to come only irregularly for his meals at the drop-in, and when he did come, he was less engaged in social interaction than in the past. The staff contacted the CPN, who visited to find that his condition had deteriorated, but was able to arrange for outpatient treatment that restored his stability. This is an example also of the importance of teamwork between different parts of the social care system reducing risk.

John and Sheila are an example of everyday supervision to provide continuity. John, an adult social services care manager, visited Anne, an elderly disabled woman, to carry out an assessment for an additional service that had been requested by Anne's family. He found Sheila, an agency care worker, eating a sandwich lunch as Anne had a cup of tea after eating a delivered meal, which Sheila had helped her with. When John arrived, Sheila was talking to a friend on her mobile phone, and then received a succession of similar calls about her social life. Doing this, Sheila was ignoring Anne.

When the end of Sheila's time with Anne arrived, she said a cheery goodbye and left, still on the phone. John arranged to come back, and left with Sheila for a brief discussion. He talked about his assessment and explained what he was doing so that Sheila was better informed about what was happening with Anne and of his role; this was a training element of supervision. He also took the opportunity to say that it was nice that she took the trouble to have her lunch with Anne, sharing this time together, starting with a positive comment, and then asked about the phone calls. Sheila received phone calls from her friends all the time while at work; it was a natural part of her life. She left her mobile phone switched on to receive calls from her agency supervisor. John asked her how Anne and the other users she worked with felt about this. It was obvious that this issue had not occurred to Sheila. John said that he made a point of being clear with Anne that he was switching off his phone while working with her, as a way of emphasizing that she had his undivided attention – a contribution to receptive caring. John suggested to Sheila that she did as he had demonstrated with Anne, because it emphasized how important Anne's well-being and dignity were by concentrating on her. Also, older people were less accustomed than young people to being in constant contact with friends and colleagues through new communication technologies. John suggested that if, taking a break, Sheila did check her phone at the beginning, she could use the content of some of the calls as the basis of a conversation with Anne. This would help Anne feel more in contact with the outside world, and build more of a relationship with Sheila and her world. However, Sheila would have to watch out that Anne was not bored or irritated by having this reminder of a world that she was not part of; this is an example of keeping boundaries.

This was in some ways an accountability, or even disciplinary, aspect of everyday supervision, but the way John handled it also included important educational and supportive elements. Sheila experienced it as a reproof from a more senior worker, so there were negative connotations for her, but it also included information that helped her to reflect on the principles of the caring role, and had positive and developmental elements too. John's demonstration of the behaviour as part of his arrival was an important way of seeing it as positive; it is best to follow our own precepts if we are going to instruct others.

The second aspect of monitoring, to meet the agency's requirements, is part of care management processes. Some monitoring results from feedback mechanisms established through the assessment and care plan in community care management of children's care. The first and most important is the personal relationship established with users and carers through early contacts with them. Carrying out the assessment in ways that build trust for practitioners and respect for their agencies helps services to achieve flexibility and responsiveness by establishing a reliable and responsive individual connection. The relationship-building aspect of service assessment and planning balances intrusion.

Monitoring and review are important for continuous reassessment. Review also usefully has the capacity to incorporate different perspectives and actions from an initial assessment, which may be undertaken in a crisis for the user. However, reviews may become institutionalized in a different way, by using them to confirm existing patterns without a serious rethink. For example, Ellis (2007) found that reviews were not used to move services for older people towards direct payments once the initial crisis that led to service provision had passed. Once service patterns are established and services are well understood, direct payments may be more easily introduced.

Quality of life

A valuable focus, therefore, of monitoring is to identify tools that may usefully explore changes in the quality of life for users and carers. Quality of life has an everyday meaning: the extent of a feeling of well-being, enjoyment of life and ability to pursue and achieve desired life aims in an individual or community. A more specialized meaning would focus on measurement or indicators of the impact of social and environment factors on the sense of well-being of an individual or community. 'Health-related quality of life' is a measurement of the impact of an illness and its treatment on an individual's sense of well-being. To extend these points to social care, care-related quality of life is a measurement of the impact of need for care and provision of care services on the sense of well-being of individuals and their social networks.

Quality of life comes up in many different services. For example, in 2001–2 the Audit Commission carried out a project to help LAs identify quality of life indicators to promote the social, economic and environmental well-being of their area, as a consequence of the new duty under the Local Government Act 2000 to work with partners to prepare a community strategy. As a result, they identified thirty-two useful indicators within three broad areas of economic, social and environmental well-being, examples being factors in the level of social and educational deprivation (Audit Commission, 2002). This draws attention to the wide range of factors that might have an impact on the well-being of someone receiving social care services. The impact of their social care needs and services needs to be disentangled from this.

Health-related quality of life measures are available for many physical conditions, and may be objective or clinical and 'holistic' (Jacobs and Rapoport, 2003). Objective measures examine issues such as mortality, rates of cure or survival. Survival measures have led to the concept of 'quality of life years' (QALYs), that is, the period that an individual might expect to survive at a particular level of quality of life. Holistic measures include patients' perceptions as well as objective information. The perceptions may be an overall sense of well-being, how well the patient is in relation to an identified condition, or how well they are able to pursue some aspect of their life, such as ordinary living, or employment. An example of a health-care quality of life study that would have relevance to social care is described in Research Box 7.1 to show the sort of research that is possible. I have selected this from a huge number of recent research studies on health-related quality of life because of its potential application to social care. It appears in a medical journal, and researches Dutch care homes using a controlled, randomized trial. In spite of this distance from the usual social care literature, it produces convincing evidence that attention to the detail of users' social experiences produces measurable benefits for them. This suggests that funding of quality of life studies covering a wide range of social care data could produce useful results informing social care practice.

research box 7.1

Food service and quality of life in nursing homes

Why this study was undertaken – To identify whether family meal service (for example sitting in groups at a table with a cloth, normal cutlery and crockery, serving themselves from a choice of dishes with staff members present and talking to residents) or pre-plated meal service (for example where divided plates are handed out by staff who do not sit down to talk) improves the quality of life for nursing home residents.

Methods – Nursing homes were divided into two categories, those with pre-plated service and those with family meals. Quality of life was measured on scales concerned with sensory, physical and psychosocial functioning, safety and autonomy. Also physical functioning in tasks requiring both large and fine body movements, body weight and energy levels were measured.

Results – Family style mealtimes were found to prevent a decline in quality of life, physical performance and body weight in nursing home residents without dementia.

Commentary – In practical terms, this study tells us that making meals in care homes a good social experience is likely to maintain older people's quality of life and physical condition, but this does not work so well with residents with dementia.

Source: Nijs et al. (2006).

The most practical place for quality of life measures in the present social care system is at the assessment stage, since government models such as SAP (see Chapter 4) aim to gain agreement among local agencies about tools to use in assessments. Quality of life measures are good for this. However, whether measures are appropriate for particular users and carers needs careful thought. Once used, quality of life measures may often be repeated when monitoring or reviewing progress. The advantage of using established measures is that they are validated on wider populations than locally devised measures. Practitioners can also devise measures for particular groups of users. As a project, teams can also develop shared measures relevant for the locality; it helps teams and practitioners maintain a focus on quality of life. Relevant quality of life issues in social care might be measures of social isolation and networks, the seriousness of relationship or other difficulties, measures of satisfaction with the services provided or combinations of services and measures of capacity to carry out activities autonomously.

Evaluation and review

Evaluation and review offer more comprehensive consideration of provision. Evaluation at the end of service provision examines the worth of the services provided to the people involved during the whole period of provision: have they helped users and, separately, carers? Evaluation contributes to the methods for considering services of similar kinds provided to everyone. Review is a process of looking back on the experience of a particular phase of the services and considering their value as a basis for future service provision – looking backwards to plan forwards.

Reviewing is an important aspect of care management in adult community care, and integral to the system for looked-after children and for safeguarding children. In the DHSS care management guidance documents (SSI/SWSG, 1991), reviewing is seen as a way of identifying service or quality shortfalls. The government guidance on inter-agency working in safeguarding children considers reviewing in two contexts, which reflect wider use of the term.

The *child protection review conference* is an example of reviewing in the context of a continuing case: the aim is to examine changes in a child's circumstances, and what actions have been taken, and explicitly reconsider what decisions have been taken (HMG, 2006: 126–7); comprehensive reports are prepared for a meeting at which the child and parents are represented. A crucial element is the sense of active reconsideration of past decisions, and whether current circumstances still justify them.

Child death review processes are an example of more formal and extended consideration of actions taken in a case, to inform decisions in other cases (HMG, 2006: chapter 7).

Child care plans for looked-after children must be regularly reviewed, under the Review of Children's Cases Regulations 1991. The Review of Children's Cases (Amendment) (England) Regulations 2004, require LAs to appoint an independent reviewing officer, among whose responsibilities are the check on the children's human rights.

Bell (2005) connects such professional practices with research, showing how the two involve similar processes of investigation. She proposes four elements of any review process:

- Context, including values that are relevant and power relations among the people involved
- Setting, including the family home, care home, day centre and community in which care takes place
- Situated activity, including the interpersonal relationships and behaviour, for example degree of distress, that occur and the factors that affect them, for example isolation, or unhelpful relationships with peers
- Self, including the biography of the people involved and the trajectory of the problems they are dealing with and the impact on them.

Policy materials and professional discussions such as Bell's suggest that reviewing should be an active, forward-looking process in which the complex interacting factors involved in the situation should be fully reconsidered.

case example

Judy was a fourteen-year-old girl who had been presenting problems at school, truanting and exhibiting difficult behaviour in the council estate where she lived. This was situated activity, affected by the environment for young people on the estate, and in turn having an impact within Judy's home. The police had been called on a number of occasions to deal with rowdy behaviour that she was involved in, together with a group of young people, some of whom were drug abusers. Judy's parents were separated, and since the separation, her mother had seemed lacking in energy. Among concerns about the values and power relationships were her apparent lack of commitment to effective responsibility as a mother: 'she's given up,' was the impression. There was also concern that Judy had too much power in the mother–daughter relationship. The mother was allowing Judy and her friends to behave in difficult ways in their home. This might have been reaction to the losses that the separation involved. The headteacher referred Judy to the child and adolescent mental health services who, after assessing her and attempting some cognitive-behaviour therapy, decided she should be referred to a school for children with emotional and behaviour disorders. Judy's mother rejected this, and the headteacher agreed to continue to try with Judy. Difficulties continued and a safeguarding children strategy meeting was held; there were ongoing concerns about her mother's capacity to care for her satisfactorily.

After some months, things were no better. Shortly before the next review, however, a social worker at the local hospital referred Judy's mother to the safeguarding adults procedure, because, unknown to Judy's social worker and the school, she was receiving treatment for cancer, and had recently been started on morphine drugs to control pain. A visiting community nurse specialist had found Judy and her friends behaving in a very aggressive way to her exhausted and sick mother, and had become concerned in case the morphine, which is a heroin-derivative, was stolen or misused by Judy and her friends. At a review meeting, this additional information changed the child protection team's assessment of the mother's competence as a parent, since it was apparent that her lack of energy was not psychological but likely to be associated with her illness. It seemed more important to support her in the power relationships, and in the home setting, attempting further treatment for Judy, while encouraging her and her mother to be mutually supportive. They also determined to be more assertive about ensuring that Judy took up her treatment, in order to protect the mother. The police also became involved to protect the mother.

This was a situation in which a change in circumstances affected the basic assessment and decisions that the various teams had made. In many reviews, significant change of this kind is not apparent, but this example draws attention to the importance of looking at all factors in the situation, rather than making assumptions about causation.

Audit

Audit means examining defined aspects of an activity by comparing it with established standards, procedures or objectives. Practitioners might use audit to look at specific aspects of a caseload, for example if some kind of work takes up more time than in the past. The auditor defines what to look at, specifies the standards or procedures to test the work against, keeps organized records of that work for a sample period and writes a brief report on the findings.

Deciding on topics to audit is more difficult than it sounds. Many people start off by thinking about a problem or category of user in their work, such as families with a drug user, or older people receiving complex services. This makes it difficult to keep control of any audit. Therefore, I find it useful to take a step back and think about the following issues:

- Audience – Whose views might the audit change? It might clarify the practitioner's own views, or persuade a supervisor to change a workload.
- Aims – This is connected with audience: what should the audience think or believe having read the audit. Is it enough that they are satisfied that useful work is going on, are extra resources justified, or does the practitioner need to defend or develop practice?

- Existing information – What is already known from statistics or documents? This might avoid doing work to repeat information that is already available, and a further audit can build on existing data.
- Defining the limits of the audit – Precisely what types of work are the focus? Understanding a small area of work well is often better than having vague information about a wide range of work.
- Something that can be counted – It is useful to find aspects of the service that can be counted, or to turn more complex information into countable aspects.
- An idea that will organize and direct the work – An idea is a hypothesis that evidence collected might prove or disprove; it may also be relevant to a longer-term programme of audit and research.

practice example

An example of this was a welfare services audit that some colleagues and I carried out, which has been published (Levy and Payne, 2003). We kept a record for three months of the outcomes of all cases taken up by the welfare rights advisers in the social work team of our hospice. We also looked backwards in a 'retrospective study' on the cases that had involved more than twenty contacts, on the assumption that many contacts implied that the cases were more complex, to see what was involved in work that is more difficult. Then, a study of referrals showed us that referrers did not consistently identify the complex cases where there were serious difficulties. As a result, we were able to show a very heavy and successful workload, which we used to argue for more resources. Also, we got a grant for a project to see whether we were missing cases, by assessing all cases, alongside those that were referred. This is still going on, but one thing we have already discovered is that our own nurse teams were good at identifying welfare needs while referrers from outside the hospice are much less likely to have identified them. While the starting point of this audit was to confirm to management and colleagues the value of the service, the 'idea' that developed was of a series of projects and studies to demonstrate that a specialist welfare rights advice service was a crucial aspect of palliative care provision. This moves in the direction of research, because it seeks to change the practice of our field of work.

Research

Research is a process of identifying and defining issues in providing care, examining them, and identifying and disseminating information that will change or improve knowledge and understanding about the topic. However, the research process is not neutral, because the topics that are studied, and the resources put into the study, reflect interest in particular topics at the time, and consequently also reflect power imbalances. For example some of the studies on community social work described in Research Box 5.1

were funded by the Department of Health to develop and explore a widely promoted model of practice and organization. However, alternative findings came from a study of service users' views on the same innovation, which were more critical, but had to be funded by the researchers themselves, through a subscription for the publication.

Research and evaluation that explore personal and interpersonal issues will often be qualitative and participatory in their methods, because this is the only way to get at the complexity of the situations that social care deals with. Effective participatory research, like practice, relies on relationships and engagement with users and carers in exactly the same way as social work (Atkinson, 2005).

The research boxes in this book, describe a range of research relevant to social care, with a variety of methods being used and a variety of interests engaged in research. Among the research methods described are the following: Research Boxes 1.1 and 6.2 use focus groups to identify the range of opinion that people have about the topic. Box 1.2 re-analyses data from an existing survey of public opinion. Box 2.2 describes an official national survey. Many studies, like those in Research Boxes 2.1 and 5.2, use interviews with people. Box 2.3 uses an action research model and non-participant observation.

They also demonstrate a range of interests in research, and the funders of particular pieces of research indicate some of the interests in them. This is particularly evident with the programmes of study. For example, Research Box 5.1 on community social work notes case studies of particular agency or staff development projects, a study from the point of view of service users, and from the point of view of the innovators of a management change. The research in Boxes 2.2 and 2.3, funded by the Department of Health, carried out and published at the same time, are similar studies of practice in children's residential care. They were funded in the early 1990s after a number of scandals in this field and the publication of the Utting Report (1997) on the same area. Research Boxes 2.1 and 6.1 were both funded by the Economic and Social Research Council, responding to theoretical sociological ideas. Although they both usefully inform us about how social care work is carried out, their main focus is on kinship relations and the sociology of the body. Smaller scale studies such as Research Box 6.2 are funded as PhD projects.

An important role for research is as part of a process of collaboration. Research Box 7.2 represents a collaborative effort by academic and agency interests in a particular locality, engaging with each other to study a topic of practical interest, which informs general theoretical interest in different roles of social care, funded by resources available to the participants. Many such projects are possible, helping to draw various interests in an area together. Using some of the techniques for examining networks in Chapter 5 may help identify interests that might work together. Sometimes it may help to identify the activity as research, because this may accumulate prestige and finance for the project. On other occasions it may be tactical to downplay the research element, focusing on the practical outcomes. Another possibility may be to create a division of labour, with more academic members focusing on research outcomes and practitioners and managers on practice and service development outcomes.

research box 7.2

Social work roles with older people

Why this study was undertaken – To enable academic and social services staff to work together to distinguish the roles social workers take on from others' roles in working with older people, partly to avoid allocating a qualified worker where someone else could do the work. This objective explicitly allowed sanction for an apparently 'theoretical' project (defining a social work role) to engage managers and practitioners in an agency.

Method – A literature review identified statements about the less-than-secure role of social workers with older people; staffing numbers in the LA involved were surveyed and compared with similar LAs. A group identified, through 'word-storming', the roles and attributes typical of a social work role, producing a 'grid', which was then tested out with stakeholders in social services and primary healthcare in the locality.

Results – Three types of activities were identified: work allocated to social workers under community care arrangements (mainly assessment tasks); work that social workers *ought* to do (such as dealing with life and transition crises of older people) although they were found not to be doing such work; and practice where social work historically claimed a role (such as dealing with discrimination and risk assessment).

The researchers propose that the grid should allow social workers to refocus their activities on medium- to long-term objectives affecting older people, rather than on immediate practical tasks, some of which could be allocated to less or differently qualified staff.

Source: Lymbery et al. (2007).

It is important to identify clearly at the outset how outcomes are to be disseminated and who gains credit and takes responsibility for achievements. This avoids difficulties arising at a late stage when participants do not feel they have received due credit. In particular, managers often baulk at the last moment about outcomes that may affect the reputation and therefore possible future financing of their agency. The enthusiasm of involvement at the start may mean that participants are not clear about how to resolve potential problems. The sharing of copyright and intellectual property rights can also be an important issue. For example, if the aim is to develop an assessment tool, and this is successful, other people may want to use it. Is the right to do so to be given free? This may be the position of some public authorities. However, a charity or private company may want to market the tool; this is unusual in social care research, but commonplace in psychology or medicine.

case example

A charity with an innovative project received a grant to evaluate its achievements. An academic on the board of trustees planned and managed this. As part of this, she planned a study of how the organization had been set up, carried out by an external researcher, who interviewed everyone involved. The rest of the evaluation used existing data on service provision and user satisfaction. When the Board read the report, concern centred on the organizational study, because it revealed several different interests in and views on the aims of the organization. The chair and chief executive complained that this information made the management and aims of the organization appear conflicted, with a consequent risk to a potential government grant. The academic pointed out that having a range of interests with different positions was true of most organizations at foundation, and the external researcher pointed out that the quotations representing the disagreement accurately reflected opinion. However, people with the role of getting the money in found the truth inconvenient. To achieve their objectives in fund-raising, they had expected the evaluation to confirm their own reality of strategic agreement rather than a process of negotiated consent.

Research can also be a significant factor in empowerment for service users and carers (Hanley, 2005). They can be involved in mainstream and academic research by being consulted about selection of criteria, factors to be examined and methods of investigation. They can also be helped to identify and carry out their own research collaboratively. This can be as beneficial for service users and carers in their personal development as it is for practitioners.

Regulatory review

A useful source of monitoring is the regulatory review required by regulators' criteria for assessment of services and the reports that they publish. These are available on the regulators' websites (Table 3.2), and can provide useful guidance on the things that can go wrong or right in social care and other services. Regulatory reports are also important as benchmarks and sources of reflection for practitioners as well as guidance for users and carers in selecting services. Advocates can also use them as a source of evidence in making cases for users.

Staff development and supervision

Most statements about human rights say that everyone is entitled to education and personal development. Hence, of course, this is an entitlement for service users, carers, the communities practitioners serve, and social and health care staff at every level. Practitioners need to think through:

- Developing and maintaining a focus on personal development for services users, caregivers and communities
- Thinking about and responding to the training and personal development needs of care staff
- Planning their own personal and professional development.

As care work is emotional labour, carers, professional and otherwise, need help to engage emotionally with people in need. Also, caring, by definition, is about development for the care-receiver, and carers' own development is required as part of the process to achieve that. Among the ways in which education and support are offered for social care workers and carers are:

- Personal support and therapy
- Informal carer, community and public education
- Professional supervision and consultation
- Management and administrative supervision
- Specific skills training
- Vocational education and qualification
- Professional education and qualification
- Post-qualifying education.

These are important aspects of improving quality of care and quality of life for users, and practitioners and carers need to be thinking through how they provide for this. Among other things, it may help to reduce stress: internationally (Coyle et al., 2005; Storey and Billingham, 2001) and in the UK (Coffey et al., 2004), social work and related professions demonstrate high levels of stress. Research Box 7.3 demonstrates how informal caring roles and jobs in social care work may interact. This illustrates the importance of agencies and managers being flexible in making time for the maintenance tasks in practitioners' lives.

---

research box 7.3

Practitioners caring for older adults

Why this study was undertaken – To look at how employees dealt with caring responsibilities for older people alongside work, by looking at people whose work also involved care responsibilities.

Methods – A screening questionnaire survey of SSDs and PCTs, collection of information from the organizations, a postal

---

survey of staff who were carers and then interviews with 44 carers and 20 managers to provide case studies.

Results – Out of around 5,000 workers in each organization, 64% and 55% of the SSD and PCT respectively were over 40 years of age and at least 10% had caring responsibilities for older adults. Many were manual workers, and did not have the income to employ paid carers. Of these working carers, 90% were women, who provided the most care, often more than 20 hours per week. The help was mainly practical and supportive. In this study, 265 carers were identified and surveyed; they juggled their caring responsibilities with their work. Their managers were key to allowing them the flexibility to manage these responsibilities. Workers built up a 'bank of trust' with their managers that they would built up time off in lieu of work done out of the usual hours, and then be allowed to use this flexibly in their caring role.

The researchers contrast the care of older people with that of children. Child care responsibilities could be organized on a more regular basis, and were a basis of pride and much social conversation, while the care of older people was more fragmented, and more private.

Source: Phillips et al. (2002).

Knapman and Morrison (1998) usefully point up issues in the supervision process, which offer helpful guidance on ways of managing regular supervision discussions:

- Deciding on the agenda, which would include cases brought by the worker and selected by the supervisor, and who does the recording of the supervision and how
- Talking about personal issues that affect the work and how to ensure they benefit rather than hinder practice
- Talking about feelings stimulated by the work, and how they may be managed and used positively in practice
- Talking about difficulties of working with colleagues and how to resolve them
- Talking about values issues, anti-discriminatory practice and confidentiality
- Feeding back clearly with concrete examples what is good and bad about practice and supervision.

These points also help people being supervised to contribute appropriate material to the shared work.

Conclusion

The argument in this chapter is that ending, monitoring, review, audit and research are all about achieving the security that social care seeks to effect for its users and carers. They are all integral to the starting point of engagement and assessment in social care, because a satisfactory ending and good results in quality of life and freedom from risk at monitoring are the outcomes that social care aims for. Users' and carers' confidence in the continuing responsiveness is a product of security of relationship, but it is also a product of attention to detail in every part of social care services. Thus, practitioners' confidence through their own development in research and reflection on their practice is also important in achieving the kind of social care that is implied by the analysis of social care established in Chapter 1. Therefore, securing practitioners' development is part of the central caring objective of securing users' and carers' development.

main points

- Endings involve loss and ambivalence; they may lead to users and carers losing a sense of security but also a loss or reassertion of control in life.
- Social care practice needs to prepare users and carers for changes arising from the end of and changes in service.
- Monitoring, evaluation and review contribute to active consideration of the needs of users and carers throughout the time they receive social care services.
- An important focus in social care is users' and carers' quality of life and its measurement.
- Audit and research processes can help to develop services and enable practitioners, users and carers to participate in planning future directions in social care provision.
- Staff development and supervision secure practitioners', users' and carers' connectedness in caring tasks.

stop and think

- Review the variety of interests and methods of research outlined in the Research Boxes of this book. How might these possibilities inform your own research practice?
- Social care may be studied at each level from GCSE to undergraduate degree. What differences can you identify in the levels and requirements?

- Look at library books for different levels of study. What are the differences in the ways similar topics are dealt with at different levels? How might this limit colleagues' work?

taking it further

- HMG (2006) *Working Together to Safeguard Children: A Guide to Inter-agency Working to Safeguard and Promote the Welfare of Children*. London: TSO.
  Well-established 'working together' guidelines; examines reviewing in child protection fairly comprehensively.
- SSI/SWSG (1991) *Care Management and Assessment: Practitioners' Guide*. London: Department of Health.
- SSI/SWSG (1991) *Care Management and Assessment: Managers' Guide*. London: Department of Health.
  These two guides reflect official views of the role of reviewing in care management.
- DCA (2007) *Mental Capacity Act 2005: Code of Practice*. London: TSO.
  The Code of Practice for the Mental Capacity Act sets out useful guidance about a wide range of rights and services for people whose mental capacity might be impaired in adulthood.

Websites
- The Care Services Improvement Website (CSIP) has, among many other resources, a useful guide to evaluating practice projects, which has the benefit of being simple but authoritative, so that its advice can be used in an argument that it is useful and important to carry out research and audit on your work.
  http://www.csip-plus.org.uk/RowanDocs/EvaluationGuide.pdf
- The patient-reported quality of life instruments database provides descriptions of a wide range of health-related quality of life instruments, some of which are general and psychosocial in their content: http://www.qolid.org/

8 The future of social care

Is good social care possible? Do we achieve it now? Can we achieve it in the future? My answers to these questions are: undoubtedly yes, yes sometimes, yes if we work at it. In this chapter, I bring together the arguments of this book and look towards the future of social care.

The shift in UK public policy since 2000 towards personalization as the basis of social care brings opportunity and risk. It recognizes an important political insight: people increasingly see public services as a commodity consumed by individuals rather than as a collective social provision and have transferred their assumptions of an individualized consumerism from other parts of the economy to public services. This means that service users expect a flexible personalized service that meets their needs, and government policy aims to 'deliver' services like this. Personalization in social care is being developed, building on experience of user-controlled direct payments for care managed by or on behalf of users themselves, rather than care being service organized and managed by officials and provided by a range of agencies contracted to LAs or by LAs themselves. This policy shift is in tension with government constraints on rising expenditure on care services because of the care deficit, which means that there are not enough resources to meet all the needs that might be identified.

How can this tension be resolved? To manage resources, the existing model of community care pushed service provision towards an administrative model of care management. Concern about risk and protection pressed care for looked-after children and for vulnerable adults towards intrusive official intervention. People who need care do not want to be 'cared for' in a dependency-creating way by social care services. The reasons for this are that they prefer family members to provide their care, they do not want official intrusion into their private lives and they want control of what happens to them when they are dependent upon others. Yet many people with the greatest care needs do not have family members who can care fully for them, so they need social care. However, for reasons of finance and public responsibility, complete control of care arrangements cannot be ceded from public authorities to individuals. Also, direct payments and independent budgeting are only proposed for community care, not for healthcare or for children and families work. This is because groups with long-term care needs have always been low priority compared with acute healthcare, and child protection requires active intervention.

The risk of personalization policy, then, is that it will be implemented by focusing on administrative processes to manage resources and risk; the opportunity is to implement it to focus on the rights of service users and carers to a significant degree of control and participation in how social care works for them. Even where protection and surveillance are also required, major areas of choice and freedom are usually possible. Service delivery is not just about how much of what kinds of services are provided, therefore, it is also about how they are provided and what outcome is achieved for the service user and their carers.

There are two basic points. One is that most people are self-caring in most aspects of their lives for most of the time. Even when they are receiving care services, even where they need protection and surveillance, many people are still significantly self-caring, and also receive important care and support from their own social networks; this is true both for children in need and for adults with long-term care needs. The second basic point is the nature of care. Chapter 1 showed that care incorporates two aspects: to be receptive and connected to people's values and to be committed to developing service users towards self-fulfilment.

The outcome of care services has to achieve these two basic points, together, if usually balancing them. Therefore, social care needs to connect self- and social network caring with receptive, developmental citizen caring on behalf of the state. Administrative care management will not do.

Chapter 2 proposed that in order to interweave citizen caring with self- and social network caring, social care practice needs to connect with, and accept as its everyday basis, the values of the user and carers. To make those connections, Chapter 3 argued that practitioners must understand and integrate organizational structures and policy developments within their social care practice. Chapters 4–7 examined current and developing approaches to practice.

Throughout the book, important themes about social care practice, which I summarized in the Introduction, emerged in different contexts. They all start from the need of users and carers to feel that their care interweaves with their social networks and therefore normalizes and connects with their shared values; people will not experience care as caring unless services achieve this. This outcome requires an understanding of the cultural, social and spiritual values that are important to users and carers, and a focus on the quality of life and qualities in life that will achieve receptiveness, connectedness and development for users.

An important concern is the intrusion of the state into people's private lives. Surveillance is different now, compared with the past. In workhouses for the poor, asylums for the lunatics and colonies for the idiots and imbeciles, it meant 'watch them because they are a risk to us all'. Now, surveillance is mainly 'watch them in case they are at risk in their social context'. Social analysis suggests that both old and new forms of surveillance are about creating and maintaining social order, making people feel safe, helping social cohesion by ensuring that people in difficulties do not cause difficulties. However, there is a genuine improvement. There is a world of difference between creating social order by locking people away from everyone else, and trying to enable people to feel safe within and connected to the people and organizations that provide them with care.

In this book, therefore, I have examined social care as a shift in service planning, based on a trail of ideas about caring roles in the social services back to the 1980s. These caring roles emerged most strongly in residential care and community care. Social care has only recently established a practice separate from but connected to social work. State social provision in the UK has pursued service provision through structural and economic reform, excluding the central role of caring as a relationship-based practice integrating practitioners, informal carers and service users with their communities. I have tried to set out in this book the practice approaches that have developed to enable people with long-term care needs to be cared for, as well as provided for.

So social care is possible. What is required is meticulous attention to the detail of people's lives, responding to the needs that they express and that we can identify, and building a continuous relationship with people so that they feel safe that we will be receptive to their needs and positive in helping them develop and plan for the future. I find, working in a hospice, that dying people have hopes for the future, hopes about their families, communities and for humankind, hope that they can die having made their contribution to life and that they are appreciated and loved. If hope is part of the experience of dying people, it is easy to imagine that someone needing social care during their life may have just as much hope for their own future, and that we can meet those hopes. Anything less is unacceptable.

While good social care is possible, unequal social care is likely, because, as demands rise with an ageing population, cost constraints will become more important. One change will be to the distinction between NHS and social care outlined in Chapter 3. The present organization of care in England distinguishes between community care and NHS continuing care. This distinction cannot be sustained in the long term, since continuing care is more generous than LA community care funding for virtually the same service; the definition of healthcare relies mainly on the provision of nursing and medical care. There is already a mechanism for paying separately for additional nursing in care homes, which is in effect a state top-up to people contributing to costs but assessed as having healthcare needs. The Health and Social Care Act 2001 provides for direct payments to service users for local authority community care services, allowing them to manage their own services; direct payments are not available for NHS continuing care. Public support for direct payments is likely to lead to a demand for similar provision to be extended to the continuing care to permit increased choice by users and their families.

The risk of this for users and carers is that care services will increasingly come to assume the social care system of contributions from users and their relatives and supporters towards care, and this must eventually spread to continuing care payments. Thus 'co-payment', with users and their families sharing costs with NHS and LA funding, will become the expectation. This is a further shift from free NHS care to means-tested social care. Once this is commonplace, pressures from periodic downturns in the economic cycle will lead to constraints on care budgets. Users and families will end up paying a higher proportion of care costs. This has always been the pattern of development in care costs. The present system of community care was introduced in the mid-1990s with the specific aim, successfully achieved, of constraining cost increases in care budgets. As needs have grown, with an ageing population, budgets have been tightly controlled and therefore care services have been increasingly rationed to those most in need, to the neglect of prevention work.

Services for children and families also distinguish between education and social care. Everyone is entitled to education, while social care is provided mainly for children and families defined as 'at risk'. Well-off families provide for their children's education and care from their own generous resources and get better education; deprived families receive limited help often in poor environments only if they are assessed as 'in need'.

For both adults and children, therefore, the care deficit will generate resource constraints that will increasingly require people's own financial contribution alongside the state's. This is already happening in a policy that requires single parents and disabled people to work if they can or have their services or benefits reduced, and older people and their families to contribute to care costs or receive poorer quality services.

In the future, what is now financial assessment for services for the poor, with more generous help if care needs are provided by traditionally free healthcare services, will shift towards an explicit responsibility for both state and family contributions to care costs. Under these economic and social pressures, inequalities are always rife. As in education, the already well off can usually ensure that they benefit the most from whatever provision the state makes, and the already deprived people receive poorer quality services.

Good social care practice, valuing and advocating for people's own values, offered to all, is one of the professional protections enabling users and carers to maintain a good quality of life when receiving social care services. Good caring practice is in the forefront of ensuring social equality in care service provision.

Abbreviations

ACT	assertive community treatment, a North American model of case management
ADASS	Association of Directors of Adult Social Services
ADSS	the former Association of Directors of Social Services
AGM	annual general meeting of a voluntary organization or company
CAF	common assessment framework (for children and young people)
CPA	care programme approach to coordinating care for people with severe mental health difficulties
CSCI	Commission for Social Care Inspection
CSED	Care Services Efficiency Delivery
CSIP	Care Services Improvement Partnership
DGH	district general hospital – a hospital providing most hospital-based healthcare in a locality, the main point of referral from a GP
DH	Department of Health, an English government ministry; sometimes rendered as DoH
EBD	emotional and behavioural disorders
GP	general practitioner, the family doctor at the centre of UK primary healthcare
ICA	Invalid Care Allowance, a now-renamed social security allowance for informal carers (the Carer's Allowance)
ICM	intensive case management
IMCA	independent mental capacity advocate
IPP	individual programme planning
LAs	local authorities, or local councils; the main providers of local government services in the UK
MAPPA	multi-agency public protection arrangements
NSF	National Service Framework
PCP	person-centred planning
PCT	primary care trust, the main local commissioning and management body for NHS community health services
SAP	single assessment process (for older people)
SCA	Social Care Association
SSDs	social services departments of English and Welsh LAs; sometimes includes similar departments in Northern Ireland and Scotland that have different names
UK	United Kingdom of Great Britain and Northern Ireland

Glossary

Advocacy – to speak on behalf of someone, in favour of their interests.

Agency – the capacity or personal and group effectiveness to achieve desired outcomes; also an organization that provides health and social care services.

Assertive outreach – care management services that maintain contact with service users to ensure they receive care, particularly mentally ill people needing regular medication or others without an organized lifestyle.

Assessment – examining the range of factors affecting an individual, group or social situation in order to prepare, plan and take action to meet social care or other service objectives.

Audit – examining defined aspects of an activity by comparing it with established standards, procedures or objectives.

Boundary – the perception of a line that forms the edge or limit that separates two connected aspects of life.

Care – practical and emotional actions, by people with a personal emotional commitment or other form of connectedness, to be receptive to others' needs and to help others achieve development towards self-actualization.

Care environment – the places within the caring arena in which care services are provided.

Care management – a range of approaches to coordinating care for service users, including organizing coherent staffing and different kinds of help to people cared for in in-patient healthcare settings, and assessing, planning, coordinating the delivery, monitoring and evaluating LA community care services; *see also* case management.

Care programme approach (CPA) – a system of coordinating multi-agency care to people with serious mental health difficulties.

Caring arena – a location and set of social relationships in which a care organization, represented by its practitioners, intersects with and intrudes upon the community, life and relationships of a person receiving care.

Caring presence – the capacity to communicate that a carer is focused on, receptive and available to meet the care needs of an individual.

Case management – an American social work process, the source of care management in UK community care, to coordinate services to a service user from a range of different agencies; latterly, particularly refers to self-directed and assertive outreach services for mentally ill people. In administrative case management (travel agent model) the manager arranges services, in clinical case management (travel companion model) the manager provides a continuing supportive relationship.

Citizen care – a social relationship in which people representing the state accept responsibility for caring for others because the care-receivers are citizens of the state.

Collaboration – the aspiration that practitioners in different services and service sectors of the economy will cooperate to provide services seamlessly.

Commissioning – authorizing a person or organization to carry out official responsibilities; by extension, establishing planning or financing services appropriate to public needs.

Communitarianism – a political philosophy that values individuals' participation in collective mutual support, seeing social provision as an exchange in which only individuals who have contributed to social capital may benefit from receiving collective support.

Community – established and institutionalized connections between people arising from commitment to a locality or interests that creates a shared identity experienced as supportive.

Critical incident – an event that makes a significant contribution, either positively or negatively, to the general aim of an activity.

Culture – an expression of the social life of an identifiable social group in its heritage, social rules of behaviour and expectations and ideas that define its identity.

Engagement – a process by which practitioners and service users become enmeshed in working together on social care issues faced by the user.

Evaluation – examining the extent to which services are achieving the best outcomes for the service user, their families and carers.

Family – social practices in which people choose to develop and enact in their personal lives ideas of parenthood, kinship and marriage.

Formal care – care provided as an organized service by or on behalf of the state by a health and social care agency.

Housing – a private area of a building that accommodates people for many of the activities of family living, in particular where people sleep.

Identity – a person's or group's continuous sense of self, derived from their experience of culture and social relationships.

Independent living – a movement initially of people with physical disabilities to reject collective living, such as residential care, that involved excessive control of their lifestyle choices by official services, and to live in ordinary housing with the user controlling, through various financial mechanisms, the employment and deployment of personal carers to provide necessary care.

Informal care – care provided unpaid by family, neighbours, friends and other people in a care-receiver's social network.

Keyworking – allocating a particular worker to be the focus of links between users and the service, particularly in residential care, or between residential care and community services.

Legislation – laws; permissive legislation allows a public authority to act, for example by providing a service, mandatory legislation requires a public authority to act.

Means test – an official assessment of the extent to which people have the financial resources to pay for a public service or should be required to pay for their own private alternative.

Mediation – a process by which an outsider helps two parties to come to shared understanding and agreement.

Monitoring – checking consistently that care or other plans are working appropriately.

Multidisciplinary – involving people drawn from different knowledge and skill backgrounds.

Multiprofessional – involving people from different backgrounds of professional training and socialization.

Need – a psychological response to personal or social experience that leads people to seek to remedy it.

Negotiation – bringing parties that have interaction with each other together where there is potential for achieving changes towards greater agreement in actions, decisions or direction.

Network – patterns of social connections between individuals and others.

Normalization – the creation of socially valued cultures and places within care environments with the aim of reducing social exclusion created by social reactions to disabilities.

Ordinary housing – a movement of the 1980s to enable residents with disabilities to live with the same degree of independence, self-caring and control of tenure that would be preferred by non-disabled people.

Participation – people with different interests each making contributions in a shared process towards an agreed objective.

Partnership – the aspiration to create cooperative relationships between personnel in different services so that they pursue the same objectives in coordinated ways.

Personalization – to change a standard format so that it suits a person or is connected with them; in social care, adapting services to the needs of a particular service user, by giving the user increased control over assessment, planning and management of the budget for the care provided.

Person-centred planning – a process of assessment and service planning that focuses on involving the service users, carers and their social networks in identifying and meeting service users' and carers' needs and integrating professional and service contributions to meeting those needs.

Place – a location, and its physical characteristics, that contributes to identity and social expectations.

Primary healthcare – the healthcare services provided at the first point of contact between citizens and the healthcare system, by practitioners associated with a patient's GP, providing assessment and most treatment.

Progressive condition – an illness that leads to a continuing worsening of a person's physical health or condition.

Quality of life – the extent of a feeling of well-being, enjoyment of life and ability to pursue and achieve desired life aims in an individual or community, and the measurement or indicators of the impact of social and environment factors on this sense of well-being. 'Health-related quality of life' is a measurement of the impact of an illness and its treatment on an individual's sense of well-being. Care-related quality of life is a measurement of the impact of need for care and provision of care services on the sense of well-being of individuals and their social networks.

Quasi-market – a system of public service provision in which competition by providers within a planned market is designed to increase patients' choice and cost effectiveness is encouraged through market disciplines.

Regulations – rules that set out the detailed way in which law and policy should be implemented.

Research – a process of identifying and defining issues in providing care, examining them, and disseminating information that will change or improve knowledge and understanding about the topic.

Review – looking back in an organized way at the progress of the case as a foundation for any future plans.

Sector – different parts of the economy covering different aspects of living, such as care, manufacturing and retail sectors, and different legal structures for organizations, such as private, public and voluntary or third sectors.

Service pathway – the route, including attempts at self-care and unsuccessful involvement with other agencies, that service users follow before applying or being referred for social care.

Social capital – the accumulated human resources of a society contributing to its social cohesion generated by citizens' participation in collective community development.

Social network – connections between individuals created by interpersonal contacts and relationships.

Spirituality – people's thinking, which may originate from beliefs or religious faith, about non-material aspects of their life that energizes them in dealing with important life issues.

Stress – the existence of events or circumstances in a care environment (potential stressors) that cause a perception that a person is exposed to risk of an adverse psychological and physiological reaction to it, which may lead to physical or mental ill-health if sustained over a long period.

Supervision – a process of engagement between a practitioner and a colleague or colleagues in shared analysis, reflection and skill development through administrative, education and personal support in practice tasks.

Supported housing – housing schemes that provide intensive care and support to people with care needs in housing built or adapted to meet their needs.

Surveillance – intrusion into private lives and decisions by enabling observation of them by public and other sources of authority.

Teamwork – working with others to develop shared values and aims.

Tenure – the legal basis by which people have the right to use a building.

The social – patterns of connections and relationships between people, in particular the social institutions and organizational setting in which such connections take place.

Third sector – an American term, increasingly widely used, for voluntary or not-for-profit organizations, implying that the first two sectors are the private and state sectors.

Total institution – a residential care setting where all or most aspects of life were provided for within one institution.

Trajectory – how illnesses or conditions develop and change over time; the progression of the combination of issues faced by a service user.

Bibliography

Ackroyd, S. (1997) Don't care was made to care. In Hugman, R., Peelo, M. and Soothill, K. (eds) *Concepts of Care: Developments in Health and Social Welfare.* London: Arnold, 19–35.

Adam, B., Beck, U. and van Loon, J. (2000) *The Risk Society and Beyond: Critical Issues for Social Theory.* London: Sage.

Adams, J. (1995) *Risk.* London: Routledge.

Adams, T. (2003) Developing an inclusive approach to dementia. *Practice* 15(10): 45–56.

ADSS (2005) *Safeguarding Adults: A National Framework of Standards for Good Practice and Outcomes in Adult Protection Work.* London: Association of Directors of Social Services.

Antonnen, A., Baldock, J. and Sipilä, J. (2003) *The Young, the Old and the State: Social Care Systems in Five Industrial Nations.* Cheltenham: Edward Elgar.

Arksey, H., O'Malley, L., Baldwin, S. and Harris, J. (2002) *Services to Support Carers of People with Mental Health Problems: Literature Review Report for the National Co-ordinating Centre for NHS Service Delivery and Organisation R & D (NCCSDO).* York: University of York.

Atkinson, D. (2005) Research as social work: participatory research in learning disability. *British Journal of Social Work* 35(4): 425–34.

Audit Commission (1986) *Making a Reality of Community Care.* London: HMSO.

Audit Commission (2002) *Voluntary Quality of Life and Cross-Cutting Indicators April 2001–March 2002: Revised Indicators Handbook.* London: Audit Commission. http://ww2.audit-commission.gov.uk/pis/doc/pi_q/F.doc (accessed: 3 December 2007).

Balloch, S. and Hill, M. (eds) (2007) *Care, Community and Citizenship: Research and Practice in a Changing Policy Context.* Bristol: Policy Press.

Balloch, S. and Taylor, M. (eds) (2001) *Partnership Working: Policy and Practice.* Bristol: Policy Press.

Barclay Report (1982) *Social Workers: Their Role and Tasks.* London: Bedford Square Press.

Barnes, C. and Mercer, G. (2002) *Disability.* Cambridge: Polity.

Barnes, C. and Mercer, G. (eds) (2005) *The Social Model of Disability: Europe and the Majority World.* Leeds: Disability Press.

Barnes, M. (2006) *Caring and Social Justice.* Basingstoke: Palgrave Macmillan.

Barton, R. (1959) *Institutional Neurosis.* Bristol: John Wright and Sons.

Bayley, M. (1973) *Mental Handicap and Community Care*. London: Routledge and Kegan Paul.

Bayley, M. J., Parker, P., Seyd, R. and Tennant, A. (1987) *Practising Community Care: Developing Locally-Based Practice*. Sheffield: Social Services Monographs.

Bayliss, E. (1987) *Housing: The Foundation of Community Care*. London: National Federation of Housing Associations.

BBC (2007) *Q&A Social Care*, http://news.bbc.co.uk/1/hi/health/4858610.stm (accessed: 6 May 2007).

Beck, U. (1992) *Risk Society: Towards a New Modernity*. London: Sage.

Bell, L. (2005) Review. In Adams, R., Dominelli, L. and Payne, M. (eds) *Social Work Futures: Crossing Boundaries, Transforming Practice*. Basingstoke: Palgrave Macmillan, 83–96.

Bell, M. (2007) Community-based parenting programmes: An exploration of the interplay between environmental and organizational factors in a Webster Stratton project. *British Journal of Social Work* 37(1): 55–72.

Beresford, P. and Croft, S. (1986) *Whose Welfare? Private Care or Public Services*. Brighton: Lewis Cohen Urban Studies Centre.

Berridge, D. and Brodie, I. (1998) *Children's Homes Revisited*. London: Jessica Kingsley.

Bland, R. (1997) Keyworkers re-examined: Good practice, quality of care and empowerment in residential care of older people. *British Journal of Social Work* 27(4): 585–603.

Booth, T., McConnell, D. and Booth, W. (2006) Temporal discrimination and parents with learning disabilities in the child protection system. *British Journal of Social Work* 36(6): 997–1015.

Bowrey, L. and McGlaughlin, A. (2007) Older carers of adults with a learning disability confront the future: Issues and preferences in planning. *British Journal of Social Work* 37(1): 39–54.

Bradshaw, J. (1972) A taxonomy of social need. In Mclachlan, G. (ed.) *Problems and Progress in Medical Care: Essays on Current Research*. Oxford: Nuffield Provincial Hospital Trust.

Brammer, A. (2007) *Social Work Law*. (2nd edn) Harlow: Longman Pearson.

Brandon, D. and Brandon, T. (2001) *Advocacy in Social Work*. Birmingham: Venture.

Brandon, D., Brandon, T. and Brandon, A. (1995) *Advocacy: Power to People with Disabilities*. Birmingham: Venture.

Brearley, P., Hall, F., Gutridge, P., Jones, G. and Roberts, G. (1980) *Admission to Residential Care*. London: Tavistock.

Brown, E., Bullock, R., Hobson, C. and Little, M. (1998) *Making Residential Care Work: Structure and Culture in Children's Homes*. Aldershot: Ashgate.

Bulmer, M. (1987) *The Social Basis of Community Care*. London: Allen and Unwin.

Burnett, J. (1994) *Idle Hands: The Experience of Unemployment, 1790–1990*. London: Routledge.

Bytheway, B. and Johnson, J. (1998) The social construction of 'carers'. In Symonds, A. and Kelly, A. (eds) *The Social Construction of Community Care*. Basingstoke: Macmillan – now Palgrave Macmillan, 241–53.

Campbell, H., Hotchkiss, R., Bradshaw, N. and Porteous, M. (1998) Integrated care pathways. *British Medical Journal* 318: 133–7.

Carers' Information Service (2006) *How to ... : A Guide for Carers in Croydon.* Croydon: Soroptimists International.

Carey, M. (2003) Anatomy of a care manager. *Work, Employment and Society* **17**(1): 121–35.

Carey, M. (2006) Selling social work by the pound? The pros and cons of agency care management. *Practice* **18**(1): 3–15.

Carpenter, J., Schneider, J., McNiven, F., Brandon, T., Stevens, R. and Wooff, D. (2004) Integration and targeting of community care for people with severe and enduring mental health problems: users' experiences of the care programme approach and care management. *British Journal of Social Work* **34**(3): 313–33.

Challis, D. (1994) *Care Management: Factors Influencing its Development in the Implementation of Community Care.* London: Department of Health.

Chan, C. K. (2004) Placing dignity at the centre of welfare policy. *International Social Work* **47**(2): 227–39.

Charnley, H. (2001) Promoting independence: a partnership approach to supporting older people in the community. In Balloch, S. and Taylor, S. (eds) *Partnership Working: Policy and Practice.* Bristol: Policy Press, 143–64.

Chene, B. (2006) Dementia and residential placement: A view from the carers' perspective. *Qualitative Social Work* **5**(2): 187–215.

Close, P. (1992) State care, control and contradictions: Theorizing resistance, change and progress in modern society. In Close, P. (ed.) *The State and Caring,* Basingstoke: Macmillan – now Palgrave Macmillan, 10–71.

Clough, R. (2000) *The Practice of Residential Work.* Basingstoke: Palgrave Macmillan.

Coffey, M., Dugdill, L. and Tattersall, A. (2004) Stress in social services: Mental well-being, constraints and job satisfaction. *British Journal of Social Work* **34**(5): 735–46.

Cooke, B. and Kothari, U. (eds) (2001) *Participation: The New Tyranny?* London: Zed.

Corby, B., Doig, A. and Roberts, V. (2001) *Public Inquiries into Abuse of Children in Residential Care.* London: Jessica Kingsley.

Cowger, C. D. and Atherton, C. R. (1974) Social control: a rationale for social welfare. *Social Work* **19**(4): 452–62.

Coyle, D., Edwards, D., Hannigan, B., Fothergill, A. and Burnand, P. (2005) A systematic review of stress among mental health social workers. *International Social Work.* **48**(21): 201–11.

Craib, I. (1992) *Anthony Giddens.* London: Routledge.

Crow, G. and Allan, G. (1994) *Community Life: An Introduction to Local Social Relations.* London: Harvester Wheatsheaf.

CSCI (2006) *The State of Social Care in England.* London: Commission for Social Care Inspection. http://www.csci.org.uk/PDF/state_of_social_care.pdf.

CSCI (2007) *Different Types of Social Care.* http://www.csci.org.uk/choose_and_find_care/different_types_of_social_care.aspx (accessed: 5 March 2007).

CSIP (2007) *Welcome to the Individual Budgets Pilot Programme Website.* http://individualbudgets.csip.org.uk/index.jsp (accessed: 27 November 2007).

Cvetkovich, G. (1999) The attribution of social trust. In Cvetkovich, G. and Löfstedt, R. E. (eds) (1999) *Social Trust and the Management of Risk.* London: Earthscan, 53–61.

Cvetkovich, G. and Löfstedt, R. E. (eds) (1999) *Social Trust and the Management of Risk.* London: Earthscan.

Dalley, G. (1988) *Ideologies of Caring: Rethinking Community and Collectivism*. Basingstoke: Macmillan – now Palgrave Macmillan.

Dalrymple, J. Payne, M., Tomlinson, T. and Ward, S. (1995) *'They Listened to Him': Report to the Gulbenkian Foundation*. Manchester: ASC and Manchester Metropolitan University.

Davies, B. and Challis, D. (1986) *Matching Needs to Resources in Community Care*. Aldershot: Gower.

Davies, M. (1994) *The Essential Social Worker: A Guide to Positive Practice*, (3rd edn). Aldershot: Arena.

Davis, A., Ellis, K. and Rummery, K. (1997) *Access to Assessment: Perspectives of Practitioners, Disabled People and Carers*. Bristol: Policy Press.

Day, G. (2006) *Community and Everyday Life*. Abingdon: Routledge.

Day, P. R. (1981) *Social Work and Social Control*. London: Tavistock.

DCA (2007) *Mental Capacity Act 2005: Code of Practice*. London: TSO.

Denney, D. (2005) *Risk and Society*. London: Sage.

DfES (2006a) *The Common Assessment Framework for Children and Young People: Practitioner's Guide*. London: Department for Education and Skills.

DfES (2006b) *The Common Assessment Framework for Children and Young People: Manager's Guide*. London: Department for Education and Skills.

DfES (2006c) *Children Looked After in England (Including Adoptions and Care Leavers), 2005–06*. London: Department for Education and Skills. http://www.dfes.gov.uk/rsgateway/DB/SFR/s000691/SFR44-2006.pdf (accessed: 31 July 2007).

DfES (2007) *Statutory Guidance on Making Arrangements to Safeguard and Promote the Welfare of Children under Section 11 of the Children Act 2004*. London: Department for Education and Skills.

DH (1990) *The Care Programme Approach for People with a Mental Illness Referred to the Specialist Psychiatric Services*. HC(90)23/LASSL(90)11. London: Department of Health.

DH (1995) *Building Bridges – A Guide to Arrangements for Inter-agency Working for the Care and Protection of Severely Mentally Ill People*. London: Department of Health.

DH (1999) *National Service Framework for Mental Health: Modern Standards and Service Models for Mental Health*. HSC 1999/223. London: Department of Health.

DH (2001) *Valuing People: A New Strategy for Learning Disability for the 21st Century*. London: Department of Health.

DH (2002) *Guidance on the Single Assessment Process for Older People*. HSC 2002/001; LAC 2002(1). London: Department of Health. http://www.dh.gov.uk/en/Pub licationsandstatistics/Lettersandcirculars/Healthservicecirculars/DH_4003995 (accessed: 01 May 2007).

DH (2003) *Fair Access to Services: Guidance on Eligibility Criteria for Adult Social Care*. London: Department of Health. http://www.dh.gov.uk/en/Publicationsandstat istics/Publications/PublicationsPolicyAndGuidance/DH_4009653 (accessed: 28 May 2007).

DH (2005a) *Independence, Well-being and Choice: Our Vision for the Future of Social Care in England*. (Cm 6499). London: TSO.

DH (2005b) *Responses to the consultation on adult social care in England: Analysis of feedback from the Green Paper* Independence, Well-being and Choice. London: Department of Health.

DH (2006a) *Our Health, Our Care, Our Say: A New Direction for Community Services.* (Cm 6737). London: TSO.

DH (2006b) *The Expert Patients Programme.* http://www.dh.gov.uk/en/Aboutus/Mi nistersandDepartmentLeaders/ChiefMedicalOfficer/ProgressOnPolicy/Progress BrowsableDocument/DH_4102757 (accessed: 18 December 2007).

DH (2007a) *Social Care.* http://www.dh.gov.uk/en/Policyandguidance/Healthands ocialcaretopics/Socialcare/index.htm (accessed: 27 May 2007).

DH (2007b) *National Service Frameworks (NSFs).* http://www.dh.gov.uk/ PolicyAndGuidance/HealthAndSocialCareTopics/HealthAndSocialCareArticle/ fs/en?CONTENT_ID=4070951&chk=W3ar/W.

DH (2007c) Trust Assurance and Safety – The Regulation of Health Professionals in the 21st Century. (Cm 7013). London: TSO.

DH (2007d) *Final Version of National Framework Decision Support Tools.* http:// www.dh.gov.uk/en/Policyandguidance/SocialCare/Socialcarereform/ Continuingcare/DH_073912 (accessed: 17 December 2007).

DH (2007e) *The Expert Carers Programme.* http://www.dh.gov.uk/en/Aboutus/Mini stersandDepartmentLeaders/ChiefMedicalOfficer/ProgressOnPolicy/ProgressBr owsableDocument/DH_4102757 (accessed: 18 December 2007).

Dolan, P., Pinkerton, J., and Canavan, J. (2006) Family support from description to reflection. In Dolan, P., Canavan, J., and Pinkerton, J. (eds) *Family Support as Reflective Practice.* London: Jessica Kingsley, 11–24.

Donald, J. P. and Brown, H. (2003) Independent multidisciplinary review of entry into institutional care. *British Journal of Social Work* **33**(5): 689–97.

Dowling, S., Manthorpe, J. and Cowley, S. with King, S., Raymond, V., Perez, W. and Weinstein, P. (2006) *Person-centred Planning in Social Care: A Scoping Review.* York: Joseph Rowntree Memorial Trust.

During S. (1993) Introduction. In During, S. (ed.) *The Cultural Studies Reader.* London: Routledge, 1–25.

Ellis, K. (1993) *Squaring the Circle: User and Carer Participation in Needs Assessment.* York: Joseph Rowntree Memorial Trust.

Ellis, K. (2007) Direct payments and social work practice: The significance of 'street-level bureaucracy' in determining eligibility. *British Journal of Social Work* **37**(3): 405–22.

Ellis, K., Davis, A. and Rummery, K. (1999) Needs assessment, 'street-level bureaucracy' and the new community care. *Journal of Social Policy and Administration* **33**(3): 262–80.

Engebretson, J. (2000) Caring presence: A case study. In Robb, M., Barrett, S., Komaromy, C. and Rogers, A. (eds) *Communication, Relationships and Care: A Reader.* London: Routledge, 235–47.

Equalities Review (2007) *Fairness and Freedom: The Final Report of the Equalities Review.* London: Cabinet Office.

Fink, J. (ed) (2004) *Care: Personal Lives and Social Policy.* Bristol: Policy Press.

Finch, J. and Mason, J. (1993) *Negotiating Family Responsibilities.* London: Routledge.

Fisher, R., Ury, W. and Patton, B. (2003) *Getting to Yes: Negotiating Agreement without Giving In: The Secret of Successful Negotiation.* London: Random House.

Flanagan, J. C. (1954) The critical incident technique. *Psychological Bulletin* **51**(4): 327–58.

Foucault, M. (1986) *Care of the Self*. Harmondsworth: Penguin.

Fowles, A. J. and Jones, K. (1984) *Ideas on Institutions: Analysing the Literature on Long-Term Care and Custody*. London: Routledge and Kegan Paul.

Fox Harding, L. (1997) *Perspectives in Child Care Policy*. Harlow: Longman.

Gardner, R. (1998) *Family Support*. Birmingham: Venture.

Germain, C. (1976) Time: An ecological variable in social work practice. *Social Casework* **57**(7): 419–26.

Germain, C. (1978) Space: an ecologcal variable in social work practice. *Social Casework* **59**(11): 15–22.

Gershon, P. (2004) *Releasing Resources to the Front Line: Independent Review of Public Sector Efficiency*. London: HM Treasury.

Gibbons, J. (1990) *Family Support and Prevention: Studies in Local Areas*. London: HMSO.

Gilligan, C. (1993) *In a Different Voice: Psychological Theory and Women's Development*. Cambridge, MA: Harvard University Press.

Gilligan, R. (1998) The importance of schools and teachers in public welfare. *Child and Family Social Work* **3**(1): 13–25.

Glasby, J. and Peck, E. (2005) *A New Vision of Adult Social Care: What Happens Next?* Birmingham: Health Services Management Centre.

Glendinning, C. (2002) European policies on home care services compared. In Bytheway, B., Bacigalupo, V., Bornat, J., Johnson, J. and Spurr, S. (eds) *Understanding Care, Welfare and Communtiy: A Reader*. London: Routledge, 240–6.

Glendinning, C. and Means, R. (2004) Rearranging the deckchairs on the Titanic of long-term care – is organizational integration the answer? *Critical Social Policy* **24**(4): 435–57.

Goffman, E. (1961) On the characteristics of total institutions: The inmate world. In Cressey, D. (ed.) *The Prison: Studies in Institutional Organisation and Change*. New York: Holt, Rinehart & Winston Inc.

Goldberg, E. M. and Connelly, N. (1982) *The Effectiveness of Social Care for the Elderly: An Overview of Recent and Current Evaluation Research*. London: Heinemann.

Goodwin D. H., Higginson I. J., Myers K., Douglas H-R. and Normand C. E. (2003) Effectiveness of palliative day care in improving pain, symptom control, and quality of life. *Journal of Pain and Symptom Management* **25**(3): 202–12.

Graham, H. (1983) Caring: a labour of love. In Finch, J. and Groves, D. (eds) *A Labour of Love: Women, Work and Caring*. London: Routledge, 13–36.

Gray, B. (2003) Social exclusion, poverty, health and social care in Tower Hamlets: The perspectives of families on the impact of the family support service. *British Journal of Social Work* **33**(3): 361–80.

Gray, J. (2005a) A voice for the UK care pathway community of practice. *Journal of Integrated Care Pathways* **9**(3): 97–100.

Gray, J. (2005b) Care pathways – are they one thing and is there a right way of doing them? *Journal of Integrated Care Pathways* **9**(1): 1–45.

Griffiths Report (1988) *Community Care: Agenda for Action*. London: HMSO.

Gursansky, D., Harvey, J. and Kennedy, R. (2003) *Case Management: Policy, Practice and Professional Business*. New York: Columbia University Press.

Habermas, J. (1984) *The Theory of Communicative Action, Volume 2*. Boston, MA: Beacon Press.

Hadley, R. and McGrath, M. (eds) (1980) *Going Local – Neighbourhood Social Services*. London: Bedford Square Press.

Hadley, R. and McGrath, M. (1984) *When Social Services Are Local: The Normanton Experiment*. London: Allen & Unwin.

Hadley, R. and Young, K. (1990) *Creating a Responsive Public Service*. Hemel Hempstead: Harvester Wheatsheaf.

Hadley, R., Cooper, M., Dale, P. and Stacy, G. (1987) *A Community Social Worker's Handbook*. London: Tavistock.

Halmos, P. (1965) *The Faith of the Counsellors*. London: Constable.

Halmos, P. (1970) *The Personal Service Society*. London: Constable.

Hanley, B. (2005) *Research as Empowerment?: Report of a Series of Seminars Organised by the Toronto Group*. York: Joseph Rowntree Foundation.

Hartley, N. and Payne, M. (eds) (2008) *Creative Arts in Palliative Care*. London: Jessica Kingsley.

Hatfield, B., Mohamad, H., Rahim, Z. and Tanweer, H. (1996), Mental health and the Asian community: A local survey. *British Journal of Social Work* **26**(3): 315–36.

Hatton, C., Azmi, S., Caine, A. and Emerson, E. (1998) Informal carers of adolescents and adults with learning difficulties from the South Asian communities: Family circumstances, service support and carer stress. *British Journal of Social Work* **28**(6): 821–37.

Hawkins, P. and Shohet, R. (2000) *Supervision in the Helping Professions*. (2nd edn) Buckingham: Open University Press.

Health Service Ombudsman (2003) *NHS Funding for Long-Term Care*. (HC 399). London: TSO.

Health Service Ombudsman for England (2004) *NHS Funding for Long-Term Care*. (HC 144). London: TSO.

HMG (2006) *Working Together to Safeguard Children: A Guide to Inter-agency Working to Safeguard and Promote the Welfare of Children*. London: TSO.

Hochschild, A. (1995) The culture of politics; traditional, postmodern, cold-modern and warm-modern ideals of care. *Social Politics* **2**(3): 331–46.

Hochschild, A. R. (2004) Emotion work, feeling rules, and social structure. *American Journal of Sociology* **85**(3): 551–75.

Holden, C. (2002) The internationalisation of long-term care provision. *Global Social Policy* **2**(1): 47–67.

Home Office (1998) *Supporting Families: Summary of Responses to the Consultation Document*. London: HMSO.

Home Office (2005) *Domestic Violence: A National Report*. London: Home Office.

Home Office and DH (2000) *No Secrets: Guidance on Developing and Implementing Multi-agency Policies and Procedures to Protect Vulnerable Adults From Abuse*. London: Home Office/Department of Health.

Houghton Report (1972) *Report of the Departmental Committee on the Adoption of Children*. (Cmnd 5107). London: HMSO.

Huby, G. and Rees, G (2005) The effectiveness of quality improvement tools: Joint working in integrated community teams. *International Journal of Quality in Health Care* **17**(1): 538.

Hudson, H. (1994) Care management: the EPIC model, a case of not grasping the nettle. In Challis, D., Davies, B. and Trake, K. (eds) *Community Care: New Agendas and Challenges from the UK and Overseas*. Aldershot: Arena, 149–59.

Hugman, R., Peelo, M. and Soothill, K. (eds) (1997) *Concepts of Care: Development in Health and Social Welfare*. London: Arnold.

Huxley, P., Reilly, S., Robinshaw, E., Mohamad, H., Harrison, J., Windle, B. and Butler, T. (2003) Interventions and outcomes of health and social care service provision for people with severe mental illness in England. *Social Psychiatry and Psychiatric Epidemiology* 38: 44–8.

Irvine, E. E. (1978) Professional Claims and the Professional Task. In Open University Course Team (eds) *Professional and Non-professional Roles 1*. Milton Keynes: Open University, 85–113.

Jackson, S. (1987) *The Education of Children in Care*. Bristol: University of Bristol School of Applied Social Studies.

Jacobs, P. and Rapoport, J. (2003) *The Economics of Health and Medical Care*. (5th edn) Sudbury, MA: Jones and Bartlett.

Jeffs, T. (1995) Children's educational rights in the new ERA? In Franklin, B. (ed.) *The Handbook of Children's Rights*. London: Routledge.

Jenkins, W. I. (1978) *Policy Analysis*. Oxford: Martin Robertson.

Jones, C. (2001) Voices from the front-line: State social workers and New Labour. *British Journal of Social Work* 31(4): 547–62.

Kanter, J. (1989) Clinical case management: Definition, principles, components. *Hospital and Community Psychiatry* 40(4): 361–8.

Kennett, C. (2000) Participation in a creative arts project can foster hope in a hospice day centre. *Palliative Medicine* 11(6): 254–6.

Klein, J. (1965) *Samples from English Cultures, Vol.1*. London: Routledge and Kegan Paul.

Knapman, J. and Morrison, T. (1998) *Making the Most of Supervision in Health and Social Care: A Self-Development Manual for Supervisees*. Brighton: Pavilion.

Leadbeater, C. and Lownsborough, H. (2005) Personalisation and Participation: The Future of Social Care in Scotland: Final Report. London: Demos.

Le Bihan, B. and Martin, C. (2006) A comparative case study of care systems for frail and elderly people: Germany, Spain, France, Italy, United Kingdom and Sweden. *Social Policy and Administration* 40(1): 26–46.

LeRoy, B., Wolf-Brangin, M., Wolf-Brangin, K., Israel, N. and Kulik, N. (2007) Challenges to the systematic adoption of person-centered planning. *Best Practices in Mental Health* 3(1): 16–25.

Levy, J. and Payne, M. (2006) Audit of welfare benefits advocacy in a palliative care setting. *European Journal of Palliative Care* 13(1): 15–17.

Lewis, I. (2006) *Dignity in Care*. (Gateway ref: 7388) London: Department of Health.

Lewis, J. and Glennerster, H. (1996) *Implementing the New Community Care*. Buckingham: Open University Press.

Likert, R. (1961) *New Patterns of Organization*. New York: McGraw-Hill.

Lymbery, M., Lawson, J., MacCallum, H., McCoy, P., Pidgeon, J. and Ward, K. (2007) The social work role with older people. *Practice* 19(2): 97–113.

McBeath, G. B. and Webb, S. A. (1997) Community care: A unity of state and care? In Hugman, R., Peelo, M. and Soothill, K. (eds) *Concepts of Care: Developments in Health and Social Welfare*. London: Arnold.

McConkey, R., Nixon, T., Donaghy, E. and Mulhern, D. (2004) The characteristics of children with a disability looked after away from home and their future service needs. *British Journal of Social Work* 34(4): 561–76.

McGrath, M. (1991) *Multidisciplinary Teams*. Aldershot: Gower.

Malin, N. (1983) *Group Homes for Mentally Handicapped People*. London: HMSO.

Marshall, M. (2003) Acute psychiatric day hospitals. *British Medical Journal* 327: 116–17.

Marshall, M., Crowther, R., Almaraz-Serrano, A., Creed, F., Sledge, W., Kluiter, H. et al. (2001) Systematic reviews of the effectiveness of day care for people with severe mental disorders: (1) Acute day hospital versus admission; (2) Vocational rehabilitation; (3) Day hospital versus outpatient care. *Health Technology Assessment* 5(21): i–iii.

Marshall, M. and Creed, F. (2000) Assertive community treatment – Is it the future of Community Care in the UK? *International Review of Psychiatry* 12(3): 191–6.

Martin, J. P. (1984) *Hospitals in Trouble*. Oxford: Blackwell.

Mayeroff, M. (1971) *On Caring*. New York: Harper and Row.

Mayo, M. (1994) *Communities and Caring: The Mixed Economy of Welfare*. London: Macmillan – now Palgrave Macmillan.

Means, R. and Smith R. (1998) *From Poor Law to Community Care: The Development of Welfare Services for Elderly People 1939–1971* (2nd edn). Bristol: Policy Press.

Means, R., Richards, S. and Smith, R. (2003) *Community Care: Policy and Practice*. (3rd edn) Basingstoke: Palgrave Macmillan.

Millard, D. W. (1992) The therapeutic community in an age of community care. In Baron, S. R. and Haldane, J. D. (eds) *Community, Normality and Difference: Meeting Special Needs*. Aberdeen: Aberdeen University Press.

Miller, C., Freeman, M. and Ross, N. (2001) *Interprofessional Practice in Health and Social Care: Challenging the Shared Learning Agenda*. London: Arnold.

Miller, M. and Corby, B. (2006) The *Framework for the Assessment of Children and their Families* – A basis for a therapeutic encounter? *British Journal of Social Work* 36(6): 887–99.

Monroe, B. and Oliviere, D. (eds) (2003) *Patient Participation in Palliative Care: A Voice for the Voiceless*. Oxford: Oxford University Press.

Morgan, D. (1996) *Family Connections*. Cambridge: Polity.

Morris, J. (1993) *Independent Lives? Disabled People and Community Care*. Basingstoke: Macmillan – now Palgrave Macmillan.

Morrison, A. (2001) Interpreting the quality of written assessments: A participative approach. In White, V. and Harris, J. *Developing Good Practice in Community Care: Partnership and Participation*. London: Jessica Kingsley, 34–48.

Newton, S. (2006) *Adult Placement: An Introduction to the Principles and Practice of Adult Placement*. Birmingham: Venture.

Nicholas, E. (2003) An outcomes focus in carer assessment and review: Value and challenge. *British Journal of Social Work* 33(1): 31–47.

Nijs, K. A. N. D., de Graaf, C., Kok, F. J. and van Staveren, W. J. (2006) Effects of family style mealtimes on quality of life, physical performance and body weight of nursing home residents: Cluster, randomised controlled trial. *British Medical Journal* **332**: 1180–4.

Noddings, N. (1984) *Caring: A Feminine Approach to Ethics and Moral Education*. Berkeley, CA: University of California Press.

ODPM (2004) *What is Supporting People?* London: Office of the Deputy Prime Minister.

Onyett, S. (2003) *Teamworking in Mental Health*. Basingstoke: Palgrave Macmillan.

Opie A (2003) *Thinking Teams/Thinking Clients: Knowledge-based Teamwork*. New York: Columbia University Press.

Packman, J. (1981) *The Child's Generation*. (2nd edn) Oxford: Blackwell.

Parker, G. and Lawton, D. (1994) *Different Types of Care, Different Types of Carer*. London: HMSO.

Parker, J., (2005) Constructing dementia and dementia care: Daily practice in a day care setting. *Journal of Social Work* **5**(3): 261–78.

Parker, R. (1981) Tending and social policy. In Goldberg, E. M. and Hatch, S. (eds) *A New Look at the Personal Social Services*. London: Policy Studies Institute, 17–32.

Parker, R. (1988) An historical background. In Sinclair, I. (ed.) *Residential Care: The Research Reviewed*. London: HMSO.

Parsloe, P. (1989) Can you care for profit? In Clough, R. and Parlsoe, P. (eds) *Squaring the Circle: Being Cared for and Caring after Firth, Griffiths and Wagner*. Bristol: School of Applied Social Studies, Bristol Paper 11, 74–85.

Parton, N., Thorpe, D. and Wattam, C. (1997) *Child Protection, Risk and the Moral Order*. Basingstoke: Macmillan – now Palgrave Macmillan.

Payne, M. (1986) *Social Care in the Community*. Basingstoke: Macmillan – now Palgrave Macmillan.

Payne, M. (1992) Routes to and through clienthood and their implications for practice. *Practice* **6**(3): 169–80.

Payne, M. (1993) New understandings of later life: Practice and service implications. In Day, P. (ed) *New Perspectives on Later Life*. London: Whiting and Birch, 1–21.

Payne, M. (1995) *Social Work and Community Care*. Basingstoke: Macmillan – now Palgrave Macmillan.

Payne, M. (2004) Social work practice identities: An agency study of a hospice. *Practice* **16**(1): 5–15.

Payne, M. (2005) *The Origins of Social Work: Continuity and Change*. Basingstoke: Palgrave Macmillan.

Payne, M. (2006) Social objectives in cancer care: The example of palliative day care. *European Journal of Cancer Care* **15**: 440–7.

Payne, M. and Askeland, G. A. (2008) *Globalisation and Social Work: Postmodern Challenge and Change*. Aldershot: Ashgate.

Payne, M. and Oliviere, D. (2008) The interdisciplinary team. In Walsh, D. (ed.) *Palliative Care*. New York: Elsevier.

Percy Commission (1957) *Report of the Royal Commission on the Law Relating to Mental Illness and Mental Deficiency*. (Cmnd 169). London: HMSO.

Petrie, P., Egharevba, I., Oliver, C. and Pollard, G. (2000) *Out-of-School Lives, Out-of-school Services*. London: The Stationery Office.

Phillips, J., Bernard, M. and Chittenden, M. (2002) *Juggling Work and Care: The Experiences of Working Carers of Older Adults*. Bristol: Policy Press.

Pickvance, C. (2003) Housing and housing policy. In Baldock, J., Manning, N. and Vickerstaff, S. (eds) *Social Policy*. (2nd edn) Oxford: Oxford University Press 486–518.

Pithouse, A. (1998) *Social Work: The Social Organisation of an Invisible Trade*. (2nd edn) Aldershot: Ashgate.

Platt, D. (2006) Investigation or initial assessment of child concerns? The impact of the refocusing initiative on social work practice. *British Journal of Social Work* 362: 267–81.

Platt Report (2007) *The Status of Social Care: A Review 2007*. London: Department of Health. http://www.dh.gov.uk/en/Publicationsandstatistics/Publications/Pu blicationsPolicyAndGuidance/DH_074217 (accessed: 6 May 2007).

Player, S. and Pollock, A. M. (2001) Long-term care: from public responsibility to private good. *Critical Social Policy* 21(2): 231–55.

Postle, K. (2001) The social work side is disappearing. I guess it started with us being called care managers. *Practice* 13(1): 3–18.

Postle, K. (2002) Working between 'the idea and the reality': Ambiguities and tensions in care managers' work. *British Journal of Social Work* 32(3): 335–51.

Preston-Shoot, M. and Wigley, V. (2002) Closing the circle: Social workers' responded to multi-agency procedures on older age abuse. *British Journal of Social Work* 32(3): 299–320.

Prime Minister's Strategy Unit (2005) *Improving the Life Chances of Disabled People: Final Report*. London: PMSU.

Pritchard J. (ed.) (2001) *Good Practice with Vulnerable Adults*. London: Jessica Kingsley.

Pritlove, J. (1985) *Group Homes: An Inside Story*. Sheffield: Joint Unit for Social Services Research.

Quinney, A. (2006) *Collaborative Social Work Practice*. Exeter: Learning Matters.

Race, D. G. (2003) *Leadership and Change in Human Services: Selected Readings from Wolf Wolfensberger*. London: Routledge.

Raiffa, H. (2007) *Decision Analysis: The Science and Art of Collaborative Decision-making*. Cambridge, MA: Belknap Press.

Ramon, S. (ed.) (1991) *Beyond Community Care: Normalisation and Integration Work*. Basingstoke: Macmillan – now Palgrave Macmillan.

Rapp, C. A. and Goscha, R. J. (2004) The principles of effective case management of mental health services. *Psychiatric Rehabilitation Journal* 27(4): 319–33.

Ray, M. (2006) Informal care in the context of long-term marriage: The challenge to practice. *Practice* 18(2): 129–42.

Reith, M. (1988) *Community Care Tragedies: A Practice Guide to Mental Health Inquiries*. Birmingham: Venture.

Renshaw, J., Hampsom, R., Thomason, C., Darton, R., Judge, K. and Knapp, M. (1988) *Care in the Community: The First Steps*. Aldershot: Gower.

Research Works (2001) *Perceptions of Social Work and Social Care*. London: DH.

Rizzo, V. M. and Rowe, J. M. (2006) Studies of the cost-effectiveness of social work services in aging: A review of the literature. *Research on Social Work Practice* 16(1): 67–73.

Robb, M., Barrett, S., Komaromy, C. and Rogers, A. (eds) (2004) *Communication, Relationships and Care: A Reader*. London: Routledge.

Robinson, C. and Williams, V. (2002) Carers of people with learning disabilities and their experience of the 1995 Carers Act. *British Journal of Social Work*, **32**(2): 169–83.

Robinson, S., Kendrick, K. and Brown, A. (2004) *Spirituality and the Practice of Healthcare*. Basingstoke: Palgrave – now Palgrave Macmillan.

Rogers, H. and Barnes, M. (2002) Caring voices: Carers' participation in policy and practice. In Stalker, K. (ed.) *Reconceptualising Work with 'Carers': New Directions of Policy and Practice*. London: Jessica Kingsley.

SAMHSA (2005) *Free to Choose: Transforming Behavioral Health Care to Self-Direction*. Rockville, MD: Substance Abuse and Mental Health Service Administration.

SCIE (2006) *About SCIE*. http://www.scie.org.uk/about/index.asp (accessed: 14 October 2006).

Scourfield, P. (2006) 'What matters is what works'? How discourses of modernization have both silenced and limited debate on domiciliary care for older people. *Critical Social Policy* **26**(1): 6–30.

Scourfield, P. (2007) Social care and the modern citizen: Client, consumer, service user, manager and entrepreneur. *British Journal of Social Work* **37**(1): 107–22.

Seebohm Report (1968) *Report of the Committee on Local Authority and Allied Personal Social Services*. (Cmnd 3703). London: HMSO.

Sellick, C. and Howell, D. (2004) A description and analysis of multi-sectoral fostering practice in the United Kingdom. *British Journal of Social Work* **34**(4): 481–99.

Sheppard, M. (2004) An evaluation of social support intervention with depressed mothers in child and family care. *British Journal of Social Work* **34**(7): 939–60.

Siegrist, J. and Theorell, T. (2006) Socio-economic position and health: The role of work and employment. In Siegrist, J. and Marmot, M. (eds) *Social Inequalities in Health: New Evidence and Policy Implications*. Oxford: Oxford University Press, 73–100.

SIESWE (2006) *About the Institute*. http://www.sieswe.org/introduction/index.html (accessed: 14 October 2006).

Simic, P. (1995) What's in a word? From 'social worker' to 'care manager'. *Practice* **7**(3): 5–18.

Sinson, J. C. (1993) *Group Home and Community Integration of Developmentally Disabled People: Microinstitutionalisation?* London: Jessica Kingsley.

Sipilä, J. (ed.) (1997) *Social Care Services: The Key to the Scandinavian Welfare Model*. Aldershot: Ashgate.

Slovic, P. (1999) Perceived risk, trust and democracy. In Cvetkovich, G. and Löfstedt, R. E. (eds) *Social Trust and the Management of Risk*. London: Earthscan, 42–52.

Smith, P. (2001) *Cultural Theory: An Introduction*. Oxford: Blackwell.

Social Care Association (2006) *Social Care Association 1949–1999*. http://socialcaring.co.uk/full_history.asp (accessed: 20 June 2006).

Spandler, H. and Vick, N. (2005) Enabling access to direct payments: An exploration of care co-ordinators decision-making practices. *Journal of Mental Health* **14**(2): 145–55.

Spratt, T. (2001) The influence of child protection orientation on child welfare practice. *British Journal of Social Work* **31**(6): 933–54.

SPRU (2000) *Introducing an Outcome Focus into Care Management and User Surveys*. York: Social Policy Research Unit.

SSI/SWSG (1991) *Care Management and Assessment: Managers' Guide*. London: Department of Health.

Stacey, M. (1969) The myth of community studies. *British Journal of Sociology* 20(2): 134–47.

Stalker, K. (ed.) (2003) *Reconceptualising Work with 'Carers': New Directions for Policy and Practice*. London: Jessica Kingsley.

Stanworth, R. (2004) *Recognizing Spiritual Needs in People who are Dying*. Oxford: Oxford University Press.

Stevenson, I. and Spencer, L. (2002) *Developing Intermediate Care: A Guide for Health and Social Services Professionals*. London: King's Fund.

Stirrat, R. (1997) The new orthodoxy and old truths: Participation, empowerment and other buzzwords. In Bastian, S., Bastian, N. and Nivaran, D. (eds) *Assessing Participation: A Debate from South Asia*. Delhi: Konark, 67–92.

Stones, C. (1994) *Focus on Families: Family Centres in Action*. Basingstoke: Macmillan – now Palgrave Macmillan.

Storey, J. and Billingham, J. (2001) Occupational stress and social work. *Social Work Education* 20(6): 259–70.

Sutherland Commission (1999) *With Respect to Old Age: A Report by the Royal Commission on Long-Term Care*. (Cm 4192-I). London: TSO.

Tasker, M. (2008) Digital art in palliative care. In Hartley, N. and Payne, M. (eds) *Creative Arts in Palliative Care*. London: Jessica Kingsley, 113–27.

Taylor, B. J. (2006) Risk management paradigms in health and social services for professional decision-making on the long-term care of older people. *British Journal of Social Work* 36(8): 1411–29.

Taylor, C. and White, S. (2000) *Practising Reflexivity in Health and Welfare: Making Knowledge*. Buckingham: Open University Press.

Taylor, S. (2006) A new approach to empowering older people's forums: Identifying barriers to encourage participation. *Practice* 18(20): 117–28.

Tilbury, C. (2007) The regulation of out-of-home care. *British Journal of Social Work* 37(2): 209–24.

Tomlin, S. (1989). *Abuse of Elderly People: An Unnecessary and Preventable Problem*. London: British Geriatrics Society.

Tönnies, F. (1955) *Community and Association*. London: Routledge and Kegan Paul.

Townsend, P. (1962) *The Last Refuge: A Survey of Residential Institutions and Homes for the Aged*. London: Routledge and Kegan Paul.

Trevillion, S. (1999) *Networking and Community Partnership*. (2nd edn) Aldershot: Ashgate.

Tronto, J. C. (1993) *Moral Boundaries: A Political Argument for an Ethics of Care*. New York: Routledge.

Twigg, J. (2000) *Bathing – The Body and Community Care*. London: Routledge.

Twigg, J. and Atkin, K. (1994) *Carers Perceived: Policy and Practice in Informal Care*. London: HMSO.

Twigg, J., Atkin, K. and Perring, C. (1990) *Carers and Services: A Review of Research*. London: HMSO.

Utting Report (1997) *People Like Us: The Report of the Review of the Safeguards for Children Living away from Home*. London: HMSO.

Venables, D., Hughes, J., Stewart, K. and Challis, D. (2005) Variations in care management arrangements for people with mental health problems in England. *Care Management Journals* 6(3): 131–8.

Wagner Report (1987) *Residential Care: A Positive Choice.* London: HMSO.

Walmsley, J. and Rolph, S. (2001) The development of community care for people with learning difficulties 1913–1946. *Critical Social Policy* 21(1): 59–80.

Walsh, F. (2006) *Strengthening Family Resilience.* (2nd edn) New York: Guilford.

Wanless Report (2006) *Securing Good Care for Older People: Taking a Long-term View.* London: King's Fund.

Warburton, D. (2006) *Evaluation of* Your Health, Your Care, Your Say: *Final Report.* London: Department of Health.

Ward, A. (2006) *Working in Group Care: Social Work and Social Care in Residential and Day Care Settings.* (2nd edn) Bristol: Policy Press.

Webb, A. and Wistow, G. (1987) *Social Work, Social Care and Social Planning: The Personal Social Services since Seebohm.* London: Longman.

Webb, S. A. (2004) *Social Work in Risk Society: Social and Cultural Perspectives.* Basingstoke: Palgrave – now Palgrave Macmillan.

Weinberg, A, and Huxley, P. (2000) An evaluation of the impact of voluntary sector family support workers on the quality of life of carers of schizophrenia sufferers. *Journal of Mental Health* 9: 495–503.

Weinberg, A., Williamson, J., Challis, D. and Hughes, J. (2003) What do Care Managers do? A study of working practice in older peoples' services. *British Journal of Social Work* 33(7): 901–19.

Weinstein, J., Whittington, C. and Leiba, T. (eds) (2003) *Collaboration in Social Work Practice.* London: Jessica Kingsley.

Wenger, E. (1998) *Communities of Practice: Learning, Meaning and Identity.* Cambridge: Cambridge University Press.

Wenger, G. C. (1994) *Understanding Support Networks and Community Care: Network Assessment for Elderly People.* Aldershot: Avebury.

Whitaker, D., Archer, L. and Hicks, L. (1998) *Working in Children's Homes: Challenges and Complexities.* Chichester: Wiley.

Whittington, C. (2003) Collaboration and partnership in context. In Weinstein, J., Whittington, C. and Leiba, T. (eds) *Collaboration in Social Work Practice.* London: Jessica Kingsley, 13–38.

Williams, R. (1983) *Keywords: A Vocabulary of Culture and Society.* London: Fontana.

Willmott, P. (1989) *Community Initiatives: Patterns and Prospects.* London: Policy Studies Institute.

Woolham, J. (2001) Good practice in the involuntary relocation of people living in residential care. *Practice* 13(4): 49–60.

Young, A. F. and Ashton, E. T. (1956) *British Social Work in the Nineteenth Century.* London: Routledge and Kegan Paul.

Author index

Subject index

and caring 18
and healthcare 2, 19
and social work xi–xiv, 8–10, 19
definitions 1–4
elements 37–49
legislation 3, 78, 61–3
multisectoral 7
perceptions of 9
policy
sources 6
see also children's social care
Social Care Association (SCA) 1, 6
social care councils 3, 58, 61
Social Care Institute for Excellence
    (SCIE) 3
social construction 82–3, 94, 101
social institutions xiii, 19, 23–5
social networks xiv, 5, 10, 23–4, 29,
    31–3, 109,138–9
social pedagogy xiii
social professions xi, xiii, 23
social security 63
social work xi–xiv, 23–4, 108, 110
    and social care xi –xiv, 6, 8–10, 23–4
    education 6
    therapeutic xii, 9

spirituality xiii, 22–3, 125–6
staff development 175–7
stigma 8, 35, 39
support 32, 139–41
supported housing 47–8, 110, 142, 153
Sutherland Commission 74, 99

teamwork 118–23
therapeutic communities 34
third sector 7, 58, 59–62, 70, 111
tick infestation 93–4
time 85, 136–7
trajectory 86–8, 147
transparency 85

users xiii–xvi, 26–9, 53–55, 62, 95, 101,
    111, 116–18, 149
    management 131
    role xiii–xiv
    valuing xiii–xiv, 27–9, 50–1, 83–4,
        130
voluntary sector
    see third sector
Wagner report 42
Wanless report (on social care) 2006 2
work 45, 115, 130, 137